THE

Intricate Art

OF

Living Afloat

THE
Intricate Art
OF
Living Afloat

CLARE ALLCARD

W · W · NORTON & COMPANY · *NEW YORK* · *LONDON*

THE PRECEDING PHOTOGRAPHS: The author and husband, Edward. *Facing the title page:* our daughter, Katy, and a young American cruising friend, Garth Snyder.

The photographs in the book are by the author and her husband, except as mentioned otherwise in the captions.

The text of this book is composed in Times Roman, with the display set in Windsor Light Condensed. Composition and manufacturing by the Maple-Vail Book Manufacturing Group. Book design by Marjorie J. Flock.

ISBN 0-393-03334-1

W. W. Norton & Company, Inc., 500 Fifth Avenue, New York, N.Y. 10110
W. W. Norton & Company, Ltd., 10 Coptic Street, London WC1A 1PU

3 4 5 6 7 8 9 0

Contents

To Edward, my love

Author's Note

~~~~~~~~~~~~~~~~~~~~~~~~~~~~~~

Now THAT I have a chance to say thank you, it's hard to know where to begin. Should I start with Edward, who burst into my life when I was twenty-two and carried me off, a green landlubber, into the blue yonder? Certainly without him this book would never even have been thought of, let alone written. And without our daughter, Katy, to experiment on, much of the information on family and education would be missing. I must also thank Margaret Banks, who, having raised her two babes aboard a cruising yacht, shared some of her innovations with me. And then there is my mother; not only was she among those who kindly read through the script, but she has also, for the past twenty years, sorted and forwarded our mail—a litmus test of love if ever there was one.

I very much want to thank my friend Dr. Shahla Eftekhari and my cousin Dr. Crispin Cobb for finding time to read through the section on health and illness and Margaret Norris for searching out the latest theories on rehydration therapy. Equally I must apologize to both Shahla and Jody Snyder for the way I took advantage of their friendship, thrusting on them the task of hunting down American equivalents of British products. For generous help in translating and checking the language section I thank Sylvie Grall, Claude Montague, Anke Will, Retze Koen, Mrs. Nixon, Jan and Marjan Klingen, Rosaria Vincenzi, Maurice Holmes, Antonia Tunnel, Ali Haykir, and Ahmet Bigali.

Thanks, too, to Wendy Holmes, who gave up the secrets of her delicious cake recipe, Paul Miller, who refreshed my memory of the Fastnet Race disaster, and Lyall Watson, who allowed me to make use of his identifying checklist on whales and dolphins. My cousin Stessa Phelps deserves an accolade all her own for the way she came to the rescue when my own slow, four-fingered typing looked set to scupper the whole project. Indeed, this book has been some years in the making, and I fear, even now, I have forgotten to mention half the good people to whom I owe thanks. Thank you.

I do remember, however, that without Eroll Bruce's initial encouragement I would never have persevered. Charles Pick has always been patient, generous, and wise in his advice. Finally, thanks go to my publisher, Eric P. Swenson, who has on more than one occasion boosted my flagging morale with his own marvelously infectious enthusiasm.

With such a set of paragons behind me, it must be obvious to all that the faults in this book are entirely my own.

Johanne. She was built in 1929 by Faarborg of Denmark.

Introduction

~~~~~~~~~~~~~~~~~~~~~

WHETHER YOU step aboard as skipper, mate, or novice deck-hand, once afloat, you become part of a different world, a world to be relished for a week, a year, or a lifetime by rich and poor, young and old alike. *The Intricate Art of Living Afloat* is a guide to that world. So come with me, and we will rid the everyday boat chores of their modern stigma of frustration. We will discover that they can be both relaxing and fun.

Here are tips on how to gut and dry fish, how to cater for a vacation cruise or a yearlong stay on a desert island. You will find ideas for earning money as you travel, advice on how to soothe the sea urchin's sting, how to wring the last drop of water from wet jeans, or how to dissolve painlessly encrusted grime from behind the ears of recalcitrant offspring.

If planning a long voyage, you will probably meet people who scorn you as hopelessly romantic, harebrained, or even, if you are carting off the children too, downright irresponsible. Ignore them; for if our own experience is anything to go by, you will at the very least never be bored. There won't be time.

As the supermarket, the automobile, washing machine, and deep freeze slip inexorably astern, do not weep. For once aboard, you will discover an amazing new life waiting for you, a life over whose unruffled depths tumbles a constant stream of change and challenge.

Yet at the heart of cruising there is a serene continuity. Long-term cruising folk are after all home-loving types, so much so that we take our homes with us. We also often spend twenty-four hours a day in them. So, incidentally, does the rest of the crew. Make sure you like them.

And who, you ask, am I to offer you advice? Nobody really. My sole qualification for writing *The Intricate Art of Living Afloat* is that after eighteen years before the mast, to say nothing of the galley sink, I still happily look forward to many more roving years to come.

My own heartfelt thanks go to all that dear fraternity of men, women, and children who put to sea in small boats and who have proved themselves unwaveringly kind and friendly. But most of all I thank my husband, Edward, who, twenty years ago, played panpipes in my mind and lured me away to learn the first lessons in *The Intricate Art of Living Afloat*.

THE

Intricate Art

OF

Living Afloat

1. The Galley

~~~~~~~~~~~~~~~~~~~~~~~~~~~~~~

ALTHOUGH the center of culinary activity afloat is only a fraction the size of kitchens ashore, there is no reason why it should not be just as convenient, in fact, more so, as everything is within easy reach.

The essentials are: something to cook on, something to chop on, and something to do the dishes in.

Something to Do the Dishes In ▪ To take the last first, a bucket has served many yachts for many years without any difficulty at all. One simply fills it over the side and adds liquid detergent.

However, for those fussy types who object to washing dishes crouched on deck in the pouring rain and for those, like me, who forget to sift the dirty water for teaspoons and washrags before tipping the lot overboard, a sink below is a boon; two sinks are even better.

They need be only big enough to take a large saucepan, but if there are two, then, in rough weather, one can be used for washing the dishes while the other drains them. This stops things from crashing to the ground. If you have only one sink, try putting a damp cloth on the drain board first. It, too, will prevent everything from skidding about.

Ensure that the sink has a nonchoke outlet pump. If you are clever and insert suitable valves, the bilge pump can be adapted to empty both sink and bilge. Some people, like Edward, prefer tapered cocks under the sink rather than normal plugs. Plugs tend to pop up just as you've filled the sink with water, or else they jam solid when you want to pump out.

Have the sink outlet pipe straight. Salt water is teeming with minute living organisms. These lodge in curved pipes where they die, decompose, and give off clouds of ghastly hydrogen sulfide, which in no time stinks the boat out.

A large-bore pump for delivering salt water and a small-bore pump for delivering fresh helps save the latter. Think twice before installing a luxury header tank with free-flowing faucets. Water that has to be pumped up with difficulty immediately becomes psychologically more precious than the stuff that runs easily out of taps. And is everybody on board going to remember to turn the faucet off before your entire freshwater supply has trickled away?

Something to Chop On ▪ For some unknown reason adequate work space is either overlooked or left as an afterthought in many galleys. Maybe naval architects can't cook. If your galley lacks flat surfaces, a removable piece of wood that fits over the sinks makes an effective additional chopping board, though it does restrict you at the time to either cutting up or washing up. To avoid accidents, make sure the board wedges in securely.

I once saw a work top with a neat trapdoor in the middle. Lift it up, and there was the garbage bin, openmouthed and waiting underneath. Normally, though, have an overhang to any permanent work surface so that the edge of the trashcan slips underneath it, thus avoiding bits of rotten tomato or chicken giblets falling on your feet.

Something to Cook On ▪ The cooker is the heart of the galley. And as if to emphasize its importance, there are no less than five main types of

Something to cook on, something to chop on, and something to do the dishes in.

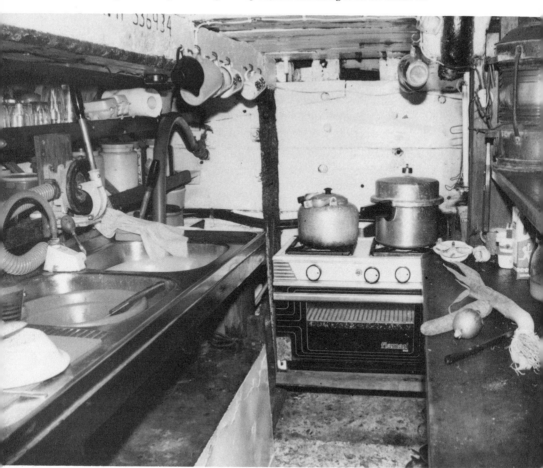

yacht stove to choose from: solid fuel, diesel fuel, gas, kerosene, and alcohol. (See also "Gasoline and Electric Stoves" on page 22.) Which you choose depends on many things: climate, cash, size of boat, safety, and patience, to name a few.

STOVES AND COOKING FUELS

Solid and Diesel Fuel ▪ If you plan to cruise in temperate zones why not install either a solid- or diesel-fuel stove? Both wood and diesel are easily available, and there is nothing quite so cozy and inviting as a cabin heated by a proper kitchen range and chimney. The oven is always hot, egging one on to bake scrumptious homemade bread and cakes while the kettle gently sings beside the hob. Wet clothes dry out in front of it; so do wet people. And if the weather suddenly turns hot, then it's easy enough to switch off and substitute a small primus instead.

The main disadvantage of the diesel stoves that I have seen is that they always call for a small amount of electricity to distribute the heat inside. This may involve more battery charging than you want and is no good at all on a pure sailing craft, though I am convinced, that hidden away somewhere must still be a diesel stove which doesn't need electricity.

I do not recommend either of the above for hot climates. Whatever their manufacturers may claim to the contrary and despite insulation, they will inevitably overheat both the tropical galley and the cook.

So there remains the choice of gas, kerosene, or alcohol.

Gas ▪ I am slightly ashamed to admit that we use gas; most dangerous and unseamanlike. I'd better say right away that it is my choice, not Edward's. The reason is quite simple. Kerosene pressure stoves don't like me, a feeling which I heartily reciprocate.

Gas is so wonderfully easy. It heats quickly, regulates effortlessly, and is there at the strike of a match. So is death if one is not careful. Boats vanish into thin air in a gas explosion. Unburned butane gas sinks, slowly filling up the bilges until eventually it reaches the level of a lighted match. However, with a careful safety routine, accidents are avoidable.

Safety ▪ First, always stow gas bottles securely on deck with no possible way for leaked gas to seep down into the cabins below. Apart from a short, flexible pieceof reinforced plastic gas piping attached directly to the gimbaled cooker, have the rest of the gas pipe made of copper. Inspect both pipes and joins regularly for cracks and deterioration. Take great care when you light the stove that the minimum of unburned gas escapes; then make sure that the whole burner is lit. Always turn the gas off on deck after use.

If you do have a leak, pump out bilges that are already dry and eventually you will empty out the gas, too. (See "Explosions" in Chapter 24, "Safety at Sea.")

Bottles ▪ Apart from the intrinsic danger of gas, the other problem is filling the bottles. Almost every country in the world seems to conspire against the foreigner by producing its own "national" gas bottle head. Unless you can devise an adapter, you will end up with a fascinating collection of totally useless and unfillable containers. However, there are occasionally gas depots near major ports where they may agree to fill "alien" bottles . . . maybe.

In the United States it is best to use one of the major oil company brands. Camping Gaz is available throughout Western Europe. It is more expensive than local gas and just as useless once you leave Europe.

When buying or swapping a bottle, test the new one by dropping a good blob of liquid—spit is ideal—onto the gas outlet. If it froths even slightly, reject it. The bottle is not only dangerous but probably half empty as well.

When not baking much in the oven, I find a fifty-pound bottle lasts five people approximately six weeks.

Stove ▪ If buying a new stove, carefully measure the available galley space first. Stoves always look much smaller in the store than on board.

Place all gimbaled stoves, no matter what their type, at the side of the yacht with the hinge-down oven door facing inward. Most boat motion is a rolling from side to side, so installed like this, the gimbals swing back and forth to counteract the roll and stop the saucepans from spilling over or slipping off. Hinge-down oven doors are essential. Side-opening ones can, in seconds, tip the whole of Sunday's dinner on the deck.

Before you buy a gas cooker, check the tap design. The best type is one with a flat-sided knob which is vertical when fully on and horizontal when switched off and which has to be positively pressed in to release gas. It is much more difficult to switch on accidentally than the circular, twiddle type of knob, and you can see at a glance if one knob is not in the horizontal off position.

There are excellent quartz gas lighters on the market now, but you should still carry some matches in an airtight container. Avoid third world matches like the plague; the wooden shaft snaps in two, or they fail to light, or if they do light, their flaming heads fly off with alarming and often painful results. You would have thought the disadvantaged of this world had enough to put up with without being forced to buy rotten matches as well.

Kerosene ▪ Next on the list is the kerosene pressure stove. (Nonpressure kerosene cookers are both dirty and smelly, turning the deck head black and the crew green.) Primus has become the generic name for all kerosene stoves working under pressure. (Although Primus now makes only gas cookers, its design of kerosene stove is still available from the firm Optimus.) Several other makes are also available.

Pressure stoves take up very little space, are economical to buy and to use. One pint of kerosene lasts approximately three hours of cooking.

The problem with kerosene stoves lies in the fuel, not in the actual stove. Good, pure kerosene is very hard to come by, and impurities cannot simply be filtered out. They build up carbon deposits, which block the jet, putting out the flame. So buy the very best kerosene around.

Lighting a Primus ▪ To light a primus, first shake it to test that there is enough fuel in the bowl. Next prick the jet to make sure it is clean.

For a pressure stove to light, the head must be so hot that the kerosene vaporizes. This heating is done with alcohol or, in the modern primus, by a tiny generator. The generator has revolutionized lighting a primus, but unfortunately it is seldom available outside Western yacht chandlers and camping stores.

With the traditional type, alcohol is poured into a little dish underneath the primus head and lit.

Filling the dish is tricky. If it is not full enough, then the alcohol burns out before the head is red-hot; if it is too full, there is a danger it will overflow, spreading a stream of flaming alcohol down the outside of the primus bowl. So I now use a wick holder meant for lighting a pressure lamp. With it well soaked in alcohol I simply clip the wick holder underneath the primus head and light it. Not only is there no danger of a spillage but also if it is removed too soon, it can be put back at once and relit without danger. (On the other hand, if things go wrong while using the dish, you must wait for it to cool down before pouring in more alcohol and making another attempt.)

Once the alcohol is alight, shut off the butterfly valve on the primus bowl so that pressure builds up inside.

Now don't take your eyes off the wretched thing for a second. As the alcoholic flame fades, give a few tentative pumps. If you get long, licking orange flames, you've pumped too soon. Release the pressure at the butterfly valve and start again.

However, it is far more likely that the kerosene will catch alight with a good, steady hissing flame, quite short and almost colorless.

Congratulations! Your primus is lit and ready for use.

To reduce heat, it is better to place a heat-resistant mat over the flame rather than release some pressure which only encourages the jet to clog up.

To increase pressure / heat, pump more, but don't forget that there is a limit to how much pressure the bowl will stand. To turn the stove off, release the pressure at the butterfly valve completely.

Have I made it all sound horribly labored? I'm sorry. The generator-heated primus really has a great deal going in its favor, and even the old-fashioned ones have thousands of loyal supporters on yachts around the world. The primus is one of the safest, most compact and economical cookers there is. Added to that, it is totally mobile.

We take ours on deck in a bucket for boiling up pitch. Others carry theirs ashore for picnics and camping. Finally, because of the relative cheapness of kerosene as a cooking fuel, it is available throughout the developing world.

Cleaning a Pressure Stove ▪ If a pressure stove suddenly goes out, check that there is enough fuel in it before cursing. Quite often, though, it goes out because of impurities clogging up the works. First try pricking the jet with a fine primus pricker. If that doesn't cure the problem, then you could have to go at Edward's more drastic "head-cleaning" operation.

Remove the head and take out the jet (a good deal more fiddly than I've made it sound). Now heat the rest of the head either over another primus or with a blowtorch. When the head is really red-hot, plunge it into a bowl of cold freshwater. Accumulated impurities in the tubes will shoot out, and with any luck, the stove will work again.

No oven goes with a basic primus but there are box ovens that balance on top; some even fold flat after use. Though not as good as a thermostatically controlled oven, with practice they can be used for any cooking and roasting that you care to do. Some kerosene pressure stoves come with proper ovens attached.

Alcohol Stove ▪ I have no personal experience with alcohol stoves. However, I am told that they light more easily than kerosene and burn with less smell, though also with less heat. They are about as safe as kerosene, but any fire can be put out with water.

Their major drawback is that unless you are living and cruising solely in the USA, alcohol (or methylated spirits, as it is called in England) is seldom sold as fuel. And to buy it from the pharmacist in tiny bottles meant only for medicinal purposes prices it right out of the market.

When using alcohol for heating washing water as well as for cooking, allow about a gallon and a half of alcohol per week for a crew of four.

Gasoline and Electric Stoves ▪ I deliberately ignored both gasoline and electric cookers in my list of possibilities. I ignored gasoline because its highly explosive fumes make it far too dangerous a fuel to carry on board for either cooking or motoring. I ignored electricity because electric stoves, when used outside a marina, can operate only with an engine running. Not only is it inconvenient to start a motor every time you want a cup of tea, but even more important, it is extremely unpleasant for everyone else (like me) who has to listen to the racket and breathe in the exhaust.

General Stove Safety ▪ As mentioned before, all gas, kerosene, and alcohol stoves should be gimbaled. When Edward's thirty-six-footer *Sea Wanderer* turned upside down in the Pacific, all the crockery fell out and was smashed, but the kettle on the gimbaled stove stayed just where it was.

In addition to gimbals, fit fiddles. These are metal bars surrounding the top of the stove, sometimes around each individual burner, to stop sauce-pans from skidding off the cooker. Although it is practically impossible to gimbal solid- or diesel-fuel stoves (because of their chimneys), they, too, must be fitted with fiddles and the saucepans filled less full.

For safety's sake I much prefer a narrow galley. Then there's always something to wedge up against in rough weather. If your galley is open to the cabin behind, sew up a foot-wide canvas safety belt and position fastenings on either side of the sink or work top so you can strap yourself in during heavy weather.

OTHER GALLEY EQUIPMENT

Crockery ▪ Most yachts come complete with their own crockery stow-age. So that the crockery doesn't bang about, the stowage has to be a close fit. That means plates etc. have to be chosen to suit the stowage, not the other way around. Because of this, we prefer tall wooden pegs rather than solid surrounds. Then, if we later want to change the size or shape of our dinner plates, we simply saw off the old pegs and glue in new ones where needed. Each pile of crockery is held in place by the bulkhead at the back and three evenly spaced pegs in front.

What to eat off depends on personal preference and on whether this is a holiday venture or a life-style. Crockery comes in metal, enamel, china, wood, or plastic.

Despite dents, tin plates last forever, let the heat go straight through them, make a fearful clatter in the galley, are cheap, and are found almost anywhere.

Enamel can be attractive, but when it is chipped the underlying metal rusts. As with tin, you risk burned lips if you drink out of an enamel mug, and eventually the handles may fall off, too.

China will break when the yacht turns upside down or when the wash of a passing speedboat shoots it off the table. But it is pretty.

Wood is beautiful, too, but difficult to clean, and it cracks if left out in the hot sun.

Good plastic is very tough and conserves heat. It does stain. (Try soaking stained plastic in a denture-cleaning powder.)

If you are fitting your boat out for weekend and vacation sailing, plastic is probably the most sensible choice. I chose china because I expect to spend the next twenty years afloat. The thought of all those thousands of meals eaten off plastic plates was rather daunting. If *Johanne* ever does turn upside down, the chances of her coming back again are such that I would be only too happy to go out and buy some new china to celebrate!

The best designed boat bowls have upright or even curved-in edges so that soup or milk doesn't slurp out. In rough weather mugs, not bowls, are better for soup.

I have two large, brightly colored plastic bowls with airtight lids which I use for holding salads and risottos, mixing cakes, proving dough, and taking food ashore on picnics and barbecues.

We now have the luxury of an oven on *Johanne* so I've bought a couple of Pyrex casseroles, though I think the pretty enamel saucepans which go equally well in the oven or on the table are really the answer to the restricted stowage problems on yachts.

Saucepans ▪ This brings us to saucepans. We all have our own favorites, but don't forget that seawater, and even sea air, incite anything that can rust to rust. Despite this, I would not part with my heavy iron skillet for the world. Instead, I treat it with extra care, washing it only when necessary and then protecting it with a smear of cooking oil.

Look for saucepans with side lugs rather than long handles. Galleys are not only small but also inclined to heave about. Long handles sticking out are a real danger to the cook, to say nothing of possibly wasting all that good food on the galley sole.

If you can afford them, stainless steel saucepans, particularly those lovely ones with copper bottoms, are ideal. Enamel pots are okay and, as mentioned in the section on crockery, can double up as serving dishes, too. Aluminum does not rust but will sprout bubbles of aluminum oxide if left with drops of salt water on it. Basically, though, aluminum is suitable for boats, provided you are not worried about what it is said to do to our brains.

Pressure Cooker ▪ One saucepan which is indispensable to any galley is the pressure cooker. We have two.

With a pressure cooker potatoes take ten minutes to cook from start to finish. Joints of meat want only twelve minutes to the pound, and a loaf of bread bakes on one moderate flame in less than an hour.

Not only does the pressure cooker save enormously on time and therefore fuel, but it saves freshwater as well. Because it cooks most things in steam, salt water can be substituted for fresh. A pressure cooker reduces the time needed for cooking lentils and other pulses till they are no more of a chore than any other food.

Vegetables correctly steamed in the pressure cooker retain more of their minerals, salts, and vitamins than in normal cooking. Using the internal separator pans provided with a Prestige pressure cooker, you can cook meat, vegetables, and a pudding all at the same time in the one pressure cooker.

Pressure cookers are also excellent for making jams, preserving fruit, and sterilizing both baby's bottles and medical instruments.

Once the food is ready and pressure reduced, the cooker will retain its heat for half an hour or more in the tropics—ideal if someone wants to finish that five-minute job before eating.

Finally, if you reduce the pressure in a bowl of clean salt water, serve up, and then put the hot cooker straight back in the bowl, in five minutes you'll have hot dish washing water as well. What more could you want?

There's another saucepan now being manufactured which is said to work like an oven but on the flame of one burner. The flame goes up through an enclosed central hole while the food is arranged inside around the edges. It is claimed to bake potatoes, vegetables, even bread and cakes.

Toaster ▪ Those of you who love toast but have no grill, do not despair. There are two types of stove-top toaster around which bring at least a hint of toast afloat. One is a metal tent which stands up over the flame with one piece of bread leaning against either side. The second is flat with a handle and two layers of metal an inch apart and punched full of tiny holes, rather like a Ping-Pong racket. The bread is laid flat on top and turned over when done. As far as I know, neither is made in stainless steel, so their boat lives are short. Because of it, I now lay my bread flat on a dry, hot, heavy skillet and toast it that way. It works fine.

Grill. Another gadget for the grill-less galley is shaped rather like a skillet, only rectangular instead of round. It has raised ridges down the middle and a moat around the edge to catch the juices. It "grills" meat, fish, bacon, or halved tomatoes from the underneath upward.

Kettle. The type of kettle with a flame trap around the base is more efficient and so heats quicker.

Cutlery ▪ Look for knives and forks made of first-class stainless steel. Lower grades resist rust for only a year or two. Check that knives are well balanced. We have some infuriating ones with extra heavy handles. They are forever toppling off the plates, scattering gravy as they go. Stock up with lots of teaspoons. Boats seem to consume them in extraordinary numbers.

However much you may shrink from the idea, a can opener comes in mighty handy on board. I recently came across an excellent one which works on a simple up-and-down wrist movement with no working parts to go wrong. The curved blade cuts cleanly and safely, pushing all the nasty jagged edges inside.

Mugs and Glasses ▪ We drink coffee and tea out of mugs. Their design is more stable than cups, and they don't require saucers. I hang them up on hooks along a beam, where they look attractive while being out of the way. The only drawback I've found is, Where do you put the teaspoon? (Maybe that's why saucers were invented.)

Nearly all cruising yachts stock up with the famous French Duralex glasses which are shatter-resistant rather than actually unbreakable.

Bottles ▪ Always try to buy unbreakable bottles. Stow them in a long, narrow locker or, if you have the room, in a plastic bottle crate. I line ours up single file along the foot of the water tank and hold then in place with a bit of stiff wire.

Refrigeration ▪ Here looms another major decision: to refrigerate or not to refrigerate?

Refrigerators are now so compact that they fit into the average cruising boat with no trouble at all. But space isn't really the problem. The question is, Is all the extra hassle really worth it?

Undoubtedly in the tropics the idea is tempting, ice-cold drinks, meat, and milk lasting longer and so on.

The trouble is twofold: one, power; the other, maintenance. For despite every effort, refrigerators always seem to break down in the end. And for some reason, once people are hooked on refrigerators, they become psychologically unable to survive without them. Sometimes a whole cruise is abandoned while frantic owners hop up and down, waiting for their next "fix" of spare parts. Hanging around in out-of-the-way places for spare parts to mend a delicate mechanism which was never intended to come in contact with salt air seems to me to belie the whole concept of cruising freedom, embracing, instead, the frustrating life of the imprisoned commuter.

The other trouble with refrigerators is that they run either on gas, which is both dangerous and expensive, or on electricity, which means long, noisy charging of batteries.

Some acquaintances of ours (I would not call them friends) charged their batteries six hours a day just to keep their food and drinks cold. They said the noise didn't bother them at all; they went ashore while the engine was running. The rest of us were not amused. Okay, that's an extreme case, but even one hour a day is too much racket for me. On the other hand, the moment someone produces a solar panel powerful enough to work a refrigerator without backup, I'll forget the maintenance, swear never to become hooked, and go out and buy one like a shot.

I have not included kerosene refrigerators here because though excellent ashore, they cannot cope with the rolling of a yacht.

If, despite all my negative comments, you still decide to buy a refrigerator (and I expect most people will), do at least check that it opens from the top so that all the cold air, and the contents, don't fall out onto the galley sole.

Icebox ▪ An alternative to the refrigerator is the icebox. This is inconvenient in that you have to buy the ice ashore, though in most warm parts of the world it is readily available near the dock. In less sophisticated places there may still be a store ashore which boasts a freezer. Take in a couple of bowls of freshwater and ask if they can be frozen for you.

Solid block ice in a good icebox will last for three to four days. Be sure the water the ice is made from is drinkable. Contaminated ice is a common source of stomach bugs.

I find our icebox very useful indeed. In cold climates it acts as a large extra locker. Then, when the temperature rises, I fill it up with ice as and when available. Our particular model has a handy little spigot near the bottom for siphoning off ice water, which, if it is clean, we drink. On our leaving the West Indies, the icebox served yet another purpose when, at our farewell party, it was filled to the brim with strong rum punch while the friendly little spigot liberally dispensed drinks from the bottom.

2. The Head

~~~~~~~~~~~~~~~~~~~~~~~~~~~~~~~~~~~~~~

LIVE-ABOARD BOATS are always fitted with some sort of head (marine toilet). The most basic is a bucket with a lid and, if you are lucky, a curtain around it for privacy.

Heads come in all shapes and sizes. Often very small ones are fitted to very small boats, presumably on the assumption that the owner's requirements will also be very small. Others are highly complicated affairs, impossible for the casual visitor to operate. This can lead to splendid scenes as the embarrassed owner shouts instructions through the locked door.

Some types of heads are prone to both leaking and breaking parts. (Our last one squirted horrible cold liquids up ones pumping arm after only a couple of years' use.) We have now installed two Lavac vacuum heads, which, for the first six years, gave us absolutely no trouble at all. The operation is simple enough for a small child to master, and the results are excellent. Some years ago Lavac switched to porcelain bowls after its previous product—fiber glass-coated aluminum ones—proved faulty. I now feel confident in recommending them to anyone who wants a simple, trouble-free (well, almost trouble-free) head.

Never put anything apart from human waste and small amounts of toilet paper down a mechanical head. Dispose of sanitary napkins, tampons, and soiled diapers separately, or they will block the valve system, which then has to be totally dismantled.

Be particularly wary of electrically operated heads with no manual backup system. It is bad enough to have the electrics fail, but to be unable to flush the head as well is an unnecessary added disaster.

That leads us to effluent storage tanks. If your boat is equipped with a holding tank, make sure it can be emptied manually as well as electrically. In the States one is, by law, forbidden to discharge untreated sewage from a boat into harbor or coastal waters. A very good law it is, too. But with that law must go all the satellite facilities: frequent sewage collection points, effluent treatment chemicals on sale everywhere, and so on. Unfortunately, in the rest of the world such facilities are not only unavailable now but likely to remain so.

So, when in countries lacking such arrangements, have a thought for the places you visit. And *never* pump out a head when you are in a marina where adequate heads are provided ashore.

Let me just add, for any foreigners thinking of sailing into U.S. waters, the U.S. Coast Guard is authorized to search all yachts, checking that you have either a proper holding tank or a special head which chemically treats and churns up sewage. If not, you are in for a hefty fine. There is one exception, however. If you still favor the old "bucket and chuck it" system, they'll let you off scot-free. Such is the logic of bureaucrats.

3. Electricity

ELECTRICAL GADGETS are fickle servants, especially on board boats. When they arrive, there's an initial, frustrating, settling-in period while you get to know their ways and sort out all the design faults they brought with them because their designers never actually had to use the gadgets they invented.

Then, for a while, they are marvelous. At the press of a button and without a word of complaint, they haul up heavy anchors, start engines, measure the depth of water under the keel, the strength of wind at the top of the mast, work out where you are, and give you light. Why, they even flush the head and steer for you . . . for a while.

The trouble is, electrical equipment has an enemy aboard: salt air.

A major weapon in the battle against salt and corrosion is to install a twenty-four-volt rather than a twelve-volt system. The extra current is often enough to break through strangling growths of corrosion on delicate wiring, especially important for electrical equipment on deck.

Ultimately your only real security lies in having a reliable backup system for all vital equipment. We once went on board a very luxurious charter yacht in the West Indies. Down below all was plush velvets and polished parquet flooring. There was only one very obvious fault. Both the heads and their holding tanks could be pumped out only electrically . . . and all the yacht's electrics had failed.

So never install an engine which does not have an alternative system to its electric starter, be it hand crank, impulse, or air.

The windlass, perched as it is on the foredeck, among flying spume and crashing waves, is one of the most vulnerable bits of equipment on board. If electric, it almost invariably breaks down. Since hydraulics are far more reliable anyway, I wouldn't accept an electric windlass as a gift. I wouldn't accept a hydraulic one, either, unless it could also be operated by hand.

If you have an echo sounder (after an electric starter, probably the most useful electrical boating toy around), do keep a proper lead line stowed neatly below.

If planning to sail long distance, consider a self-steering gear rather than an autopilot. Along with suffering from the usual drawbacks of all electrical equipment, autopilots are a merciless drain on batteries when they are operating under sail. If you do decide on a wind-powered self-steering gear, however, avoid those with a servoblade. Every tale I read of servoblades has them snapping in two like third world matches.

Remember, too, when leaving home and loved ones for far distant lands, that your ship-to-shore radio is as prone as anything else to electrical faults. In fact, it only needs the batteries to go flat for electrical equipment aboard to die. So warn relatives not to panic if they don't hear from you. It could be nothing more than a dynamo or alternator collapse. (See also "Radio" in Chapter 24, "Safety at Sea.")

If you invest in satellite navigation, bear in mind that until there is constant satellite feedback, it will never be perfectly accurate. Sat. nav. has shown yachts on land when they were actually bobbing around at sea and, unfortunately, vice versa. So keep your sextant well polished and be sure you know how to use it.

One expert skipper, in charge of half a million dollars' worth of yacht, insisted on turning off all the electrical wizardry aboard for twenty-four hours of every voyage, ensuring that the crew could navigate and steer without it.

That puts electricity on board just where it should be, a wonderful convenience never to be totally relied on or taken for granted.

4. Lighting

Electric Light ▪ Talk of electric light presupposes an engine and good batteries. If you have both, then electric light must be the leading contender for lighting on board, but do ensure that the lights run off twenty-four volts, not twelve (See Chapter 3, "Electricity.")

Fluorescent bulbs give a bright, though harsh, light. They are easy to replace as ordinary household bulbs work perfectly well in the twenty-four-volt fitting.

Pressure Lamp ▪ The best-known pressure lamp is probably the Tilley. It, too, gives a harsh, bright light and suffers from all the common ailments associated with impure kerosene. However, pressure lamps produce an excellent reading light and can be carried anywhere you like on the boat. Keep a good supply of spare mantles and also a couple of spare vaporizers, the former because they are so fragile and the latter because they can be hard to come by. Pressure lamps give off a heat which is pleasant in temperate climates, not so pleasant in the tropics unless they are used on deck.

If heading for the tropics, check that your lamp has the special insect guard which stops bugs from flying inside the glass and breaking the fragile mantle.

How to light a kerosene pressure lamp. First make sure you've enough fuel by giving the lamp a gentle shake. Next tighten the valve at the base of the plunger. Now take the alcohol-soaked wick lighter (we keep ours permanently steeped in a small jar of alcohol so it doesn't go brittle), and fix it under the glass lamp cover. Light the wick.

When the mantle at the top is red and glowing and the wick flame is beginning to die down, open the little knob just under the lighter by turning it counterclockwise. Now give a gentle pump. If the mantle turns whiter and the lamp hisses, pump several more times until the light no longer increases. Your lamp is lit.

The manufacturers warn against overpumping. They say that with too much pressure the bottom of the fuel tank may burst off. Frankly I almost wish they hadn't mentioned it. Now I sit in ever-increasing gloom until a braver soul than I comes along to do the pumping.

During the evening the pressure inside the bowl will drop. Give it a couple more pumps and it will shine bright again.

If, after that first tentative pump, soft flames lick up rather than white light, close the little knob by turning it clockwise. Heat the mantle a bit longer before trying again.

Sometimes the light fades not from lack of pressure or fuel but from dirty kerosene blocking the jet. This will be evident if, on pumping, you fail to improve the light.

Try turning the little knob off and on very quickly. This pushes a needle into the jet to clean it. But you must be very quick indeed; otherwise the light will go out completely. Always have a match and flashlight ready in case. If the light does go out, strike the match at once; then hold it as close to the mantle as possible without touching it. With any luck it will relight.

If it does not, you will have to start again with the wick and the alcohol, first twisting the knob back and forth several times to make sure the jet is really clear.

It is important never to touch the mantle, for once it has been used, it becomes as fragile as gossamer.

To turn the light off, twiddle the small knob clockwise as far as it will go. The light will die away from lack of fuel. We also release the pressure by opening the valve on the plunger. This is not strictly necessary, but otherwise kerosene occasionally oozes out.

In the event of a flare-up, turn off the knob and release the pressure at once. Because such a flare-up is possible, never leave a pressure lamp unattended.

Kerosene Wick Lamp ▪ Wick-burning lamps include hurricane lamps, at least one of which should be on every yacht, and also the traditional bronze gimbaled lamps with their beautiful mellow light, perfect for an evening chat, not so good for reading by.

Hurricane lamps come in many makes, some of which blow out in the merest zephyr while others, such as a good Dietz, keep going in a gale.

We always use a hurricane lamp for a riding light. There are several reasons for this: They do not drain the batteries, they can't blow a bulb, but most important, in anchorages backed by electric lights onshore, the yellow warning glow of a hurricane lamp is much easier to pick out against the white and greens of the town.

A wick should burn in an even, straight line. If one corner burns higher, it will cover the inside of the glass with soot. Inspect the wick before lighting it. Often a match end, rubbed over the edge of the wick, will remove any charring. If it is really crooked or badly burned, cut the wick straight again with a sharp pair of scissors. Keep water from splashing on the fragile glasses of bronze lanterns.

One final general comment about cabin lighting: position the lights so none shines out onto the helmsman, thus ruining his night vision.

5. Heating

~~~~~~~~~~~~~~~~~~~~~~~~~~~~~~~~~~~~

IF YOU ARE SAILING in the colder parts of the world, various types of solid fuel and diesel stove are available. They not only warm and dry the boat but can be used for cooking as well. (See "Stove and Cooking Fuels" in Chapter 1, "The Galley.") If you have more variegated cruising in mind, look for a smaller heater to use only on cold days and evenings.

Kerosene is probably the most economical heating fuel, but it is not so easy to find in the West as in the developing world. We have a couple of kerosene wick stoves which are satisfactory as heaters although they do not dry the atmosphere like wood or charcoal. Also, remember that with any chimneyless stove, it is most important to ensure that there's enough ventilation down below. Otherwise on a cold night, with everything tightly battened down, the stove will gradually burn up all the oxygen, asphyxiating the crew members in their sleep.

Gas stoves are dangerous insofar as gas is explosive, but it is a good deal easier to find in Western countries than kerosene.

In addition to our kerosene stoves, we have a small wood-burning heater. Edward swears he gets hotter before the fire's lit, chopping all the wood for it, then he ever is once it is finally burning. Not quite fair, for once it gets going, it gives off a good heat and dries the air well, as does any stove with a chimney.

There are also kerosene pressure stoves. Their chief drawbacks are that, like a primus cooker, they are susceptible to impure kerosene and flare-ups so must not be left unattended for long.

My personal choice for cold-water cruising would be a solid-fuel stove, such as a Shipmate, which both heats and cooks; a kerosene wick-heater; and a single primus as a standby for those places that occasionally have real summers.

6. Water

PEOPLE CAN survive more than a month without food but only a few days without water.

Once you quit the land and take to the sea, you will find your whole attitude to water undergoing a radical change. Suddenly it becomes more precious than platinum. So let's look at some techniques for conserving this most treasured of earth's gifts.

For a start always have two entirely separate supplies of water so that if one tank leaks or becomes contaminated, you have another one to fall back on. Try to keep the water in both tanks at approximately the same level; otherwise, by Murphy's Law, the second tank is bound to spring a leak just as you drain the last drop from the first.

I also like to have a couple of full jerry cans at the ready in case we have to abandon ship. Some people store all their water in jerry cans distributed evenly around the boat.

On ocean voyages the traditional freshwater allowance is half a gallon per person per day. That's pretty tough. Four pints to drink, with nothing left over for cleaning your teeth.

Nowadays, at least in the tropics, doctors recommend a minimum of six to eight pints of drinking water per person per day to combat dehydration and heat stroke. (See Chapter 14, "Health and Illness.") If possible, carry a further 50 percent in reserve in case of accidents to either water tank.

Water Supply • There are two main ways of watering ship: from the sky and from the shore.

During two years of cruising in the West Indies we used shore water only for washing clothes. We did everything else in pure rainwater. But to do that you must be well armed, whether at sea or in port, for the great moment when it comes.

As the dark clouds gather, grab every container you can lay hands on: barrels, buckets, saucepans, the inflatable dinghy (preferably scrubbed clean first), the baby's bath, washbowls, anything at all which might conceivably be pressed into service and, at sea, tied down so it won't scoot overboard.

A piece of canvas or plastic sheeting, slung above the foredeck so that is sags in the middle, makes a great water catchment area at sea, as does the awning in port.

When the clouds finally spew down their precious burden, quickly rush your containers under all the best water chutes. Save the first, brackish water for clothes washing (perhaps in the inflatable). As soon as the water tastes okay, lead hoses to your water tanks or empty jerry cans, and siphon off from the buckets on deck.

Even at sea, provided there's no strong wind or heavy swell, you may actually catch water faster than you can siphon it. Once we caught 150 gallons of glorious pure drinking water from a single mid-ocean downpour.

Now is also the time for that heavenly shower you've been dreaming about. Strip off and soap up. Work those salt-laden locks into a fine foaming peak of shampoo. Everyone else aboard will be happy too—for it's almost guaranteed to stop the rain in mid-lather.

If you are designing a boat for cruising, incorporate a drainage system that catches water off the cabin top. But remember to scrub the top first before running any rainwater into the tanks.

In port put up your awning and see where it sags most. Cut a hole at the lowest point on either side, and sew in short cloth funnels. From these lead your hose pipes directly to the tanks below.

The other main source of water is the shore. Nowadays most ports in the world have safe drinking water, but before filling up, check that it is palatable as well as pure. At a historic port in Europe we once watered ship without doing a taste test first. That port authority could make its fortune bottling its water by the ounce and selling it as "Genuine Sixteenth Century."

Water Sterilizing ▪ Where the shore water is suspect and the local rainfall low there are various ways to sterilize drinking water.

Try purifying tablets, but test them first because some taste disgusting. Two drops of 2 percent tincture of iodine to one pint of water also kill most bugs. Or you can purify water by boiling it, but that wastes valuable fuel.

Finally there's potassium permanganate. Add just enough to turn the water slightly pink (the merest pinch); then let it stand for fifteen minutes. After this the water is ready for drinking. If the water turns brown, it is unfit to drink no matter how long you leave it. If you put in too many crystals, the water will turn red and may give you a sore throat as well. Add water until it turns pink.

That said, I must own that the last time we bothered to sterilize drinking water was seventeen years ago in what was then Portuguese Timor. There, more than 70 percent of the population had amoebic dysentery and our daughter, Katy, was less than a year old.

While we are on the subject of sterilizing, don't forget local produce. Never eat raw fruit or vegetables from a street stand or at a restaurant unless you wash and peel them yourself. If uncertain about salads at home, soak everything in a pink solution of potassium permanganate for fifteen minutes. Though not 100 percent proof (nothing is), it kills off most germs.

Washing: People ▪ If you are spending your vacation in marinas, then this section does not apply to you. You can nip ashore any time for a shower and take over the marina Laundromat for your dirty clothes.

In more out-of-the-way anchorages washing tactics vary considerably. How much salt water you use depends very much on the yacht's freshwater supply and whether you are port-hopping or crossing an ocean.

When coasting, I never use salt water but instead ration myself to half a basin of freshwater per wash, just enough to sluice off the grime and sweat. In the tropics we augment proper washing with swims and bucket baths of seawater. Not only do they keep us vaguely clean, but they fend off the dreaded specter of heat stroke as well. (See Chapter 14, "Health and Illness.")

When water is seriously limited, as on an ocean passage, freshwater showers become a luxury, while baths are good only for storing onions, and even then the onions may stain the bath.

In fact, it is perfectly possible to wash yourself in salt water. I press the dishwashing liquid into service as soap though some shampoos also lather well. I have been told that liquid detergent gives you cancer, but then, it seems to me, there's precious little that doesn't these days. Still, if you are worried, apart from shampoo there are saltwater soaps on the market specially designed with the well-to-do yachtsman in mind.

If you hate the sticky feeling after a saltwater wash, nab a mug or two of freshwater and rinse yourself off with that.

For a hot wash either heat up a small amount of water in the kettle or else, on hot days, hang a black plastic shower bag in the sun for a few hours; but don't scald yourself when you open the nozzle.

Most Western yacht clubs welcome overseas visitors and allow visiting crews to make the most of their facilities. Spain is an exception. There most of the yacht clubs are in reality very exclusive social clubs with little to do with sailing and everything to do with status. The last thing they want is grubby yachties sullying their immaculate marble halls. However, with luck, that same grubbiness will remind other friends ashore to invite you up for a bath.

Washing: Hair ▪ To be a success, hair washing really does need some freshwater. To use the minimum, put two pints into a flaring, steep-sided bowl. Then wet your hair, letting the excess run back into the bowl. Now lean over the side of the boat, or over a deck bucket if it's rough, and rub in the shampoo. (I find tube shampoo best at sea. It can't fall over or spill.)

Rinse all the shampoo off with salt water. Finally rinse out the salt by bailing freshwater from the original bowl, a little at a time, over your hair, letting it run onto the deck and firmly squeezing out the salt water still in your hair between bails. If you can spare four pints of freshwater, then the saltwater rinse is unnecessary.

In ports where no showers are available ashore, I have sometimes taken my shampoo and towel to a public lavatory and washed my hair there. Tote a thin plastic bag and a lump of putty along, too. Public basins seldom have plugs. If the water is cold, pack a vacuum flask of hot freshwater as well.

Washing: Dishes ▪ Once the freshwater tanks are topped up for a long cruise, your chief aim must be to keep them that way.

At sea or in deserted bays wash dishes in salt water plus a good splash of liquid detergent. Then leave everything to drain for a while before drying up; otherwise the drying-up cloth gets horribly salty. But do wipe mugs and glasses before putting them away or your more forthright guests will want to know where you bought your intriguing new brand of salted coffee.

An alternative is to washup in salt water, then rinse everything in a shallow bowl of fresh, allowing one bowl to last the whole day.

None of the above applies in port. There are harbors in this world where simply breathing in the rising stench seems guaranteed to bring on a premature demise. As for the water itself, it is obviously only fit for dying in. In such places I save the fresh rinsing water from one meal to act as washing-up water for the next.

If doing the dishes in a bowl rather than a sink, once again do remember to run your fingers through the water before chucking it over the side. I know of one man who stocked his whole cutlery tray with spoons and forks he'd dredged up from harbor bottoms with a strong magnet.

Washing: Clothes ▪ When coasting, I wash all clothes in freshwater, mostly ashore. Nearly every anchorage with houses has some sort of freshwater supply, and even isolated bays sometimes offer superb washing facilities. One of my favorites was in a deserted corner of northern Spain. There a stream tumbled down through the trees and over a rocky ledge before cascading into a rock pool near the beach.

Even more exciting is scrubbing clothes in a river. Not only do you stand with water, and maybe fish, swirling around your legs, but there's also that sudden buzz of adrenaline as you dive off downstream after a truant scrubbing brush, bar of soap, or pair of socks.

Many villages in the developing world have special shady spots set aside for doing laundry. The local people are usually most welcoming and eye my extraordinary efforts at the tub with quite as much fascination as I get from watching them flailing their sarongs against rocks or pounding skirts with smooth stones to get them clean. (It's worth investigating local theories on cleaning clothes before letting someone loose on your favorite evening shirt.)

To be honest, however, such picturesque settings are the exception not the rule. Everyone has his own pet way for doing the washing. Below, I describe how I do it. It may give you some ideas; it may not.

First dissolve some detergent, then distribute it among several buckets of freshwater either collected previously from the shore or caught from the sky. Provided you remember to clean the inside of the dinghy before a cloudburst, it makes a wonderful scrub tub. We once collected so much water in ours that I managed to do a huge wash, including three large bedcovers, without going ashore at all.

Bioactive detergents, while excellent for loosening dirt from soaking clothes, are possibly bad for your skin and certainly, like all detergents, bad for the environment.

Now, sort the washing into whites, coloreds, and frankly filthy. Then put them in separate buckets to soak. Never soak woolens, elasticized garments, or anything you think might run.

After the clothes have soaked for anything up to five hours, pick out one garment at a time, and brandishing a nylon scrubbing brush and a bar of soap, give it a good scrub on the cabin top.

To my surprise it wasn't long before I discovered that gently rubbing the dirt out of clothes until they look clean is a wonderfully soothing and satisfying occupation. On the other hand, there's nothing like a good, aggressive scrub to relieve tension, but it is best to do that on tough jeans or old towels. My favorite type of brush, by the way, is nylon, multi-pronged but not very stiff. Animal bristles are either too hard and wear the clothes out or too soft and no use at all. Shield both nylon and bristle brushes from hot sun.

Having scrubbed everything as clean as possible, wring it all out and drop it back into the emptied buckets. Load the buckets plus a large sheet of strong, clean plastic into the dinghy. The shore party is ready for departure. Head for the nearest source of freshwater. Many fishing villages have a faucet right on the dock; others have a well in the center of town. In more sophisticated places you may once again have to make for the public lavatories; they provide excellent laundry facilities.

Once arrived, make yourself at home. If working in the open air, spread the plastic sheet on the ground beside the well or faucet; then tip the contents of the buckets onto it.

If the local water supply is ample and the drainage around the faucet adequate, rinse everything in overflowing buckets of clean water before finally wringing them out and again piling them on the plastic sheet to keep clean.

Often, though, water is not plentiful or there is nowhere for the dirty water to run to. Then I use a more tedious rinsing routine.

It goes like this. Quarter-fill each bucket and proceed to rinse everything bit by bit, with a system of wringing out each and every garment very hard *before* each rinse.

As each bucket of water turns cloudy, relegate it to primary rinsing, saving the next clean water for the final rinse, still wringing the clothes out very firmly between each rinse.

You now see what I mean about tedious. But I do think the extra effort is worth it. For with this process, one big bucket of freshwater, rationed out a little at a time, is enough to rinse a fair-size wash. It not only saves the village water supply but stops one from stirring up a quagmire around the village faucet as well.

Once everything, including the plastic sheet, has been rinsed transfer it back into the dinghy, wave good-bye to the interested sightseers, for you will undoubtedly be considered a "sight," and take everything back on board to be dried. (See Chapter 15, "Clothing," for tips on drying, ironing, and stowing laundry.)

Clothes Washing at Sea • If possible, wait for rain. Catch all the first brackish water which comes off the sails; then use it to do the laundry in the same way as you would a frugal wash ashore. If, however, there's not a cloud in the sky yet your clothes are revolting, then you'll have to make the most of what little freshwater can be spared.

Clothes constantly washed and rinsed entirely in salt water feel horribly uncomfortable, rough, and thick, and they never dry properly because the salt in them constantly absorbs moisture from the air. Salt also rots cloth. So, although it is quite possible to wash clothes in neat salt water with liquid detergent or shampoo taking the place of soap, I have evolved a method which uses a minimum of freshwater while giving at least passable results.

This time don't soak the clothes at all. Instead, fill a bucket with salt water. Briefly dunk the first thing to be washed in the water; then scrub it thoroughly, substituting either diluted shampoo or liquid detergent for soap. But watch out. Liquid detergent may remove the dye as well as the dirt!

When everything is scrubbed to your satisfaction, rinse it all thoroughly, but quickly, in salt water. Finally put whatever freshwater can be spared in the bottom of the buckets and, using the same system as before—wringing every garment out very thoroughly before putting it into the next bucket—get as much of the salt out as possible. (See Chapter 15, "Clothing," for tips on wringing out clothes.)

I never use salt water for washing big water- and therefore salt-retaining things like towels and jeans. For those I usually wait for the next downpour though I have been known to stuff them all under a bunk till the end of the voyage. It only needs one salt-laden towel to ruin a whole bucket of fresh rinsing water.

Grease Stains ▪ When it comes to removing oil and grease from clothing or people, Swarfiga is an excellent commercial standby. Rub it very thoroughly into the dry stain until you see it has lifted the grease. Then immediately scrub it all out. It works miracles. However, I have known Swarfiga destroy the waterproofing on oilskins. Another, much older remedy for removing tar and oil is to soak the area in oil of eucalyptus until the stain looks runny. Then wipe a wet bar of soap over it to remove the softened oil before giving the while garment a good wash in soapy water. That is, unless the garment is for dry cleaning only.

Salt Water for Cooking ▪ To save on freshwater at sea, cook vegetables in a pressure cooker with salt water up to the trivet. When ready, put the cooker in the sink and reduce pressure with salt water. (See "Pressure Cooker" in Chapter 1, "The Galley.")

Both rice and pasta can be boiled in partly salt water. (See Chapter 8, "Eating Afloat.") But for heaven's sake don't overdo it. I remember one appalling meal. We were very low on water so I tried cooking spaghetti in neat seawater—not a success.

Make the most of any freshwater left over from cooking. Rather than throw it away, thicken it into stock for soups or gravy, and do the same with the nutritious liquids drained from canned vegetables.

One final tip: You'll waste less freshwater if you make tea with a cup and a tea bag rather than a pot and tea leaves. With the latter some liquid is always chucked out with the leaves.

7. Storing Up

The Quantity of Stores ▪ What and how many stores you buy depends on two things: your immediate objectives and the size of your boat.

If the plan is for a two-week vacation cruise, stopping in a harbor or marina most nights, then Chapter 10, "Vacation Planner," is for you. With those basic stores aboard it will only be a question of popping ashore for fresh food when necessary.

If, on the other hand, that same vacation is to be spent gunk holing in remote bays, then Chapter 9, "Menus for Ten Days," might prove a more helpful guide. If you also want some ideas on preserving your fresh fruit and vegetables, then read on.

When you are contemplating longer passages, a detailed stores list is a must. But no need to overdo it. Before my first ocean crossing I got in a complete panic, certain we would all starve because of my catering incompetence. I sat up late into the night working out a ten-day menu. Two such menus, modified, appear in Chapter 9.

Once I had the menus, I worked out in minute detail what staples and canned goods would be needed to provide that ten days of food for four people. Next I multiplied the result by how many groups of ten days we expected to be at sea: four. Finally I added a third as much again in case of delays, ending up with an item-by-item list of stores I considered indispensable to the survival of four people setting out on a possible fifty-five-day voyage.

It worked perfectly. No one starved. But what an effort!

Nowadays, having, among other things, stored up for a yearlong stay on a desert island, which never came off (then what do you do with all that flour?) and for a trip of a hundred days from Singapore to Suez, which did, I'm much more relaxed. I have devised a delightfully simple system based on "cans per day for four."

Again, start by estimating how long the trip will take, and add on one-third extra for safety. Then allow the following basic number of cans per day to cover lunch and supper for four people:

> Three sixteen-ounce cans of vegetables
> Two sixteen-ounce cans of fish or meat
> One thirty-two ounce can of fruit

Add to this your staples, such as rice, pasta, potatoes, onions, pulses,

and milk, plus your cheeses, soups, crackers, drinks, and flavorings (see the following list). Include whatever it is you eat for breakfast, and a crew of four should complete the voyage with good health and contented stomachs.

For example, on *Johanne* we eat muesli for breakfast. Then, when we are four aboard, I open two cans of vegetables plus one of meat or fish for lunch, combining them with staples such as rice or potatoes. We either have soup to start with or a milk pudding to follow. For supper we eat one can of vegetables and one of meat, plus more staples, and we finish off with a large can of fruit.

I also like to carry extra supplies of rice, dried milk, oats, and beans for sprouting "just in case." No, I'm not desperately nervous. I am willing to learn from experience. We once expected a trip to last thirty-five days and finally reached our destination seventy-five days later. I was glad of those extra rations.

Below is a rough guide to the quantities of staples needed to satisfy normal healthy appetites.

Quantities of margarine, cooking oil, and instant coffee are particularly dependent on the cook's and crew's preferences, so check how much you use per day before storing up.

Our sugar ration works out at about two tablespoons per person per day including cooking. This is already quite a lot, but again, check with the crew before storing up. You could be shipping a sugar freak.

Flour quantities depend entirely on your culinary ambitions. Some people bake bread every day; others wouldn't recognize dried yeast if they saw it. Flour is also necessary for sauces, cakes, and cookies.

How many eggs you buy depends on whether you eat them for breakfast.

When assessing quantities from advertisements, be pessimistic. If the manufacturers claim their packet of soup makes four large helpings, I would expect it to make two. The same applies to dried vegetables and fruit.

Shelf Life ▪ Before dashing out to buy enough stores to last a decade, bear in mind that many foods have a shelf life, though rice, for one, lasts for centuries. Dried milk, flour, and instant mashed potatoes all have an approximate shelf life of six months, provided they are kept in airtight containers. Once they are opened, raising agents quickly lose potency and so are best bought in small bags or cans. As for crispy breakfast cereals,

How many stores you buy depends on your immediate objectives and the size of your boat.

STAPLE	QUANTITY	NUMBER OF PEOPLE	LASTS
Cooking oil	1 pt.	4	1 week
Instant coffee	1 lb.	4	2 weeks
Margarine	1 lb.	3	1 week
Milk powder	1 lb.	1	10 days
Oats (for muesli)	1 lb.	1	8 days
Pasta	12 ozs.	4	1 meal
Potatoes	12 ozs.	1	1 meal
Rice	12 ozs.	4	1 meal
Sugar	1 lb.	1	1 week

they go soggy in no time. (In third world countries, where only maladapted expatriates eat them anyway, dry cereals are soggy before they even arrive.) They also take up far too much locker space.

To be fair, however, the last cereal package we bought did at least give us a good laugh. We were anchored off the African coast when, in a moment of weakness, I gave in to Katy's pleas; she wanted to enter the painting competition advertised on the package. Back aboard we studied the rules only to discover that the closing date for entries had passed . . . two years before. The flakes were none too crisp either.

Canned goods, unless they are acidic like rhubarb, last at least one year, if not two.

Freeze-dried goods, unopened and undamaged, will last twelve months or more.

Canned or Dried? When you buy stores for a long passage, you must choose between those that take up space and weigh a lot like cans and items that are dehydrated and therefore need lots of water added to them. Which you select hinges on your stowage and water tank capacity as well as on personal preference. You may decide, like us, to compromise and take some of each.

Freeze-Dried Vegetables and Fruit ▪ Buy dried peas and onions in quantity. They last well and are excellent both on their own or added to rice and stews. Dried apple is delicious and extremely quick to prepare. Instant mashed potatoes varies considerably from brand to brand and, once opened, has a short shelf life. I provide some ideas for making it more palatable (and boy, does it need it) in Chapter 8, "Eating Afloat."

While we're on the subject of dried foods, don't forget ordinary dried beans and lentils. They keep indefinitely, and with a pressure cooker, you can quickly produce highly nourishing soups and stews from these simple pulses. And how about taking alfalfa, soy, or mung beans for sprouting? That way you have a fresh salad every day of the trip. (See Chapter 8.)

Milk ▪ My own preference here is for a good instant dried milk. It tastes quite like the real thing, mixes easily, and lasts well. It is also very versatile. You can mix as much or little as you like so it won't go sour, and it can be added to recipes either reconstituted or neat. But dried milk does presuppose adequate water tanks.

Evaporated milk, once opened, does not keep for long. It should be diluted with an equal part of water unless it is consumed thick, as a cream substitute, when it is delicious. It will curdle if mixed with acidic fruit.

Sweetened condensed milk is often favored by those with a sweet tooth. It has the advantage of not going off once opened. I use it for making milk puddings. Never give sweetened condensed milk to babies.

When you are coast-hopping and if you have room to spare, Longlife milk is bulky but good and needs no water added.

Cream ▪ Longlife cream is excellent. Canned cream has a definite tinny taste. See Chapter 8 for help in disguising it.

Soups ▪ Soups can be both healthy and interesting. For a filling main meal try mixing a basic soup with a can of vegetables plus rice, pasta, or potatoes. Or drop in some eggs and poach them, unbroken, in the liquid. Soups are ideal on cold dark nights at the helm, and even in the hottest parts of the Red Sea we found a good salty soup most welcome.

I personally prefer the taste of canned soups to dried and have fun experimenting with mixing together different varieties: cream of chicken with asparagus; red bean plus mushroom.

For night watches in cold climates I boil up a couple of vacuum flasks of water, and then it is up to the person on watch to decide whether to add it to instant coffee or instant soup. Instant soup is nothing like as good as the real thing; in fact, I reckon it's pretty indigestible. So, if I am cooking soup for supper anyway, I make enough extra to fill one of the flasks. Tiller Soup (see Chapter 8) has always been a favorite with sailors.

Canned Meat and Fish ▪ Canned stewing steak and ground beef form the basis of a variety of meals: steak for stews, curries and pies; ground beef for pasties, chili con carne, spaghetti bolognese, and shepherd's pie. I never buy cans of ready-made stew because they consist almost entirely of gravy and colorless vegetables with a rare piece of meat thrown in to satisfy the consumer protection people.

Often the gravy in canned meat has a rather unpleasant taste. (See Chapter 8 for tips on improving it.)

Canned fish will go farther if a sauce is added, as will canned meat. Avoid buying large quantities of fish in tomato sauce: the sauce palls quickly, and the fish is not nearly so versatile as that canned in oil or brine. Don't forget that small cans of such delicacies as shellfish, squid, and kippers offer an interesting addition to risottos.

Canned Vegetables and Fruit ▪ Canned vegetables are inclined to taste either watery or tinny, but shop around because some are excellent. Buy as many varieties as possible and ring the changes. Canned sweet corn is always popular. Mixed vegetables go well in casseroles, curries, soups, risottos and potato salad. Canned tomatoes are said to retain their vitamins better than other canned vegetables, while canned spinach and broad beans taste just like the real thing.

When abroad, check out local canned foods. Malaysia and Kenya both have excellent ones while Argentinian corned beef is the mainstay of many a lone sailor. But always sample one can before buying in bulk. Chinese canned fruit is luscious, but their canned pork is, to Western taste, virtually inedible, consisting almost entirely of soft white fat.

On long voyages I like to carry a few special foods for celebrations plus little extras such as asparagus, ham, and anchovy-stuffed olives for well-timed morale boosters.

Drinks (hot) ▪ For some inexplicable reason people's drinking habits undergo dramatic changes once they put to sea. A perfectly sober tea drinker may suddenly turn into a jittery coffee addict and vice versa, or everyone may switch to hot chocolate and all my reserves vanish (one crew cleaned out my whole two years' supply of dried mint in a single weeklong mint tea binge), so take a large and varied store of beverages. Tea bags save on freshwater if you put one in each cup and add the boiling water.

Drinks (cold) ▪ Plain water flavored with tangy citrus is most quenching in baking calms. Warm, gassy drinks are not for hot days, though some say they are good for seasickness. Tea, coffee, and Ovaltine can all be drunk cold. Fruit juice is both refreshing and nourishing but bulky to stow. Finally, there is alcohol of many types for those who like a little extra comfort in their bunk.

Whenever possible buy drinks in unbreakable cans or plastic bottles.

Buying and Keeping Fresh Food ▪ Fresh foods are the luxuries of an ocean passage and part of the pleasure of a gunkholing vacation. The art is to ensure that they last as long as possible. This hinges in part on temperature. The survival times in the tropics are less than half those in temperate climates. (Scientific experiments in Nigeria showed that spinach picked in the early morning had lost 90 percent of its vitamin C by midafternoon.)

So rule number one is that all produce must be bought as fresh as possible. That means none of your giant supermarket foods. I once stocked up from a huge supermarket in Puerto Rico. Never again! Within two days nearly everything had turned to rotten slime, unable to survive normal outside temperatures. The survival times given below are therefore for fresh produce bought from ordinary local markets in the tropics. In temperate climates you can safely double the times. In either climate always choose fruit and vegetables individually, a little underripe and without blemishes.

Vegetables ▪ *Potatoes* last about five weeks if they are stowed in well-ventilated darkness. If left in the light, they turn green as a result of an increase in the poison solanine. Never eat green potatoes. Buy them brown, firm, and shootless (spring is a bad time to buy potatoes in bulk). I always load up with a whole sack of potatoes before a long voyage, then check frequently for rot. One sniff suffices.

Onions survive better kept in the light, which retards sprouting. Before buying, check that onions are really firm at both ends with no shoots showing. Once onions have sprouted, they quickly rot inside. Well chosen, onions last even longer than potatoes.

Garlic keeps for months and is a good source of vitamins. It was garlic bought in Spain which saved the lives of Magellan's officers when they crossed the Pacific. There is also a possibility it reduces the levels of blood cholesterol.

All foods must be bought as fresh as possible *(taken in Turkey).*

Tomatoes may be bought both red and green and firm or hard to the touch. Store them stalk upward. The green ones will last several weeks.

Green beans, green peppers, and cucumbers do not last long in the tropics but will survive two to three weeks in cooler climes. Green peppers, threaded on strings and dried in the sun, will keep indefinitely, but most of their rich vitamin C content will be lost by drying.

Cabbage lasts well. Check the stalk frequently. If it is at all soft, cut it out; then store the cabbage stalk up so it dries out. Store cabbages in an openwork plastic or wicker basket for ventilation.

Carrots should be fat. Thin ones shrivel in the heat. In the tropics try standing them upright in a bowl with a plastic bag covering but not touching them. This helps conserve their moisture.

Squash and pumpkin are the very queens of vegetables. Stored separate from each other in airy racks, they seem to last forever. Once opened, they quickly go bad, so buy small ones.

Sweet potatoes, taro, and yams all begin to shrivel after a week.

Fruits ▪ *Citrus* fruits will last several weeks. Limes, being small, go hard after one week. Weigh up grapefruits before buying them. Test them in your hands; the heavier they feel for their size, the more fruit they have inside.

Bananas are a delectable bore. Buy a whole bunch and they all ripen together. Turn to Chapter 8 for some ideas on what to do with them.

Apples keep well, provided they have not been frozen or mishandled. Store them separately.

Soft fruit which is easily bruised is best left behind.

Fresh Fish ▪ If you do happen to land a big un in the tropics, it will keep if you cook it twice a day. Alternatively salt, dry, or pickle it. (See "Cleaning Fish" and "Salting Fish" in Appendix G, "Fish.")

Fresh Meat ▪ Cordon Bleu cooks, please don't throw a fit when I tell you that if meat is well cooked twice a day, it too will keep in the tropics. (In cold climates it needs cooking only once a day.)

I always requisition the pressure cooker, with its higher cooking temperatures, for this job. After bringing the meat up to pressure, I then cook it for one to five minutes. (If the meat is insufficiently heated, germs actually breed rather than die, and severe food poisoning can follow.)

I do not suggest overcooked meat for a dinner party, but if you have bought a large joint or caught a nine-foot shark, it is certainly one way of preserving it.

Another way, if the weather isn't too scorching hot, is to hang freshly bought meat on a hook in the rigging.

Choose the meat carefully. It should be in one solid chunk with no loose flaps and preferably no fat. If possible, buy it on a breezy, sunny day. Then, when you hang it up, the outside quickly forms a hard, dark red skin while inside, the meat becomes beautifully tender. Ensure that the meat hangs in an airy place with nothing touching it. If drying properly, the meat will not smell at all or attract flies. Take it below if it rains.

In countries without refrigeration, meat is sold freshly killed, hence is very tough. Hanging it helps tenderize it. We once kept a hunk of raw beef in the rigging for twenty-three days before eating it. Five to seven days are ideal.

In the tropics an alternative tenderizer is pawpaw. Smear it over the meat, and then leave it in a cool place for eight hours.

If raw meat is just beginning to go off it can sometimes be revived by being given a good wash and rub with salt water. If it then smells perfectly fresh again, it is edible. Pressure-cook it at once.

Good-quality salami and smoked meats last for months if hung up.

One way of preserving freshly bought meat is to hang it in the rigging.

Whenever possible, suspend fresh food in air: onions in sacks, plaits, or old stockings; bananas hung by the stalk; and the same for pineapples. Those nylon string bags sometimes provided by supermarkets are fine for suspending vegetables from a hook. I store cabbages and pumpkins slung under a beam in a well-ventilated plastic laundry basket.

Eggs ▪ The storage of eggs is surrounded by a great and glorious myth: that eggs go bad very quickly. On a recent trip we bought ten dozen eggs from a supermarket, did absolutely nothing to them, and six weeks later we had had only a couple of bad ones.

If you want to preserve eggs longer, then choose them individually and with care. (Careful selection is probably the most important single factor in fresh food preservation.) Make sure that the eggs come straight from a chicken, not from a refrigerator. Eggs which have pinpoints of translucence on their shells are already stale. Reject them, for they will go bad quicker.

Some people turn eggs every day to keep the yolk from sticking to the shell. I prefer to stack my eggs point down. The yolk then drifts slowly up to the rounded top end and sits under the air sac instead of adhering to the shell. The boat's rolling also helps.

Some people put eggs in a muslin bag, then lower them for ten seconds into boiling water. This hardens the very outer white and seals off the interior. Others cover eggs in oil or Vaseline. Thor Heyerdahl smeared his eggs with a lime paste.

For really long-term preservation (desert island candidates, please note), store eggs in a solution of water glass (sodium silicate, either powder or syrup, plus water), but don't forget, boats roll and water spills.

To prevent eggs from breaking, I place them on layers of egg trays in a cardboard box.

Cheese ▪ Firm cheeses survive a little longer if cut in cubes and immersed in olive oil. Alternatively, wrap a block of cheese in vinegar-soaked paper, and then put it in an airtight box with a couple of lumps of sugar. Beautiful soft French cheeses are available in cans, but in the tropics they won't keep past the first meal without refrigeration. I once came into the galley the next morning to see an exquisite Brie taking off under its own maggot power.

We found Greek feta cheese has exceptional lasting qualities. The shopkeeper doubted it would survive three days out of a fridge. We bought four pounds anyway, popped it in a plastic bag in an airtight box, and took it right down the broiling Red Sea with us. It stayed good to the last morsel.

Butter and Margarine ▪ In temperate winters well-salted butter will keep for several months without refrigeration. Once one moves south, however, butter, even in cans, tends to liquefy. If buying canned butter, try shaking the tin gently, close to your ear. If you hear any liquid on the first shake, then there is a good chance the butter inside is rancid. As a rule we switch to canned margarine when it gets hot.

Bread ▪ Shore bread, unless black and very solid, will last only a few days. There are several alternatives. You can substitute crackers or buy packages of rye and wheat crisp breads, both highly nutritious, though about as much fun to eat as a pack of cards. Double-baked bread is very hard and rusklike and lasts almost indefinitely if kept dry. Later those with sensitive gums can soften it up by dunking it in tea or coffee.

My own solution is to carry crackers and to bake bread if and when required. Bread mix is convenient when available; otherwise dried yeast and plain flour will do. Dried yeast is worth stocking up on because it can be hard to track down. Buy it in the smallest cans possible because each time a can is opened the yeast loses some of its potency.

If you have no oven try cooking bread in your pressure cooker. (See Chapter 8.) If you cannot be bothered to churn out real bread, then scones and soda bread using baking powder are quick and easy and can be made either in the oven or in a heavy skillet on top of the burner.

With your cans, dried provisions, staples, and fresh foods safely bought, don't forget all those flavorings which add that extra spice to life.

Flavorings ▪ Buy lots, and use them often; salt and pepper, herbs and spices all in tightly sealed jars, jams, honey, syrup, pickles (especially popular at sea), olives, sauces, vinegar, sherry, wine, brandy, candied peels / fruits / cherries, soy sauce, tomato paste, Parmesan cheese (if you've room, take it), plus nuts, raisins, candies and cookies for snacks at the helm. We also treat ourselves to a couple of squares of chocolate after supper each night.

Nonedibles ▪ Then there are all the nonedible stores, such as liquid detergent, soap, toothpaste, head paper (some people use amazing quantities), tampons, shampoo, detergent powder, Handi Wipes, paper towel, aluminum foil, disposable diapers, scrub brushes, boxes of matches in an airtight container, mosquito coils, batteries for everything and to spare, medicines, spare flashlight bulbs, cooking fuel, diesel fuel, spare parts, and more.

Specialties ▪ It won't be until after you've left that you'll discover which foods are unique to your homeland. Then, to your astonishment, you will find that foods you thought everyday items are quite unknown in other parts of the world. So ask returned wanderers what goodies they advise you to stock up on. Here are just a few of the foods which I have missed abroad: real jam with fruit in it, ketchup, angostura bitters, baked beans, Worcestershire sauce, gravy browning and mix, maple syrup, cornmeal, and peanut butter.

Discount ▪ Once the stores list is ready and if money is short, go around the local markets and supermarkets comparing prices. Ask for the manager, spin a good yarn, and try for a discount. And don't be fooled by advertisements. In Piraeus, the port of Athens, one supermarket advertised in huge letters that it gave a 10 percent discount to all yachts. Great! On investigation I found that the 10 percent discount in no way covered the 15 percent markup already put on each item.

If you manage to wangle access to a wholesale caterer, then you will make big savings on bulk buying.

Transport ▪ Once the food is bought, transporting it to the boat is not always easy. When storing up for a long voyage away from home, you obviously hire a taxi or pickup or hijack a car-owning friend. But for everyday shopping, it's more often shank's mare—my shanks, too. After years of lugging vast loads of vegetables and fruit sometimes a couple of miles from the market to the boat, I abandoned my pride and bought myself a granny shopping cart. It was such a success that I now have two, one for each hand.

When buying a cart, make sure it folds flat and give it an extra coat of paint as these carts seem particularly prone to rust.

If you don't want a cart, how about a fold-up bike? We have had great fun with ours. Not only are they useful for humping shopping and gas cylinders back to the boat, but they are also a good way to see the countries one visits.

Stowing Stores ▪ Once all the stores are gathered on the dock, you have two ways of dealing with them.

In cold climates, provided there's room, you can immediately move the lot aboard to be sorted. But in the tropics this is the moment to mobilize the front line of your cunning anticockroach strategy.

First, don't allow any cardboard boxes on board unless they are completely debugged. Cardboard boxes harbor both cockroaches and their eggs, which later hatch out. Submerge all bananas, another favorite home for happy roaches, in a bucket of seawater, or lower them into the sea. Any insects will gradually float out or drown.

Now to the real test of your patience. To be quite certain no cockroaches or eggs come on board, strip the labels off the cans and then write the contents on with indelible marker. Frankly I have neither the patience nor the time for such labors; instead we spend both time and patience fighting cockroaches. (See Chapter 21, "Pests.") It is a great help to buy cans with the type of content imprinted in the actual metal, but there are not all that many brands around that do it.

Cans ▪ Along with the egg myth goes another one that says cans must be stripped of labels, names, and varnished, roach problems or no, just to stop them from rusting.

I have never done anything to ours and regretted it only when I have accidentally overstocked in a massive way. (I once ordered a case of tomato paste cans only to find that there were three hundred to a case, not the two dozen I had expected.)

The only place where cans definitely do need the full treatment is in the bilge. Even if it's dry when you put them in, it is well to take every precaution, if only to prevent the possibility of soggy labels clogging the bilge pump in an emergency.

Where else you stow cans varies according to the sort of cruising you have in mind.

If you are coasting, it is easiest to stash all the staples near at hand and then have the cans distributed around the remaining locker space. With luck you will have no call for them at all as good fresh food should be available ashore.

For longer distances I like to have one locker for meats, another for vegetables, and so on. Whatever you do, make a list of where everything is. I once lost a precious can of maple syrup for two years! When thinking about stowage, don't forget jerry cans. I store all my rice, oats and mueslii in them. Sugar, too, stows well this way. My main flour supply I store in a small plastic barrel, and whenever possible, I buy it in one-pound plastic bags.

If, when in developing countries, you have to buy flour from an open sack, treat it as follows. Collect a wide-necked storage container; a small barrel or large cookie tin will do. Now sieve the flour into the container to remove the larger grubs and weevils. Then pound the flour down as firmly as you can. I continue until all the flour is a rock-hard compact mass—all, that is, that is not up my arms, in my hair, and on the floor.

The theory, my own, rather brilliant, I thought, is that if the flour is pounded solid enough, the weevils cannot breathe, therefore cannot grow. It works pretty well, too. Flour which normally keeps a month or so before being totally infested has lasted me more than a year. The only trouble is that I have since discovered it's not my brilliant idea at all. As long ago as 1627 Captain John Smith's *Sea Grammar* advised that ship's stores should include "fine wheat flour close and well packed." The whole thing, in fact, is old hat!

Everyday supplies of tea, sugar, milk and flour I stow in large, gaily painted empty cans which have airtight plastic lids. The cans last about five years, when it is simple enough to replace them with a new batch. Otherwise, pliable, rather than brittle, plastic is best for containers. And have them square rather than round. They waste less space that way. Jerry cans are also efficient space users.

If you have a long ocean passage ahead, consider assigning one complete berth, the sides suitably built up, to storing bulk foods like jerry cans of rice.

Heavy-Weather Stores ▪ I reserve one whole locker for heavy-weather stores. Easy to lay my hands on, they are also easy to prepare and easy to digest. Hot soups are at the top of my list. Creamy ones like chicken or mushroom stay down well, though some people prefer tomato or salty beef stock. Serve tiller soup in mugs to avoid spilling and spoons. Condensed soups are quicker to heat up and more digestible than the dried variety. Ground beef or whitefish and rice all provide excellent extra ballast. Crackers are both filling and soothing.

Finally, try to eat "little but often" in bad weather. (See "Seasickness" in Chapter 14, "Health and Illness.")

8. Eating Afloat

A GOOD DEAL of what is eaten on boats, particularly on long voyages, comes out of cans or packages. This can lead to a monotonous sameness of taste, so add fresh vegetables to canned or dried casseroles. If there are none, not even those great stalwarts the onion, garlic, or bean sprout, then try adding mixed herbs, Worcestershire sauce, or, best of all, a good slurp of red wine. Homemade gravy also peps things up a bit.

Canned carrots which taste either watery or tinny improve considerably when they are chopped thin and cooked up in a parsley sauce. Slice *canned potatoes*, and toss them in dried mint and melted butter. *Spinach*, well drained and tossed in margarine, is very like the real thing. Canned *broad beans*, if you like them, are particularly good and go well in a white sauce.

Instant mashed potatoes may be made a little more appetizing by adding half a bouillon cube to the boiling water and letting it dissolve before adding the milk and potato powder. A good dollop of margarine, a pinch of garlic salt, even a little ground nutmeg all help disguise that dreary, powdery taste.

Did you know you can make *mayonnaise* by mixing vinegar with sweetened condensed milk if you've run out of eggs? Sounds disgusting, doesn't it, but I was amazed to find that I actually preferred it to some of the over-oily store products.

Most yachts have some sort of cookbook aboard already, although really cookery cards are far more practical. They lie flat, take up hardly any space on the work top, and are easy to clean. Better still, make your own. Copy favorite recipes from cookbooks at home onto index cards; then cover them with clear plastic. They can then be kept permanently on the boat.

The Intricate Art of Living Afloat is not a cookbook, and I am certainly no cook; but I have scattered a few recipes throughout this chapter. They are recipes which recommend themselves both for their ease in the making (anything that takes longer than thirty minutes is a dead loss as far as I am concerned) and for their popularity in the eating. *Oat crisp* is one of them.

If, like us, you start your day with homemade muesli, try adding some oat crisp to give it an extra bit of crunch.

For this you need one-quarter cup (2 ounces) margarine and one-quarter cup (two ounces) sugar for every one cup (three ounces) oats.

Melt the margarine in a heavy skillet. Mix in the sugar, and add the oats. Stir well until all the oats are moist. Continue to stir the ingredients over a moderate flame until the oats turn a pleasing honey brown color.

Empty them out onto a large baking tray to cool. Stir them occasionally to stop the crisp from sticking together. Once the crisp is absolutely cold, either mix it with ordinary oats for breakfast or put it in an airtight jar for a topping to puddings and fruit or simply for a quick snack when you feel peckish. Fruit and nuts add richness.

Talking of richness, I am sorry to say that *canned cream* is strangely cloying. Mix it thoroughly with a few drops of vanilla extract and a little sugar. Taste until it is right but not until there is none left.

To thicken canned cream and make it stretch, mix up a small amount of cornstarch and water. Cook it until it is well set. Allow it to cool. Transfer it to another bowl, and slowly add the canned cream until it is well mixed in. The cornstarch should not constitute more than one-quarter of the bulk of the cream.

Cream whips better if an egg white is added to it.

Dried milk makes things creamy when a large amount is dissolved in a little water; add to mashed potato, soups, or sauces.

Make two holes in the lid of an *evaporated milk* can so that air is sucked in one and the milk runs out the other.

When you are on a long trip, prepare two meals in one. For instance, have potatoes for supper, and cook enough for the remainder to be used in a potato salad or fry-up the next day. The same applies to rice and spaghetti, both of which make an excellent base for vegetable salads. In winter they can form part of a filling soup.

Tiller soup has infinite variety. Use a basic soup or soup mix or the stock from previous cooking or the liquid strained from canned vegetables. Allow half a pint of liquid for each person. If using a soup mix, follow the packet instructions.

While the liquid is still cold, add any of the following uncooked foods: dried peas, dried onions, rice, pasta, or cracked wheat. Allow half a handful per person. Bring the soup to the boil, and then simmer it for fifteen minutes to allow everything to cook. Some canned soups cannot be boiled, in which case cook the staples first and stir in the soup afterward. Add extra water or evaporated milk if it looks a bit thick, or stir in a cornstarch paste to warm, not boiling, soup if it is too thin.

If using rice, pasta, or potato left over from the previous meal, add them in the last five minutes, along with whole raw eggs if making that particularly delicious variation egg drop soup.

Serve tiller soup in mugs, half full. This is a rough cold-weather dish, good for morale and prevention of seasickness. One favorite combination is tomato soup with rice and chunks of fish cooked in it. For the tropics a thin, salty broth base is better.

*Rice.*To my mind rice is unrivaled as a staple. It forms the basis of so many dishes and, stored properly, lasts forever.

My mother cooks beautiful rice by putting the grains into a large saucepan of boiling water. But on a boat large saucepans of boiling water are at a premium. So try this method for cooking rice. It uses the minimum of fresh water.

For every two people you need cooking oil, one cup of long-grain rice, one cup of freshwater, and one scant cup of salt water.

Now put a dash of oil in a saucepan or heavy skillet which has a lid. Measure into it the cleaned rice (see Chapter 21, "Pests," for a rice-cleaning system).

Fry the rice gently for a few minutes without browning. Add the water; the exact quantity varies with the rice. Stir with a fork, and cover.

Cook on a high heat until the rice boils. Quickly turn the heat to simmer. Simmer the rice for twelve minutes without lifting the lid. Now the rice should be cooked, though times, like the quantity of water, vary with each strain of rice.

There is one other ingenious way of cooking rice which uses practically no fuel at all. Put one cup of rice in a wide-necked vacuum flask. Add three cups of boiling salted water. Screw the cap on tightly, and leave it for two to three hours. If you do this at breakfast time, you will have cooked rice ready for two people at lunch.

However, this is only of use if you want plain rice. With the saucepan method you can fry some onion in the pan before adding the rice. Freeze-dried peas or green beans, thrown in right after the cold water, will be cooked when the rice is. (Add a little extra water to allow the vegetables to rehydrate.) Toward the end of the cooking, stir in chopped tomatoes, green or red peppers, and leftover meats, and you have a risotto ready made.

To jazz up rice for a dinner party, fry chopped fresh mushrooms in butter, and stir them into the cooked rice. Then, in the same pan, fry blanched almonds sprinkled with salt until they are golden brown. Stir them in, too.

Another dish ideally suited to entertaining large numbers of people on small boats is a paella. Everything except the rice can be prepared beforehand. The essential ingredients are chicken, ham, some shellfish, and peas. If you can trace black olives, fresh mushrooms (canned will do in a pinch), and a few drops of angostura bitters, then it will be a real feast. Try to make the paella so it has more goodies in it than rice.

Cold rice makes an excellent summer salad when it is mixed with cold vegetables and French dressing.

Even that is not the end of the wonders of rice. How about this everyday dish which is different, popular, and quick to make? To serve four people *rice with bananas,* you will need two cups of rice, six rashers of back bacon, butter, four ripe bananas, four to eight eggs, salt, and pepper.

Cook the rice as before. Meanwhile, chop the bacon into small squares. Fry them in butter till crispy. At the same time chop up the bananas into quarter-inch-thick rings. Put the crispy bacon on a plate. Fry the banana rings in butter until golden (use margarine if you must but butter really does taste much better in this dish).

When the rice is cooked, season it, add the bacon and bananas, and cover to keep warm. Fry one or two eggs per person. Serve the rice mixture onto plates, and top with the fried eggs.

If you only have one burner, fry up the bacon and bananas as above. Put them together on a large plate, and use it as a saucepan lid while cooking the rice, putting the real lid on top of the plate to keep everything hot. When the rice is cooked, add the bananas and bacon, and keep the saucepan warm with a thick towel or blanket. Fry the eggs and serve as before.

If you are not already convinced of the versatility of rice, here's a dessert to finish up with.

Anyone who likes *creamed rice pudding* will be glad to hear that the pressure cooker makes it beautifully. Follow the instructions carefully, though, because milk under pressure is volatile stuff.

To make enough for four people collect together a small knob of butter, one pint of water, four to five soup spoons of sweetened condensed milk, and one-third cup (two ounces) of Carolina rice.

First melt the butter in the pressure cooker to stop the rice from sticking to it. Mix in the water and sweetened condensed milk, and bring it quickly to the boil in the open cooker. Add the rice. Stir the rice until the milk is again boiling and beginning to rise up the inside of the cooker. Lower the heat until the rice is just bubbling in the bottom of the pan.

Put on the lid, and raise the pressure to fifteen pounds *without* increasing the flame. Pressure-cook for twelve minutes. Reduce pressure slowly at room temperature, and you'll find a marvelously creamy rice pudding inside waiting for you.

Pasta. Although pasta doesn't rate as high as rice, it still has more uses than bolognese, lasagne, ravioli, and macaroni cheese. Try it in soups or with hot mixed vegetables coated in a sauce flavored with cheese or Tabasco. Or again, have it cold with mixed vegetables and mayonnaise as a salad.

Crumble. Another good filling standby is crumble. It acts as a topping for either a vegetable casserole or fruit.

For the crumble topping rub one and a half cups (six ounces) of margarine into three cups (twelve ounces) of plain, preferably whole wheat flour until it is like fine bread crumbs. If you plan to make *vegetarian crumble* (our daughter Kate's favorite seagoing dish), stir in half a packet of celery soupmix as well. I have given pretty large quantities of flour and margarine as we all love crumble. Halve the quantities if you prefer.

Once you've rubbed the margarine and flour together, put the mixture into a dry, very heavy skillet.

Cook without any additional fat, turning the crumbs all the time to prevent burning. It will take about seven minutes to cook. When the mixture is crisp and light brown, remove it from the skillet.

In port I make the underlying casserole with fresh vegetables, but at sea I fry some onions and then throw in canned baked beans, carrots, tomatoes, and mushrooms plus the rest of the package of celery soup.

For a *fruit crumble,* mix one scant part fat and sugar with two parts flour. Rub to crumbs, and cook as above. Sprinkle over stewed or canned fruit. In England rhubarb, apple, or blackberry and apple are all very popular fruit crumbles.

This stove-top method of making crumble not only saves time and fuel but I think makes a more crunchy crumble than one baked the normal way in an oven.

Eggs. When breaking eggs, crack each one separately into a cup or else get in the habit of giving a very gentle crack first and then a sniff before adding the egg to the main mixing bowl. A bad egg will quickly reveal itself. I do sometimes wonder, though, what our poor guests think as they watch me surreptitiously sniff at each egg before adding it to their dinner.

To check for bad eggs when making *oeufs aux officiers,* however, you will have to float the uncooked egg in water or check the shell for large patches of translucence. This is because it is made from soft-boiled eggs. Oeufs aux officiers is really more of a lunchtime snack than a hearty meal. (Edward's name for it derives from the fact that officers eat in a mess and this is one.) Well organized, it takes as long to prepare as it does to boil and peel an egg.

For each helping you will need: one slice of bread and butter, one or two eggs, one diced tomato, chopped green pepper or leftover peas (optional), knob of margarine or butter.

Soft-boil the eggs until the white is just firm but the yolk still definitely runny.

While the eggs are boiling, chop the bread into inch squares, and put them in a breakfast bowl. Add the diced tomato, plus the green pepper or green peas. Top with a knob of margarine or butter. Once the eggs are ready, remove them from the water. Holding one egg wrapped in a paper towel, decapitate it and pour the hot contents onto the knob of margarine so it melts. Scoop out the remaining white, not forgetting the bit left in the lid. Repeat with egg number two. Then stir up the whole into an egg-impregnated mess (the officers).

For this dish to be a success, the eggs have to be really hot and the yolks really runny. The quantities may be adjusted to the appetite of individual officers, who should all be commanded to decapitate their own eggs as that is the only tedious part of the process.

Bread. If you have no bread ready for this tasty dish, then why not make some? No, no, really, don't shudder like that. Making bread is actually very easy—and fun. Something children enjoy helping with, too. And it is no good saying you haven't an oven. Bread bakes almost as well in a pressure cooker as in an oven.

One word of warning before you start: If you wear any rings, either remove them or tape them over. Kneading is a messy business; hence its appeal to children. It is less sticky if you oil your hands first.

Now follow any bread recipe from a good cookbook. Remember that temperatures are very important. Yeast is a living organism. Make it too hot, and you kill it; too cold, and it never gets going at all. On a boat you will probably be using dried yeast (one-half ounce of dried yeast equals one ounce of fresh yeast), so heat the water until it feels pleasantly hot to your fingers, before you pour it over the granules.

When you come to knead, do it swiftly and firmly, squeezing and stretching the dough to spread the yeast around. Dough which has been kneaded enough is pliable and elastic with a certain lightness and resilience. If the dough feels stodgy and dead, it could be due to the original temperature of the water or the age of the yeast as much as to the kneading.

When the dough is ready for its first proving (rising), put it back into the mixing bowl and enclose the whole lot in a large plastic bag (the bag keeps out any drafts). Find a warm place for it to rise (68°F is the perfect temperature; 85°F is too hot).

On cold days I heat some water in the pressure cooker, turn the flame off, and suspend the bowl of dough above the water inside the warm cooker with the lid on.

Proving until the dough doubles its original size may take one hour, or five, or ten, but it must double to be successful. The longer it takes to rise, the better the bread will taste . . . or so they say.

After kneading a second time, prove the dough again for about twenty minutes. A French baker taught me a handy trick for knowing when this proving is complete. Take a little bit of the dough. Roll it into a ball, and pop it into half a glass of fresh water. The ball will sink to the bottom. When it rises to the top, the main dough will also have risen and be ready for baking.

Now, if you have no oven, put the dough into a greased pressure cooker tin, cover it with two, deeply pleated layers of greased greaseproof paper, and tie it down firmly. (The pleats are to allow the dough to rise.) Have an extra length of string looped over the top to form a lifting handle.

Pour one and one-half pints of boiling fresh water into the cooker (salt water will do in a pinch, provided it cannot get under the paper). Put the trivet into the cooker, and stand the bread tin on top. Close the cooker, and steam the bread on a *low* flame for ten minutes. Now bring the cooker up to fifteen pounds pressure, and pressure-cook the bread for thirty minutes. Reduce the pressure at room temperature. Incidentally this same pressure cooker method "bakes" cakes as well.

Bread is cooked if it sounds hollow when tapped on the bottom. Pressure-cooked bread tends to be damp on top, so dry it under a grill, in a hot oven, in the tropical sun, or upside down on a hot skillet.

Chapaties. If bread takes too long and, anyway, you want something for tea *now,* make chapaties. They are terrific eaten hot with butter and jam or, of course, with an Indian curry.

For a good batch take two cups (eight ounces) of flour (whole wheat or self-raising is best) plus a little salt water to mix. Mix the flour with enough

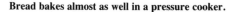

Bread bakes almost as well in a pressure cooker.

salt water to make a flexible dough. Roll it into two-inch-diameter balls. Now roll out each ball till it is wafer-thin; use an empty wine bottle if you have no rolling pin.

Heat a heavy skillet without oil until it is hot. Drop the chapaties one by one onto the skillet, cooking each side until it is slightly brown before turning. Each one takes about two minutes to cook. What I call a good recipe.

Drop scones. One final quick bread substitute, which I think is heavenly eaten hot and topped with butter plus a squeeze of lemon or scrape of honey, is drop scones.

Use either two cups (eight ounces) self-raising flour *or* two cups (eight ounces) of plain flour plus one and one-half teaspoons of baking powder. You will also want one tablespoon margarine, three level teaspoons of baking powder, one-fourth cup (two ounces) of sugar, one egg, one cup of milk, a pinch of salt, and, if you want, three level teaspoons cinnamon or mixed spice.

Put a heavy skillet on to heat with one tablespoon of margarine brushed over it. Sieve the flour, baking powder, salt, and spices into a bowl. Beat the egg and milk together, and gradually add it to the dry ingredients till it forms a smooth, thick cream.

Drop dessert spoons of batter onto the hot skillet. They spread on cooking, so keep the drops well separated. Watch until the top is covered with bubbles; then turn the scones, quickly cooking the other side. Put the scones on a plate, and butter them immediately. Eat them hot.

While we are indulging ourselves, how about these two variations on a theme, the theme being rich, sweet and terribly bad for you? Naturally it is also quite delicious and does not need an oven.

John's birthday cake. For one, seven-inch version of John's birthday cake collect together one-half cup (four ounces) of margarine, one-half cup (four ounces) of sugar, four tablespoons of maple syrup or cane syrup, one-half cup (two ounces) of cocoa, a few drops of vanilla extract, and six ounces of crisp bread crumbs (either make toast and crush it up, or break up one package of toast).

Melt the margarine and sugar together, stirring. Remove from the heat. Stir in the syrup, cocoa, and vanilla extract until smooth. Add the crisp crumbs. When they are well coated with the cocoa mixture, press the lot into a greased seven-inch cake tin, and leave overnight in a cool place.

Next day make the icing as follows. Collect together one-half cup (four ounces) of margarine, four tablespoons of maple syrup or cane syrup, one-half cup (two ounces) of cocoa, and a few drops of vanilla extract.

Melt the margarine, and remove from the heat. Stir in the syrup, cocoa, and vanilla essence. Beat till smooth. Spread over the cake, and leave in a cool place to set.

If feeling good, or poor, halve all the ingredients except the crisp crumbs.

For those with a more sophisticated, less sugary palate, here is an equally scrumptious alternative, fed to me recently by a friend.

Wendy's Tiffin cake. You will need one-half cup (four ounces) of margarine, two tablespoons of maple syrup or cane syrup, two tablespoons of cocoa powder, one tablespoon of sugar, two or more tablespoons of rum, one cup of regular raisins or sultanas, and eight ounces of plain sweet cookies, crushed.

Melt together the margarine, syrup, cocoa, and sugar, stirring all the time. Remove from the heat. Stir in the rum, dried fruit, and crushed cookies. Mix well. Press into a greased jelly roll tin, and leave in a cool place overnight.

Bean sprouts. On a much more healthy note, how above sprouting beans? Have you ever wished you had a garden on board where you could grow fresh vegetables during a long sea voyage? No, maybe not. Nevertheless, bean sprouts are still the answer to the sailor's need for fresh food. Below is my method for sprouting Chinese mung beans at sea, but the basic principle is the same with any sprouting bean.

Take one tablespoon of mung beans for each person. I look through them very carefully for stones, then clean them thoroughly by putting the beans in a bowl and covering them well with salt water. Any that float I throw out—along with bits of twig and dead weevils.

Strain the cleaned beans, and put them in a medium-size glass jar. Add enough freshwater to cover them well. Leave the jar somewhere safe for twelve to twenty-four hours depending on the outside temperature (it takes longer to sprout beans in the cold).

If you want to increase their vitamin C content, place the beans in the light. To increase the vitamin B, put them in the dark.

After twelve to twenty-four hours strain off the soaking liquid, rinse the beans well in freshwater, and replace them, strained, in the container. The beans should now be damp but with no free liquid around them. A little muslin cover protects the sprouts from dust while allowing them air. In order to save on freshwater, I pour on just enough to cover the beans and swill it around well. After the second day I start a new batch, using the same rinsing water for both lots.

In temperate zones rinse the beans once a day; in the tropics, once every twelve hours.

After two or three days the green seed cases will come free, and a root plus two tiny tongues of fresh green leaf should appear. The sprouts are ready to eat, though you may prefer to let them grow a bit bigger before harvesting your crop. (In cold climates it can take five days to reach this stage.)

Fry bean sprouts in soy sauce for a couple of minutes to make them more digestible. Add them to risottos, omelets, casseroles, and soups to give an extra juicy crunch to the meal. Eat them raw as a salad.

Chinese mung beans are tiny, take up very little storage space, and are a constantly available source of fresh food on a long sea voyage. Soy or mung beans are one of the most nutritious foods yet discovered. They offer most of the vitamins and minerals plus protein. Captain Cook took along beans for sprouting on his voyage to New Zealand.

Lettuce. Still on the subject of fresh vegetables, if you want *to keep lettuce* without an icebox, put it in an airtight, plastic bag, suck all the air out, and close the bag tightly. If the lettuce has already gone limp, try putting it in cold seawater with a peeled and chopped raw potato.

Tips. To chop fresh parsley or mint, place the broken-off leaves in a small glass; then, slowly rotating the glass, cut them with scissors. To *peel onions without tears,* put a teaspoon in your mouth before starting. You may look a bit funny, but it is remarkably effective. Before we fly off to the tropics one final, even more practical bit of advice: *To stop plates from slipping* when you're serving food on a rough day, place a damp cloth under them.

TROPICAL EATING AFLOAT

For those of you arriving in the topics for the first time my advice is to hotfoot it down to the market and see what's on display.

Among the vegetables there will be little you do not recognize. But the tropics are a paradise for luscious fruits of amazing variety. Following are some of the more common tropical foods and a few ideas on what to do with them. If you come across others, then ask the sellers how to eat them; they'll be only too happy to help you. Many countries also put out recipe books for tourists. You never know, you may uncover a whole new cuisine you didn't realize existed.

Tropical Fruits ▪ *Bananas.* So what's unusual about bananas? you ask. Well, nothing. It is just the problems they pose when your whole stalk turns ripe at the same time. Then they become a delectable bore. So . . . slice and dry bananas on trays in the sun for later use. They'll taste a bit like figs. Mash them into banana bread; turn them into fritters and pancakes and curry. Slice them up in milk and jam or honey. Fry them in butter; then eat them as a vegetable, or add brown sugar and a squeeze of lemon for a fantastic dessert. Squash them in custard or on bread and butter. Yup! You're right. I've faced many a bunch of ripe bananas in my time.

Breadfruit. Although this is a fruit and grows on trees, breadfruit is often used as a vegetable. It is round and normally about half the size of a soccer ball. It has a rough, scaly skin, lime to dull green in color. Breadfruit is a starchy food with not too much taste. It is best roasted in embers before being swamped in coconut milk. However, if you don't have any embers around, try this recipe for *breadfruit hash*. A dish similar to corned beef hash, it improves the breadfruit enormously.

For four people you'll need one medium breadfruit, two onions, cooking oil, margarine, salt and pepper, some nutmeg (optional), an egg (optional), and coconut or evaporated milk.

Skin the breadfruit and boil until soft. Meanwhile, chop up the onions, and fry in oil in a heavy skillet. Turn the cooked, soft breadfruit into a

Slice surplus bananas, then dry them in the sun.

bowl. Add the onions, a knob of margarine, and seasoning to taste. An egg, too, can be beaten and added if available. Mush everything together.

Melt some oil in the skillet, and when it is hot, ladle on the hash. Cook on a high heat, holding the hash down with a spatula. Sprinkle with coconut or evaporated milk. When the underside has browned, turn it all over and repeat with the other side.

Cooked cabbage, corned beef, or bacon all improve the hash. Serve with some juicy vegetables such as ripe tomatoes, and pour on extra milk if desired. Cooking time is approximately thirty minutes.

Breadfruit also makes excellent french fries. An extra-rich variety is produced if you wait until the uncooked breadfruit is soft and overripe. Scoop out half teaspoonfuls of the raw pulp, and drop them carefully into deep fat as for french fries. They come up marvelously crispy and extremely rich. To turn this into a breadfruit pudding, simply make a caramel sauce and pour it over the top and eat as a dessert topped with coconut cream. But do remember never to deep-fat-fry at sea or on a stove which is not gimbaled. Even in a calm anchorage be sure to use a very deep saucepan with only, at most, an inch of fat in the bottom.

Coconut. When I think of the tropics, I think of rustling palm fronds and the thud of coconuts as they hurtle like cannonballs to the ground. (Never sit under a palm tree.) But in fact, the coconut must be one of the most versatile foods around, different parts being edible at different stages of its life cycle.

A green or jelly nut is one that still has a green outer husk. When opened, it is awash with a completely sterile and safe liquid which is refreshing to those who like it. Some people call this juice coconut water; others, coconut milk. Since it looks like water, I will stick to that name, and reserve "milk" for the white liquid, which I'll describe in a moment.

With any luck your jelly nut will also have a thin coating of translucent jelly (hence its name) around the edges. This is heavenly, though best eaten with a spoon.

As the coconut gets older, the shell hardens, and the liquid solidifies into a thicker jelly and then into the proper coconut meat.

If you buy or are given a coconut, husk and all, you must first remove that husk. (Don't forget that coconut trees belong to someone just as peach trees do. Ask before you lift a coconut off the ground.) The best tool for dehusking a nut is a pointed metal stake stuck firmly into the ground. A sharpened hardwood stake, though not as good, might also do.

Hold the nut sideways like a football; then bring the fatter end of the husk down hard on the pointed stake, trying to penetrate the husk. Once you are successful, twist the nut back and forth to tear off one section of husk. Once one has been removed, it is easier to repeat the process with the rest, inserting the stake in the new opening provided. Dehusking is an art which requires quite a bit of practice and strength; either that or patience.

If using an ax instead of a stake, start at the pointed end of the husk, which is where the nut is, and chop down to the shell.

To break open the exposed shell, arm yourself with an unbreakable glass and a heavy hammer. Place the nut on a rock or thick plank, and hit it hard with the hammer. Quickly whisk the glass underneath to catch the gush of water which will spurt out all over your hands. If particularly prized, the water can be carefully drained off first.

To do this, find the coconut's three "eyes." One of them is soft and easily penetrated by a corkscrew. Make a hole as big as possible so that air can get in to let the coconut water glop out.

Once you have the nut broken open, there's quite a lot you can do with what's inside. If you leave the meat on the shell, you can make coconut milk and cream.

The best tool for this is a proper coconut grater found in hardware stores in any coconut-growing country. Failing that, try using a fork. The idea is to grate all the coconut meat off the shell, making it into tiny crumbs, which you collect in a bowl. Once it is grated, pour on two cups of very hot water (one cup if you are making coconut cream), and leave it to stand for half an hour.

Next squeeze the meat and water between your fingers so that the water gradually turns milky. (Remember to wash your hands first, or it's more likely to turn gray.) Continue squeezing for about five minutes. Now strain the milk off, preferably through a muslin bag, but alternatively, sieve the mixture and then press out any remaining liquid with the back of a spoon.

And there you have it, rich coconut milk or cream. Pour either over fruit salad or puddings. It is also good added to soups or as a liquid in which to poach fish. Mixed in with taro, yams, or breadfruit (see above), it turns those rather tasteless foods into something altogether more appetizing.

Alternatively, once the shell has been broken open, prize the meat out with a knife. This is another skilled job; I've a fair-size scar on my thumb to prove it. Once free, the meat can then be eaten as is or turned into cocktail snacks. Try grating the coconut into very fine slivers. Now roast them in a heavy skillet sprinkled with salt. Once they start turning brown, take them out, and you've a mouth-watering snack ready to hand around.

An even more advanced coconut, one which is about to take root, has a succulent and extremely rich growth inside, the future root, which is also edible.

As we are talking of "rich," a treat known as "millionaire's salad" also comes from the coconut palm. But the tree has to be killed to provide it. Thus only millionaires are supposed to be able to afford the delicacy. It is made by shredding the soft white heart found near the inside base of the tree. However, in my opinion, the only exotic thing about "millionaire's salad" is the price; the taste is totally nondescript.

Coconuts are a rich source of protein. They also contain some vitamins, and their juice or water is said to be particularly good for children suffering from dehydration. But the meat eaten in any quantity is difficult to digest as we found to our cost when trying to live à la Robinson Crusoe on a desert island. One further word of warning: Coconuts are totally banned from the diets of people suffering from high levels of cholesterol.

Durian. The durian is a pineapple-size fruit with very hard, sharp spines like a horse chestnut. According to the *Shorter Oxford Dictionary,* the durian has a "strong civet odor." What the compilers mean is it stinks like a urinal. Durian grows in the Far East, where many believe it has aphrodisiac properties. Don't be put off by the stench. Cut the durian into slices like a melon. Force a teaspoonful into your mouth, and sample its exquisite taste. I would only sample it, though, for it, too, is very rich. It makes wonderful ice cream.

Guava. This fruit is the shape and size of a small lemon. It has a smooth yellow or pinkish skin with a pretty, crown of leaves like a rose hip. It has tiny, very hard seeds—death to the teeth. When very ripe, guavas are soft and may be eaten raw. Otherwise stew and sieve them for crumbles, fools, and purées. Guavas also make excellent jam and guava cheese. They are said to contain more vitamin C than any other tropical fruit.

Jackfruit. This is an enormous fruit, sometimes eighteen inches long with a rather prickly exterior and a dirty yellow color when it is ripe. Inside, the flesh is sweet and somewhat like pineapple in texture. Jackfruit seeds are the size of small new potatoes and, when boiled, taste like chestnuts.

Lime. Small, round fruits the size of squash balls, limes should be treated the same as lemons though their vitamin content is less. Lime is excellent sliced into cold tea and for lime meringue pie as well as for fresh lime juice. Use two limes to one lemon in any recipe. I like lime juice as a basis for fruit salads. Remember, as soon as fruit is cut, it quickly loses its vitamin C, so make your fruit salad at the last moment.

Mango. Mangoes are either grafted or wild. It is hard to tell for certain which is which until you struggle to pick the stringy bits of flesh from between your teeth. Then you know yours was wild. Even then mangoes are a truly luscious fruit. Very sweet and juicy, they vary in color from yellow to peachy red when ripe. Even green ones are sometimes ready if they are soft. But feel them gently or they will bruise. Mangoes are the size of large avocado pears and are very messy to eat. Our method is as follows.

Select a mango which is slightly soft to the touch and without brown blemishes. Wash it. Collect a plate, a sharp knife, and, if you're wise, a teaspoon.

Hold the mango so it balances on its most pointed end with its narrowest aspect facing you. Now cut it as if in half from top to bottom, but pass the knife a little to the right of center, cutting so close to the stone that you remove all the flesh from its widest part.

Swivel the mango on its point, and do the same to the other side. You now have two oval sections lying on the plate and a narrow piece containing the stone still in your hand.

Grip the exposed sides of the stone with index finger and thumb. Make two cuts right across the skin on either side of the navel, and peel off the remaining skin in one strip. Still holding the stone, suck off all the glorious yellow pulp before you discard it. This is your just reward for doing the cutting.

Provided the skin has been well washed, the remaining two segments can also have the pulp gently levered off the skin with one's teeth. However, to prevent tasty juices from going to waste down your chin, it is better to dice the pulp while it is still attached to its base of mango skin. Then lever off the die with a teaspoon. This is certainly more civilized if you are giving a dinner party and avoids the need for a strip wash afterward.

Mangoes go well in fruit salad, with custard, and with curry. If you are keen on bottling, they also make excellent chutney.

Mangosteen. This is a deep purple fruit the shape and size of a large tomato. It is a native of the Far East. The purple rind is hard and brittle but easily cracked open by fingers eager to get at the delicious, slightly sharp white segments of fruit inside. Each segment holds a large pit which is not eaten.

Orange (and lemon). In some countries oranges may not be orange-colored at all but green. They are just as good. Any sour citrus fruit should be dipped into a few grains of salt. All the tartness disappears.

If you have no lemon squeezer, roll the fruit firmly back and forth, cut it in half, insert a spoon and squeeze on that.

Pawpaw or papaya. This fruit is about the size of an elongated pineapple and slightly soft when ripe. The skin is quite smooth and varies from yellow or pink to pale green-yellow when ripe.

Slice the pawpaw up like a melon, and remove the black pips. A squeeze of lime and some sugar greatly enhance the flavor of the orange or pink flesh.

If the pawpaw has been bought *very* hard and green, add it to stewing steak in a casserole. It tenderizes the meat and tastes rather like marrow.

If the pawpaw has been bought even harder and greener, dice it and stew it in sugar. The result resembles stewed apple.

The skin of the pawpaw is used for medicinal purposes. (See Chapter 14, "Health and Illness.")

Pineapple. You will already be familiar with pineapples, but I find they keep best suspended from their crowns. They tend to go bad if left sitting in one spot.

To tell if a pineapple is ripe, give it a gentle squeeze and a good sniff. If it smells strongly of pineapple, it is ripe. Pulling out a leaf from the crown is another test, but I find smell more reliable and less prickly.

To prepare a pineapple, chop off its head and tail. (If you know a local person with land, he might be grateful for the heads, for they can be replanted to produce new pineapples. Just put them to one side until collected.)

Having topped and tailed the pineapple, I then cut the skin off in strips from top to bottom. The central core is sometimes edible, but often it is too fibrous.

Plantains. Plantains are very similar in appearance to bananas, so beware. They can be distinguished from bananas by the sharp angles on their outer skins. In the Seychelles they are aptly called square bananas. Plantains are usually large and are eaten fried in butter or oil as a vegetable or can be made into fritters after first being cooked.

Rambutan. This Southeast Asian fruit looks like a red, hairy strawberry, and they hang several to a twig. The red (or yellow) hairy shell is broken open with fingers and the fruit inside, rather like a litchi, is sucked off its pit. The pit tastes bitter so don't bite into it.

Soursop and custard apple. These two fruit are almost identical in taste, but they differ considerably in appearance. The soursop is the size of a medium-size melon with a bright green, spiny skin. The custard apple is the size of an apple with a weird green skin divided up rather like a pinecone before it opens.

Inside, both have succulent, slightly tangy white flesh and many large, shiny seeds, which have to be sucked around and then spit out.

Tropical Vegetables ▪ These are far less varied and interesting in the tropics than are the fruit. Most countries actually import such temperate vegetables as potatoes, onions, and carrots. However, there are a couple of vegetables worth noting.

Greens. Green-leafed vegetables looking something like spinach are often found in the markets. Some are just as good, too, but others are very bitter indeed. These become edible only if you change the cooking water several times. Since this throws out most of the goodness and wastes freshwater as well, I buy greens only if I am sure they are tasty. I have cooked local lettuce which was too bitter to eat raw and found it quite pleasant.

Sweet potato, yam, and taro. All these root vegetables are similar in their starchiness. As such they are better added to stews than eaten separately. Sweet potatoes also make good french fries if cut very thin and then fried. If boiled, all three can be mashed up with lots of margarine or coconut milk or used in corned beef hash.

9. Menus for Ten Days

THE MENU suggestions which follow are both for the cruising vacation cook who wants the emphasis to be on vacation, not cook this time, and for the novice crew / cruiser who is worried that there may not be enough stores for that first long trip.

No doubt you will want to make lots of alterations, cutting out dishes people dislike, adding delicacies if the budget allows. We, for instance, always have a large can of fruit to finish off our evening meal.

When compiling these ten-day menus, I had several thoughts in mind. First, they should be nourishing and well balanced, so they include a good variety of vegetables and very little fried food or saturated fats. They should be inexpensive; hence there is only one serious meat meal a day. They should still contain sufficient protein, so I substituted peas and beans when fish and meat were not used. Finally, the menus should suit the conditions likely to be encountered on a small boat at sea.

Nothing on the menus calls for an oven, and everything can be prepared on one burner. You will notice that I have several times included staples in the evening meal which, if cooked in double quantity, can be reheated for the following lunch.

Under each meal I have written the cans or servings required, and at the end I have made an approximate list of the stores necessary to feed four people for lunch and supper over the ten days, including such staples as margarine and flour.

Naturally it is far better to use fresh ingredients whenever possible; when we are in port, my can opener becomes redundant, but here I have listed everything in packets or cans so that the menus apply equally well to a ten-day or a seventy-day trip. I have, however, used fresh potatoes and onions throughout. Remember that potatoes, at least in the tropics, last only about forty-five days. After that you will need to substitute dried or canned potatoes.

I have not mentioned breakfast at all as it is such an individual meal. We have one cup of muesli each, but if you like a cooked breakfast and toast, then you will want to add extra eggs and toast packets to your shopping list. You may also need extra flour or cookies for afternoon snacks.

Finally, I had better perhaps warn you that vacation visitors reckon we eat far too much aboard *Johanne*. Hardworking crew members do not.

MENUS FOR TEN DAYS IN *COLD WEATHER*

On these menus "large" equals a thirty-two-ounce can, "medium" equals a sixteen-ounce can, "small" equals a six- to eight-ounce can, and * indicates all the dishes which will be improved by the addition of nutritious and crunchy bean sprouts.

D A Y 1

L U N C H	S U P P E R
vegetable crumble*	corned beef hash
fruit with cream	peas*
. . .	. . .
1 medium baked beans	1 medium corned beef
1 medium carrots	3 pounds potatoes
1 package celery soup	4 servings peas
1 small mushrooms	
2 fresh onions	
evaporated milk	
flour	
margarine	
1 large fruit	
cream	

D A Y 2

L U N C H	S U P P E R
Russian salad	fruit or vegetable curry*
sardines*	. . .
chocolate semolina	1 medium butter beans
. . .	1 medium fresh carrots
1 medium mixed vegetables	1 small tomatoes
1 medium beets	2 fresh onions
1½ pounds fresh potatoes	1 medium apricots, optional
2 cans sardines	12 ounces rice
mayonnaise	
semolina	
cocoa, milk	

D A Y 3

L U N C H	S U P P E R
split pea soup	fish pie
rice*	spinach
cheese and crackers	• • •
• • •	1 large fish
½ pound split peas or	1 large spinach
4 servings pea soup	1 hard-boiled egg
1 cup rice	1 fresh onion
4 servings cheese and whole wheat	white sauce
crackers	3 pounds fresh potatoes
margarine	

D A Y 4

L U N C H	S U P P E R
stewed beef	vegetable risotto*
potato croquettes	• • •
mushroom sauce	4 servings peas
fruit and custard	1 small tomatoes
• • •	1 small mushrooms
1 large beef	2 fresh onions
1 mushroom soup	1 pound rice
3 pounds fresh potatoes	
1 large fruit	
custard	

D A Y 5

L U N C H	S U P P E R
tomato soup	ground beef
leftover risotto*	potatoes
cheese and crackers	broad beans in white sauce
• • •	• • •
4 servings tomato soup	1 large ground beef
leftover risotto	1 large broad beans
4 servings cheese	white sauce
4 servings whole wheat crackers	3 pounds fresh potatoes

D A Y 6

L U N C H	S U P P E R
Spanish omelet*	fish casserole*
fruit crumble	• • •
• • •	1 large fish
8 eggs	1 medium carrot

1 medium tomatoes
1½ pounds fresh potatoes
2 fresh onions
1 large fruit
flour
sugar
margarine

4 servings peas
2 fresh onions
2 pounds fresh potatoes

D A Y 7

LUNCH

vegetable soup*
semolina
sultanas

• • •

4 servings vegetable soup
1 medium peas
semolina
sugar
milk
sultana raisins

SUPPER

meatballs
spaghetti*

• • •

1 large meatballs
1 medium sweet corn
1 small tomatoes
1 fresh onion
12 ounces spaghetti

D A Y 8

LUNCH

spaghetti
mixed vegetables
white sauce*
fruit

• • •

1 large mixed vegetables
1 fresh onion
12 ounces spaghetti
white sauce
1 large fruit

SUPPER

shellfish risotto*

• • •

1 small prawns
1 small clams
1 small tomatoes
4 servings peas
1 fresh onion
12 ounces rice

D A Y 9

LUNCH

chicken soup
sweet corn*
cheese
crackers

• • •

4 servings chicken soup
1 medium sweet corn
4 servings cheese
whole wheat crackers

SUPPER

chili con carne

• • •

1 large ground beef
1 small tomatoes
1 medium baked beans
12 ounces rice
chili sauce

D A Y   1 0

LUNCH	SUPPER
fried eggs	frankfurters
rice	potatoes
tomatoes*	fried onions
blueberry fool	spinach
• • •	• • •
8 eggs	1 medium frankfurters
1 medium tomatoes	1 large spinach
12 ounces rice	2 fresh onions
1 medium blueberries	3 pounds fresh potatoes
custard	

INGREDIENTS FOR FOUR PEOPLE FOR
TEN DAYS IN *COLD WEATHER*

CANNED VEGETABLES

Baked beans, 2 medium
Beets, 1 medium
Broad beans, 1 large
Butter beans, 1 medium
Carrots, 3 medium
Mixed vegetables, 1 large, 1 medium
Mushrooms, 2 small
Spinach, 2 large
Sweet corn, 2 medium
Tomatoes, 2 medium, 5 small

CANNED FISH AND MEAT

Beef, corned, 1 medium
Beef, ground, 2 large
Beef, stewed, 1 large
Fish, 2 large
Frankfurters, 1 medium
Meatballs, 1 large
Sardines, 2

SOUPS

Celery, 4 servings
Chicken, 4 servings
Mushroom, 4 servings
Pea, 4 servings (if no split peas)

Tomato, 4 servings
Vegetable, 4 servings

CANNED FRUIT

Apricots (for curry), 1 medium
Blueberries, 1 medium
Fruit of choice, 4 large
Add 10 cans if planning on fruit for
    supper as well.

OTHER INGREDIENTS

Cheese, 16 servings
Cocoa, 2 tablespoons
Cooking oil, about 6 fluid ounces,
    preferably olive oil
Cornstarch, 2 to 4 ounces for gravy
    thickening
Crackers, 16 servings
Custard, 8 ounces
Eggs, about 18
Flour, 1½ pounds
Garlic, to taste
Margarine, 1 pound
Milk, 11 pints, or 2 large cans of
    sweetened condensed milk plus 3
    pints of ordinary milk

Mung beans, up to 60 servings
Onions, about 15
Pasta, 1½ pounds
Peas, dried, 16 servings
Potatoes, 20 pounds
Rice, 4½ pounds
Sauces, to taste

Seasoning, to taste
Semolina, 8 to 10 ounces
Spices, to taste
Split peas (optional), ½ pound
Sugar, 2 ounces or 1½ pounds if using
  plain milk for milk puddings
Sultana raisins, a handful

Plus needs for breakfast and afternoon snacks

MENUS FOR TEN DAYS IN *HOT CLIMATES*

On these menus "large" equals a thirty-two-ounce can, "medium" equals a sixteen-ounce can, "small" equals a six- to eight-ounce can, and * indicates all dishes which will be improved by the addition of nutritious and crunchy bean sprouts.

D A Y 1

L U N C H	S U P P E R
sardines	curried beef
potato and pickle salad*	rice*
fruit	• • •
• • •	1 large beef
2 cans sardines	1 medium carrots
2 pounds fresh potatoes	1 small tomatoes
pickles	1 fresh onion
olives	12 ounces rice
mayonnaise	
1 large fruit	

D A Y 2

L U N C H	S U P P E R
oxtail soup*	fish pie
semolina	spinach
apricots	• • •
• • •	1 large fish
4 servings soup	1 fresh onion
3 servings peas	3 pounds fresh potatoes
1 cup rice	1 large spinach
1 fresh onion	1 hard-boiled egg
1 medium apricots	flour
semolina	margarine
milk	milk

D A Y 3

L U N C H	S U P P E R
Russian salad	spaghetti bolognese*
eggs*	• • •
sultanas	1 medium ground beef
custard	1 medium tomatoes
• • •	1 medium mushrooms
1 large mixed vegetables	12 ounces pasta
1 medium beets	
4 hard-boiled eggs	
mayonnaise	
custard	
sultana raisins	

D A Y 4

L U N C H	S U P P E R
tuna salad*	frankfurters
fruit	mash
• • •	• • •
1 tuna	1 medium frankfurters
1 medium tomatoes	1 medium sweet corn
12 ounces pasta	3 pounds fresh potatoes
black olives	2 fresh onions
French dressing	
1 large fruit	

D A Y 5

L U N C H	S U P P E R
sardine salad*	chili con carne
cheese and crackers	• • •
• • •	1 large ground beef
2 cans sardines	1 medium baked beans
1 medium sweet corn	1 small tomatoes
1 medium green beans	chili sauce
1½ pounds fresh potatoes	12 ounces rice
4 servings cheese	
whole wheat crackers	

D A Y 6

L U N C H	S U P P E R
salami	vegetable crumble*
tomatoes	• • •
rice*	1 medium carrots
prunes	1 medium baked beans

custard
• • •
salami
1 medium tomatoes
8 ounces rice
1 medium prunes
custard

1 medium mushrooms
2 fresh onions
flour
margarine
1 package celery soup

D A Y 7

L U N C H	S U P P E R
clear egg drop soup	tuna hot pot*
butter beans*	• • •
pancakes	1 can tuna
• • •	1 large mixed vegetables
4 servings clear soup	12 ounces pasta
5 eggs	white sauce
1 medium butter beans	spices
2 servings peas	
flour	

D A Y 8

L U N C H	S U P P E R
salami	ground beef
pasta salad*	vegetables
fruit	• • •
• • •	1 large ground beef
salami	1 medium broad beans
8 ounces pasta	3 pounds fresh potatoes
1 medium mushrooms	white sauce
1 medium sweet corn	
1 large fruit	

D A Y 9

L U N C H	S U P P E R
cold meat	prawn risotto*
salad*	• • •
cheese and crackers	1 can prawns
• • •	3 servings peas
1 cold meat	1 small tomatoes
1 medium green beans	1 small mushrooms
1 fresh onion	1 fresh onion
1½ pounds fresh potatoes	12 ounces rice
mayonnaise	
4 servings cheese	
whole wheat crackers	

D A Y 1 0

LUNCH	SUPPER
fish cakes	eggs
tomatoes	potatoes
blueberry fool	spinach
• • •	• • •
1 large fish	4–8 eggs
1 medium tomatoes	3 pounds potatoes
3 pounds fresh potatoes	1 large spinach
1 medium blueberries	
1 pint custard	

INGREDIENTS FOR FOUR PEOPLE FOR TEN DAYS IN *HOT CLIMATES*

CANNED VEGETABLES

Baked beans, 2 medium
Beets, 1 medium
Broad beans, 1 medium
Butter beans, 1 medium
Carrots, 2 medium
Green beans, 2 medium
Mixed vegetables, 2 large
Mushrooms, 3 medium, 1 small
Spinach, 2 large
Sweet corn, 3 medium
Tomatoes, 4 medium, 3 small

CANNED FISH AND MEAT

Beef stew, 1 large
Cold meat, 1 medium
Fish in brine, 2 large
Frankfurters, 1 medium
Beef, ground, 2 large, 1 medium
Prawns, 1 can
Sardines, 4 cans
Tuna, 2 cans

SOUP

Clear soup, 4 servings
Oxtail

CANNED FRUIT

Apricots, 1 medium
Blueberries, 1 medium
Fruit of choice, 1 large (or 10 if having fruit for supper, too)
Prunes, 1 medium

OTHER INGREDIENTS

Cheese, 8 servings
Cooking oil, about 4 fluid ounces, preferably olive oil
Cornstarch, 2 ounces for gravy thickening
Custard, 12 ounces
Dried peas, 8 servings
Eggs, 14 to 18
Flour, 2 pounds
Garlic, to taste
Margarine, 1½ pounds
Mayonnaise, to taste
Milk, 11 pints, or 2 large cans sweetened condensed milk plus 3 pints ordinary milk
Olives and pickles, about 6 servings
Onions, about 7
Pasta, 3½ pounds

Potatoes, 17 pounds

Rice, 3½ pounds

Salami, 8 servings

Semolina, 4 ounces

Sprouting beans, up to 5 servings

Sugar, 1 pound if using plain milk for milk puddings

Sultana raisins, 2 handfuls

Vinegar, to taste

Whole wheat crackers, 8 servings

Plus needs for breakfast and afternoon snacks

If angling for a discount, find out whether it's the size of the order which earns you the reduction or the buying of individual items in bulk, a whole case at a time. If it is the latter, it may be worth suffering a bit of monotony and cutting down on the variety of cans offered on these two menus. For instance, all meats could be the same and the sizes of cans standardized. In most meat dishes I have allowed 1 large (or two medium) cans per meal. If money is tight, make do with one medium can, and substitute some beans or lentils. Adults only need three and one-half to four ounces of protein a day. Children need more. Twenty percent of beef is protein.

If you decide to skip the menus and use the more simple Cans per Day for Four system, here is a general guide to how it works:

L U N C H

1 medium can meat / fish

2 medium cans vegetables

soup or pudding

S U P P E R

1 medium can meat / fish

1 medium can vegetables

1 large can fruit

Plus rice, pasta, potatoes, bean sprouts, and / or onions

Whichever system you decide on, check Chapters 7 and 10 for other flavorings, staples, and nonedible goods you will need.

10. Vacation Planner

PLANNING a weekend or vacation cruise? Worried you'll leave something vital behind? Here are a few lists to jog your memory. One shows the foods and nonperishables that can safely be left aboard between visits (provided the visits are no more than a month or so apart). The others you will want to take down to the boat each time you go.

FOOD AND NONPERISHABLES TO BE LEFT ON BOARD

Remember, everything deteriorates with time, especially on boats. Remove all perishables when laying a boat up for the winter. Keep all dry staples in airtight containers. Anything that is particularly liable to deteriorate I have marked with an asterisk.

LIST A / FOODS

Angostura bitters	Drinks, in cans	Olives
Baking powder*	Flour*	Pasta
Bay leaves*	Garlic	Pepper
Cloves	Garlic salt	Pickles
Chili powder	Gravy browning / mix*	Pickling spice
Cocoa*	Instant mashed pota-	Rice
Coffee*	toes*	Salt
Cooking oil	Jam	Semolina*
Cornmeal	Ketchup	Soup cubes
Cornstarch	Margarine, in cans	Soy sauce
Curry paste	Mayonnaise*	Sugar
Custard powder	Milk, dried*	Sultanas and raisins
Dill*	Mixed herbs	Tabasco sauce
Dried mint	Mustard	Tea*
Dried parsley	Nutmeg	Tomato paste
Dried beans*	Oats, in cans	Vinegar

Plus a selection of canned fruit and vegetables for the first couple of nights

LIST A / NONPERISHABLES

Aluminum foil	First-aid kit	Scouring powder
Beach towels	Fishing gear	Sewing kit
Bedding	Games	Sextant
Books	Handi Wipes	Soap
Charts	Liquid detergent	Sunscreen cream
Children's toys	Matches in airtight con-	Toilet tissue
Cling wrap	tainer	Toothpaste
Clothes hangers	Navigation books	Toilet cleaner
Clothespins	Paper towels	Writing materials
Cookery cards	Sanitary napkins / tam-	
Detergent powder	pons	

FOOD AND NONPERISHABLES
TO TAKE DOWN EACH VISIT

List B can be ignored if there are shops near your mooring which will be open when you arrive.

LIST B / FOODS

Bacon	Cheese	Meat
Bread	Eggs	Milk
Butter	Fresh fruit and vegeta-	Onions and potatoes
Cereals	bles	

LIST C / NONPERISHABLES

Address book	Money, checks, credit	Spectacles
Binoculars	cards	Sunglasses
Children's toys	Oilskins	Toothbrush
Clothes	Passport, if necessary	Toothpaste
Diary	Prescription medicines	Towel
Facecloth	Sea boots	Wristwatch
Flashlight	Sheath knife	
Hobbies: paint box,	Sleeping bag (maybe)	
camera, etc.	Snorkling gear	

Anything from the boat which has been repaired or washed at home

_____

_____

_____

_____

The space above is for your personal list of extras such as those things required for the children.

List C also acts as a rough guide to those planning to fly off to a bareboat charter abroad or to those starting a new life crewing around the world.

If you are fitting out a new boat, these three lists combined should help clutter the boat up nicely!

11. Garbage

ALONG WITH modern food and living goes modern garbage, and anyone who has done any sailing at all will know just what a worldwide menace garbage has become.

Ideally all refuse should be recycled, but recycling plants are expensive and scarce. That is no excuse for choking the world's oceans with floating trash. So here are a few thoughts on the tender loving care of the sea.

For a start, when you are in port, *always* put your garbage in the rubbish bins ashore. Never tip it surreptitiously over the side after dark. Once you are at sea, things are a little different, but even then some basic rules apply.

Never ever throw anything plastic overboard. Plastic is not biodegradable. It does not as a rule sink. It just bobs around on the surface, looking for its friends, and alas, they are not hard to find.

Ten years ago in the western Mediterranean, despite the fact that floating plastic bags are difficult to spot, we were almost never out of sight of at least one. Sometimes underwater currents miles from land amassed nightmare rivers of filth and plastic.

Already the stuff travels in hordes. It is only a question of time before plastic refuse will be forging footpaths across the oceans.

As well as being unsightly, plastic bags are particularly hazardous to boats because they wrap around propellers and clog water intakes.

So at sea I collect large plastic bags and fill them with the rest of our plastic and aluminum rubbish (washing it clean first). Then I save it all until we come to a port with litter bins. Even in mid-ocean, thousands of miles from land, *never* throw plastic into the sea.

The same applies to sump oil. The odious pollution that oil causes is well known, yet some yachtsmen still dump it overboard, thinking, "That little bit won't matter." It does. One finds great globs of congealed oil on even the most remote coral strands, and every drop thrown out adds more.

We collect our sump oil and take it ashore. If no local person has a use for it one can always seal the container tightly and put it in the garbage bin.

The rest of one's rubbish is less of a problem as, to my mind, the seabed is no worse than the land as a dump site for degradable garbage. On land rubbish dumps take up precious space, they stink, they encourage rats, flies, and disease, and they take a very long time to decompose.

On ocean passages, therefore, I fill all empty glass bottles with water and sink them, unbroken. Gradually the sea will work on them, returning them to their original state of sand.

I puncture nonaluminum cans four times in the side, twice near the top and twice near the bottom. The holes ensure that the cans sink rapidly and don't float around on the surface for months. Once sunk, they, too, will slowly disintegrate into their component minerals.

Vegetable matter thrown overboard will soon recycle through fish and scavenging birds. We caught a fish shortly after lunch one day. Its stomach was full of the overgrown bean sprouts I'd jettisoned a moment before!

When you are anchored in a remote bay, the picture is different again. Think before throwing cans and bottles over the side. Have you space to keep them until the next garbage bin? Are you anchored in deep water, over weed or mud, or are you perhaps poised beside a fairyland of coral? If the latter, why not take your garbage out to sea in the dinghy and dump

The worldwide menace of garbage.

it there? Alternatively there may be a suitable place ashore to bury it or even to burn it. (Don't start a forest fire in the process!)

If you must jettison garbage in an anchorage, wait till the tide is ebbing so at least it is carried farther out to sea. And if it is empty cans you are dumping, have a thought for fellow yachts and crush the open lips of the cans together before throwing them over the side. This prevents anchors from dropping into the open mouth of the can and dragging. Farfetched? Not at all. It has happened to us three times in five years, and we have seen it happen to many other people as well.

One final word of warning from the world of experience: If you are hurling rotten tomatoes out through the galley porthole, do check where the dinghy is first.

When throwing things away, do bear in mind that what seems like rubbish to people from an overaffluent, chuck-away society may be of great value to resourceful people in poorer parts of the world.

In Africa all sound cans with lids that make them water- and antproof are much in demand. Good glass bottles with screw caps will store water or kerosene. All toys are welcomed by children who have none, as are good clothes your own children have grown out of.

All garbage bins are carefully picked over in poor countries, so if you want to give something away but have no one in particular in mind, leave it beside the garbage bin. It will soon be gone.

The other side to this garbage recycling is the danger that a child might pick up something poisonous, so never throw pills or poisons in a trash can.

Now, to my final tip on the subject of rubbish. Just as in poor countries it is worthwhile for local people to rummage through cruising people's garbage, so in affluent countries it is worthwhile for the relatively impoverished cruising person to rummage through the garbage bins of fancy marinas.

We found charts for the whole of our trip to Holland and Germany in one refuse dumpster, and in Gibraltar we came across a luxury motor yacht about to throw out its whole folio of charts for the Mediterranean. We now have a whole folio of charts for the Mediterranean.

12. Living Together

MOST CRUISES are abandoned not because the vessel has been cast upon cruel rocks or wrecked by hurricane-force winds on hostile shores but quite simply because, after a few weeks together, the crew cannot stand the sight of each other.

Four people sailing a thirty-two-foot boat across the Atlantic will, in all probability, see and hear very little of one another, what with different rosters and the need for sleep. Those same four people port-hopping along the coast of the United States will be falling over each other day and night. They will have to adapt and pull in their feet.

On a short cruise you can hold your breath, knowing that it will soon be over. But when it is your one vacation of the year, something you've been dreaming of through long, hard days of work, it would be a crying shame if that vacation did not live up to expectations.

The adage "If you want a crew, marry her" is not as chauvinistic as it sounds, or at least I hope it isn't, for it is based on the sensible premise that if two people have lived happily together ashore, there is some chance they will do the same afloat. However, this is not a guaranteed road to success. Ashore spouses often only see each other and their offspring in the evenings and at weekends. And even then they can escape for a walk in the park or a chat with a friend. On a boat there is no escape unless you go up the mast. You are all living together for better or worse.

And if I may be permitted a little sexism myself, I would add that some men make it quite definitely "worse." For they become strangely metamorphosized when they step on board a boat. Suddenly quiet, sensible, easygoing guys become all snapped orders, raised voices and profanity. I have finally put it down to sheer panic, and I suggest soothing them with motherly, clucking noises, though now that more and more women are taking the helm as either skipper or as equal partner, maybe this strange male aberration will die out.

Since Edward and I have to take on extra crew for long trips but like to live *en famille* in between, we have had more than our share of getting along at close quarters with friends and strangers alike. At the time of writing we have had more than fifty crew members of eleven different nationalities aboard *Johanne,* 90 percent of whom have been a success. Despite that, I still have no magic formula for selecting a crew.

Some people favor a week's shakedown cruise, sailing and living together, before making any final decision. It may be a week well spent. But remember everyone will be on his or her best behavior. With everyone optimistic irritating habits may be overlooked as you hope against hope that the great adventure will succeed.

I would never consider lack of experience a drawback in a crew. Provided they are intelligent, practical, and eager to learn, novices may actually fit in better than those who think they know it all and cannot adapt. There was one owner who asked all prospective crew members the sole question "Do you play piquet?" For him this apparently irrelevant question wasn't irrelevant at all.

Reviewing characteristics which irritate you and checking them off against your future companions may also pay dividends.

Do you like to smoke, drink, listen to stereo music, live it up in the evenings? Our idea of a perfect anchorage is one where there is not a house in sight and the only sounds are made by the sea and the birds and the wind in the rigging. We would drive the poor "bright lights and disco" man to distraction. Luckily there are always plenty of people, young and old, who share common goals.

Everyone finds some habits difficult to stomach. Edward can't stand laziness while I seethe inside if people are faddy. I am most wary of those who say they eat everything . . . except meat. We once spent fifty-seven days drifting around the Indian Ocean with a couple who ate everything "except meat." It was only after we had left land well behind and after they had helped me spend six hundred dollars on canned stores that they added that they didn't actually eat canned food, sugar, white flour, or any other such poisons either. After devouring all the fresh fruit and vegetables, they ended up living off pasta with olive oil twice a day plus raw garlic for breakfast.

Other traits which bother people living in close proximity are unconscious habits like nail biting or nervous laughter, different standards of cleanliness or senses of humor, untidiness and thoughtlessness.

But feeling that someone is not pulling his or her weight, not doing a fair share of the work, probably causes more resentment than any other single factor. This applies equally to the owners' slacking as to the rest of the crew.

There is also the problem of division of labor along sexist lines. At sea more than anywhere else men and women, husbands and wives can watch each other at work. (Did you know that there's a perfectly good English word to describe men and women who cohabit whether they are married

Many women resent being bundled off into the galley and quite rightly too.

or not? They are feres, pronounced like "fairs." A nice friendly word meaning mate or companion. Much more straightforward than that ghastly "live-in lover," which sounds like an inferior servant, or the coy "fiancé.")

Many women resent being automatically bundled off into the galley and quite rightly, too, if what they want to do are the other unpleasant jobs on board like cleaning out the sump oil or fixing the engine. But if engines aren't your scene either, try a cool look at the situation before getting too het up.

So the men are sitting in the cabin discussing what ails the engine while you wash up their dirty dishes in cold seawater. The questions to ask, are: (a) Can you fix the engine yourself? and (b) Would you be willing to go groveling underneath it, getting covered in oil and filth? If the answer to either question is yes, then dry your hands and join in the discussion. If the answer is no, then take a kinder view of the job in hand and be thankful someone else is willing to fix the wretched motor.

To my mind who does exactly what is totally irrelevant. All jobs aboard have to be done, so all jobs are equally valuable. The only real difference is that some are fun and some foul. It is up to you to see that they are distributed fairly.

I know Edward dislikes scrubbing clothes and fixing engines. So do I, but I can scrub clothes, I can't fix engines. I dislike going aloft while I love going out on the bowsprit to hand down the sails. Indeed, I probably grab more than my fair share of bowsprit work. I hate steering in jerking calms, so Edward often relieves me early. I love chipping metal and he doesn't, so I do all the chipping on board. I hate cooking and I don't drink tea or coffee, so Edward makes the tea and coffee, and I do the rest.

Finally, if you see someone doing a difficult job, don't just sit and watch fascinated. Offer to help. Often you will be turned down, but you will have defused that "Why am I the only one who ever does any work on this boat?" feeling.

A good crew is a group of people all pulling the same way, together.

Youngsters can also cause ructions. If you plan to crew on a boat with children, first check that you like them and that, broadly speaking, you agree with their upbringing. If taking crew on, try to explain how much of the children's upbringing is shared and how much your own prerogative.

In my own experience American men are much better with children than their English counterparts. They treat children as ordinary human beings who happen to be a bit smaller.

I love to discover everyone's birth date so we can celebrate, for I like to believe all our crew are members of our family while on board.

In some ports it is not safe to leave the boat unattended. This problem is easily solved with a fair system of anchor watches. But when possible, we like to have personal invitations extended to include everybody.

On the other hand, living in a confined space, constantly in the company of other people, makes some solitude desirable. So, if possible, all the crew members should have a place on the boat where they can be private, even if it is only a curtain pulled across the entrance to their bunks so they can lie there unobserved.

If there are children on board, stop them from nagging crew members who want to sleep or read or think. Everyone wants peace and quiet at times. Children must learn to respect this.

A good crew is a group of people all pulling the same way. *Tim Agerback photograph*

To ensure the success of communal living, some cooperation is necessary. People habitually coming late on watch, not doing their share of bilge pumping, dishwashing, or whatever the task is inevitably build up tension.

Some skippers are more despotic than others, though this is often hard to tell ashore. Edward, for example, while quite relaxed in port, is very much in command when *Johanne* is under way and dislikes it if people do not do as they are asked when they are asked. Such traditional command does not appeal to some people, who, however ignorant they may be about the sea, feel that things should somehow be more "democratic." Such people would obviously be happier on another boat.

I might add here that one of the findings of an inquiry into the Fastnet Race disaster of 1979 (fifteen dead, twenty-four yachts abandoned) was that despite the crew members' being experienced sailors, those crews with a clearly defined chain of command stood a better chance of survival in an emergency than "democratic" ships. Maybe, after all, the old skippers in days of sail knew what they were about.

If you are signing on a couple as crew, do first discover if they get along together. No point in having other people busting up your crockery.

Finding crew is usually pretty easy. Most ports with other yachts in them have one or two "hitchhikers" who want a change of scene. It is sensible to inquire discreetly why, remembering that there are two sides to most stories. Sometimes an advertisement in a local yacht club or harborside café will raise volunteers. Otherwise just ask around.

If planning a foreign cruise, spare a thought for the nationalities of those in your prospective crew. A crew member with an Israeli passport can have trouble in Arab states; one with a South African one may have difficulty most places. What is perhaps even more unfair is that people from third world countries arriving by sailboat on the shores of richer nations can be met with endless hassle by bureaucrats, who are terrified that they are potential immigrants.

Discuss finances in full before setting out so that there is no confusion later on. When you sail overseas, it is well to realize that by international law, the owner of the yacht is liable, under certain circumstances, to pay for the repatriation of his crew members. For this reason it is wise to ask all crew members to deposit with you the price of a single air fare from the cruise destination to their home countries before setting sail, however, we ourselves have never done so. On the same basis many large airlines give hefty discounts to seamen either being repatriated or returning to their ships. This also is worth investigating although often the discount on a charter route is greater than the seaman's rebate. On longer or more unusual routes the airline discount can more than halve your bill.

Differing nationalities of crew members should only add to the interest of the trip. When we sailed from Sri Lanka to Malaysia we took with us as crew one German woman, one French woman and one Dutch man. The actual trip took one month, but we stayed together for six.

It will be unnecessary to tell most readers *never* to disparage the country of anyone on board (or off it, for that matter). However much people may revile their own country, they don't want to hear foreigners pulling it apart.

A final tip for contented cruising: don't ship anyone aboard who has a tight time schedule. To be gliding gently along at one knot under a perfect blue sky and then be reminded that someone is in a hurry because he has booked his return flight is definitely not conducive to collective happiness.

To sum up, I now look for maturity (no connection with age) in people before embarking with them on a long voyage. Maturity decides whether a crew member is self-assured and tolerant enough to cope with the give-and-take of close communal living. There are enough problems and challenges to be overcome sailing small boats without having to nurse along other people's faltering egos. The other important attributes, in my eyes, are practical common sense, a willingness to help, and a sense of humor.

Many points which apply to selecting a crew also apply to selecting a skipper. But this time find out first if s / he can sail, an attribute considerably more important in skippers than other crew members.

There are a frightening number of people who buy boats and go cruising and yet know absolutely nothing about the sea and may equally well never learn. We met a good example recently.

This skipper / owner knew almost nothing about sailing and lacked self-confidence as well. His wife hated the sea and boats and had no confidence in her husband. Because the skipper was unsure of himself, he did not want a knowledgeable crew that might scorn his seamanship, so he set off to cross one of the world's oceans with a reluctant wife and two other crew members whose sole recommendation was that they had never sailed in their lives before.

If you are crewing, it is much better to decide beforehand what sort of cruise you want, even write it down, so that during those hours of romantic talk in the bar of far-off places with evocative names, you are not so carried away you sign on for something which will be a disappointment to you.

If you are an experienced sailor and discover the skipper is not, it is probably best to leave. I know of several seafarers who have been asked to help novice owners sail across the Atlantic, teaching them the ropes en route. Beware!

The fact is, however ignorant the owners are, the boat is theirs! After a very few days they take umbrage at the slightest suggestion from their crew. So look for a skipper who knows as much as or more than you. If that's difficult, then it's time you either bought your own boat or became a skipper yourself.

Check on a vessel's seaworthiness before signing on, and sound out the owners' attitude to sea safety. Listen around the waterfront. If someone has left the crew, ask for the story, not forgetting that it will have two sides as well. See if anyone comments on the boat or her sailing abilities.

Ask what is expected of you in the way of work and financial support before deciding to take on the job. If the owners say "share expenses," find out exactly which expenses they mean. Do they simply mean food and fuel (the most common combination), or do they mean minor repairs as well? If sharing the cost of food and fuel, you will probably be expected to chip in with any work that needs doing in port. After all, you are not a charterer paying a thousand dollars a week. If offered free board and lodging as well as free travel (rare these days), then you will be expected to put in fairly regular hours of work, the traditional arrangement being four hours per day.

None of this applies to charter yachts. If working as crew on a yacht which is earning money, you, too, should be paid. After all, you will be expected to work damned hard.

Crew members who disappear ashore as soon as the cruising boat reaches port and return only in time for the onward passage may find the boat has left without them. Crewing involves sharing both the ups and downs of sailing. You are relying on the boat to get you to your destination, so lend a hand to keep her seaworthy.

However, there is another side to this. Many boat owners adore pottering and fixing; they do it happily all day every day. Unless informed otherwise, these skippers assume you have the same single-minded enthusiasm. It is wise to mention casually the day before if you plan to go off on a day's expedition ashore. Unless there's a deadline to meet, the skipper is unlikely to object; it's just that he wouldn't have thought of it himself!

Once you have found your ship, ask what to bring along apart from wet-weather gear. There is, for instance, a particular danger if a beginner wants to learn to navigate on the ship's only sextant. Knock it once, and the whole expedition is in trouble. Ask about bedding and clothing, too. Otherwise "List C" in Chapter 10 should serve as a rough guide.

Bear in mind that the boat is the skipper's home. Just as you would not walk into someone's house and criticize the wallpaper or the meals, don't step aboard and object to the way everything is run. There's an old saying from windjammer days which applies as well today: "Different ships, different long splices." Every boat has its own ways. There's generally a good reason for them.

Always carry a secret fund of money that is enough to fly you home from your farthest destination in case you decide the skipper or the rest of the crew are intolerable or if an urgent message arrives from your family summoning you home.

I have heard some truly horrific tales of skippers and their feres. One friend was attacked by a screaming woman pointing a loaded spear gun at his navel. Another sailed across the Atlantic with a despotic lunatic who allowed his crew only one cup of fresh drinking water per day while he himself shaved in a bowlful of freshwater.

Yachts seldom stick to a schedule, and winds seldom blow as they should. If you are in a hurry, go by tramp ship or airplane.

In times of stress or during bad weather avoid complaints of the cold, the wet, and the lack of sleep. Everyone is in the same boat. No one is worse off than the others. By whining you are forcing an extra burden on your companions while failing to pull your weight. Now is the time to weld together a marvelous bond. As you all struggle together in adversity, so, later, you will be able to laugh together in the warmth of relief and success which follows.

Believe it or not, this chapter is not meant to put you off. Only, a compatible crew is as important an ingredient as the boat itself in creating a successful, enjoyable voyage. Cruising is a wonderful way of life, and crewing is one of the most carefree life-styles imaginable. Hop on a boat, and your travel is free. Help along the way and maybe chip in with your share of the food, and you can see the world and meet a host of interesting people. Then, when you want a change of scene or to go in a different direction, you just announce you'll be leaving in a week, and off you go.

The best things in life, such as a happy relationship or a contented crew, call for a positive effort to maintain them. Both demand consideration and concern from all those involved. If you feel irritated, search your own mind for the underlying cause. It is as likely to turn out that the roots of friction are laid deep in your own psyche as in the other person's. Sailor, know thyself.

13. Family Afloat

BABIES

IF, AS WELL AS BEING a crew member, you happen to be the skipper's wife, then there is a good chance that little skippers will soon appear, if they haven't done so already. As soon as they do, Grandmama or the next-door neighbor will inform you that you are doing a terrible thing, taking the baby to sea. (Let me hastily add that my own mother was magnificent, never made a murmur. In fact, despite suffering considerable discomfort, she has joined us on four continents of the globe.) As for those dreary pessimists, I'd just point out that the most dangerous part of the trip will be the drive down to the marina.

Most babies thrive on sailing boats. There are no hideous noises to dampen their hearing, no car fumes to fill their lungs, and at the end of the day a gentle rocking motion sends them to sleep. And if by chance you do have to run the engine, that, too, is a surefire way to transport them to the land of Nod.

Feeding ▪ The first two things that come to mind when contemplating babies on boats is feeding and diapers, so let us deal with those first.

Milk. Breast-feeding small babies is the obvious answer, on boats or anywhere else. That way you are absolutely certain that the milk and its container are sterile and that the baby is getting the one and only food on God's earth perfectly suited to human infant digestion. What is more, it is fortified with the mother's own antibodies. There are no problems of sterilizing bottles or mixing formulas, no worry about whether the next village or country will have the formula the baby likes best.

Sadly, though, there are always some mothers unable to breast-feed their children. In that case, once you find a formula that suits your baby, buy enough to last the whole vacation or, if on a longer trip, enough for the next six months. (Formulas sometimes go stale.) Avoid long-lasting sweetened condensed milk; the high sugar content is bad for babies.

Bottle sterilizing is the same as ashore, though in some countries sterilizing agents are not available. Don't worry, your pressure cooker makes an excellent sterilizer.

See that you have a few spare bottles plus a good supply of nipples in case of breakage at sea.

Solids. As the baby grows, so will its appetite. If you like them, canned baby foods are on sale in an amazing number of countries, both developed and developing. However, I don't believe our daughter, Katy, suffered without them. I weaned her anchored off Portuguese Timor, where such luxuries as potted baby foods were unheard of. She flourished instead on fresh fruit, vegetables, and meat all ground to a purée in a Mouli (a sort of manual liquidizer used by the French to mush up their soups). The only problem with the Mouli is rust. I washed the blades in freshwater, then dried them out on the stove, greased them all over before sealing everything in an airtight plastic bag. They still went rusty.

Of course, it is more work to prepare food this way, but you do know what has gone into it and that your child is eating a fresh, balanced diet.

That said, ground instant cereals are a godsend if the baby's hungry, the weather's foul, and you're expected on deck in ten minutes.

Diapers • *Cloth.* If this is your vacation, stock up on disposable diapers and worry about where you will stow them later.

For the longer cruise, diapers are certainly a problem, a problem that I must admit I never really solved, my response representing more of a skirmish around the foothills than a conquest of the peaks. My solution was virtually to dispense with them altogether. This was possible only because Timor was so hot. I tied diaper liners around Katy like bikini pants and then let her play under an awning on deck. A bucket of salt water and a deck brush quickly washed away the urine. The liners dealt with the rest.

To be fair, my "liner" system was bred out of necessity rather than idleness. All but two of Kate's terry-cloth diapers had been stolen, and no such thing as thick diapers existed in Timor. In addition, freshwater was at a premium and diaper liners need very little.

However, even in the tropics, proper cloth or disposable diapers are pretty well essential at night and when out visiting. They are essential all the time in cold climates.

To clean dirty cloth diapers when under way, tow them astern, but do make sure you have attached them really firmly to the line.

To sterilize them, either use a sterilizing agent in a bucket of freshwater or boil them in a large pan on the stove. Yes. Living with a baby on a boat demands vast quantities of freshwater.

In the tropics dry diapers in the sun. It helps to sterilize them. In colder countries still hang them out in the fresh air for a good blow, having first wrung out as much of the water as possible. (See Chapter 15, "Clothing.") If it is raining, however, they will have to come below to be draped all around the cabins.

Diapers ▪ *Disposable*. This is the moment when couples suddenly decide that the extra bulk and expense of disposable diapers are after all worthwhile. But disposable diapers are generally on sale only in affluent societies. If tracked down in developing countries, they cost a fortune. Yet to stock up on disposable diapers in large quantities on a small boat is often impracticable; they simple take up too much room. But if you do plump for them, buy the largest size available to avoid "leaking," with all the extra hassle and washing that involves.

Throw soiled diapers overboard at sea. They will soon sink. In anchorages without shore facilities put soiled diapers in a bucket of seawater until they sink, then throw them overboard. That sounds revoltingly unhygienic. It is. But no more so than pumping out the head. If you are port-hopping, then save the diapers in an airtight plastic bag for disposal at the next port. Never flush disposable diapers down a head or even down a toilet ashore if there is any chance that it runs into a septic tank.

If the baby has to wear clothes and especially at night, put on those silky soft variety of plastic pants. The others soon become uncomfortably brittle.

A plastic tablecloth to cover the baby's mattress is a lifesaver (or at least a mattress saver). If getting a lot of wet bottom sheets, try running up some small drawsheets similar to those used in hospitals. They need be only eighteen inches wide, just enough to cover the area where the baby's bottom lies. Sew tapes or elastic underneath to hold the drawsheet firmly around the mattress. With a strip of plastic well secured between drawsheet and bottom sheet you will save equally on washing water, elbow grease, and drying times.

Keeping Warm ▪ With all that pure sea air, babies should be healthier than ever on a boat. In cold countries make certain the baby is warm enough on deck; check hands, feet, and tummy from time to time. But don't wrap the poor mite up so much it can't move. Wool bootees and a wool and nylon vest next to the skin, followed by a warm Dr. Denton, should exclude any drafts. A waterproof hooded cape is often easier for a baby to wear than something with sleeves.

When going ashore in the dinghy in cold or rough weather, be careful to protect the baby well. Katy and I used to muffle up completely inside a great length of oilcloth with one little hole left open for air.

Keeping Cool ▪ In the tropics very different precautions are called for. A baby's skin is extremely delicate and should be exposed to the sun slowly but regularly. Even under an awning the reflected glare from the water can burn.

A sensible regimen is to put the baby in the sun for five minutes on the first and second days: one day front, the next back. On the third and fourth days increase this to ten minutes unless the baby tends to burn.

In cold countries make sure the baby is warm enough on deck *(Katy, 4 months old, and her father Edward Allcard).*

Continue this gradual approach until the baby is a nice brown all over. Even then there is no need to overdo it. Brown skin is not necessarily healthy skin. The sun's rays really do cause skin cancer, so even adults should avoid too much of them. There is also growing evidence that one bad bout of sunburn in childhood can lead to skin cancer in later life. So take sunshine, like everything else, in moderation.

That said, there is nothing like a bit of sunshine to heal sore bottoms and diaper rash. But strong direct sunlight can damage a baby's eyes. So don't forget that both the sun and the boat move. A baby that was carefully left in the shade at one moment may, after a slight shift of wind, be in the blazing sun the next. A good hat which shades both face and neck is a must once a baby sits up.

Thin, loose, long-sleeved dresses are ideal for both sexes in the tropics, particularly while the baby grows acclimatized. Buy them in fine cotton or a cotton and polyester mix. Nylon prevents the body from sweating freely.

Seasickness ▪ Sadly it is all a myth that babies are never seasick. Katy proved that most convincingly at six months—all over a friend's new yacht. The danger is dehydration. In Africa dehydration kills thousands of infants every year.

If the baby cannot keep down milk, try glucose and warm, slightly salty water in a bottle. (See "Rehydration Therapy" in Chapter 14.) If this, too, is returned, then head for the nearest port. If you are in mid-ocean, keep trying with the liquids and hope that the weather will ease up. Even constant tiny sips from a teaspoon help.

Consult your doctor before leaving home to see if there is any anti-emetic he recommends giving a seasick baby in an emergency.

Babies Abroad ▪ Taking youngsters abroad has many advantages not only for them but for you, too. Wherever you go your children, (unless quite impossible) are a passport, pretty well guaranteeing a warm and friendly reception. Even awkward immigration officials soften at the sight of a baby aboard.

I love to watch child-rearing customs overseas. There is so much for us to learn, so much we have collectively forgotten. I am sure the African and Asian habit of carrying babies everywhere with them (now gradually catching on in the West) produces happier, more secure children. How seldom one hears small, healthy children crying in such countries, compared with our own, so often condemned to the solitary ritual of crib or carriage.

On the other hand, some Chinese spoon-feed their children up to the age of five. (I suspect chopsticks have something to do with it.) In Singapore I used to watch fond mamas, bowl and spoon to the fore, chasing around their backyards in hot pursuit of athletic little darlings. I quickly decided that that particular custom was not for me . . . we have no backyard.

At mealtimes Kate sat in a child's automobile seat. It had a tray in front and a metal frame which allowed it to stand free on deck.

Entertainment ▪ Babies need to be amused and stimulated wherever they are. On boats the parents are seldom far away, their voices heard reassuringly close. This closeness between parents and children is one of the great blessings of family life afloat. It can also be one of its major drawbacks. If wee sprog decides to exercise her lungs on a thirty-footer in the middle of the Pacific Ocean, there's nowhere much you can escape to.

Boats are ideal for suspended mobiles. The rocking of the waves and the fluttering of the breeze keep them constantly in motion. I made one for Kate from the letters on a cornflakes package, then proudly strung them across her bassinet. The only trouble was she ate them.

All the usual safe rattles and finger toys are as suitable on a boat as in a house, but giant teddy bears belong strictly ashore.

Beds ▪ Sleeping accommodation for babies is no problem. I have seen them stowed (not stuffed) in open drawers, on shelves (as they cannot sit up, headroom does not matter), and on small mattresses on the cabin sole.

Kate slept in her bassinet on the cabin sole until she was almost a year old.

Babies should be free from drafts and drips in cold climates and given lots of ventilation in hot ones; otherwise they will suffer the misery of prickly heat. (See Chapter 14.) The most important thing, wherever they sleep, is a good bunk board so that they cannot fall out. If it is made of plexiglas allowing a clearer view of the world, so much the better.

Transport ▪ A collapsible stroller is a great boon, for carting the shopping home, if nothing else. Also, invest in a baby carrier or sling for shore expeditions and on the boat, too, if you feel so inclined.

TODDLERS

While the first concern with babies is food and diapers, toddlers mean one thing: mobility.

Mobility ▪ Here I include crawlers because it is the fact of their new-found mobility that adds that extra flutter of apprehension to everyone's life. What is she up to now? Considerations of food, clothing, and diapers alter little, but once your wee lass or laddie can get around, the real fun begins. Down below the main danger is that she will find her way to that fascinating, swinging stove with the pretty flickering flame burning so brightly.

Either you must be quite sure you are always there when cooking or you must erect a childproof barrier between infant and stove. One of the most tragic sights in a hospital is that of badly burned children, especially when you know that the accident and the agony could have been prevented. For that reason I would definitely opt for a barrier of some sort, for you never know when you may suddenly want to dash on deck.

As in a house, all drugs, cleaning fluids, paints, solvents, and glues must be kept out of reach of children, and, if the skipper is a fussy type, it may be wise to lock the sextant up as well.

Most of the dangers for a toddler, however, are found on deck. How to cope with this depends partly on the boat, partly on the toddler. To start with, we popped Katy in the cockpit. That was fine until one day a loud thud and pain-filled bellow announced that she had learned to climb out—albeit headfirst.

Then we rigged up a playpen on the side deck. Here life was much more exciting for the dear child. Boat babies quickly learn, through a process of rapid elimination, which of their toys sink and which float. Harassed parents quickly learn to tie everything on with bits of string.

To give Kate greater freedom, while still a crawler, we tried buckling her into a harness with a lifeline made fast down the center of the boat. But it caused terrible frustration each time she became entangled in the line or could not reach what she wanted. I still think there is a place for such an arrangement but not until the child is old enough to disentangle itself.

We finally bought a large amount of fishing net and tied it firmly top and bottom to the boat's lifelines starting near the cockpit and going forward of the mainmast (*Sea Wanderer* was a ketch) and back the other side. It gave Katy ample freedom to wander while protecting her from the dangers of tiller and anchoring gear.

I have often seen this method used since and only once met a toddler enterprising enough to scale the wobbly netting and fall overboard.

Life jackets are another solution to the "child overboard" dilemma. However, they are better suited to a vacation boat child than a long-term one. While life jackets may be a novelty for a few days, they are fiendishly uncomfortable things to live in day in and day out. If you do feel happier with infant in life jacket, and infant doesn't seem too miserable about it, do at least test the jacket out in the shop. Get the child to sit down and bend at the waist; quite often both exercises are impossible.

Under way, when children fortunately seem to be less active, I would favor a harness and lifeline. As the weather gets rougher and the danger of toppling overboard increases, the toddler usually becomes quieter and more inclined to lie in its bunk playing or sleeping. Finger puppets, simply made from scraps of felt, are good company, as are much loved cuddly toys.

Entertainment • There's no need to take the whole playbox along when you go on vacation. Toddlers are easily amused. Two buckets, one full of water, one empty, plus something to bail with, can occupy an infant for hours. Sieves, spoons, and saucepans add to the sport, particularly if someone forgets to tie them on board. Cardboard boxes, once they've been debugged (see Chapter 7), give endless entertainment: climbing in and out; making houses and boats or even hats out of them. Any toys brought aboard should float, not take up too much room, and preferably be made of nonrusting wood or plastic.

Another idea for sunshine days is a paddling pool on deck. Try either a large plastic baby's bath (useful later on for doing the washing), or if you have the room inflate the rubber dinghy or even a real paddling pool. Quite large children will enjoy splashing about in it. But they are slippery things, so keep a watchful eye on the little ones.

Cleanliness • Keeping toddlers clean is as difficult on a boat as anywhere else. That irresistible lump of shining black grease that Mom has just given to the shackle—there's surely enough for two and to spare. And what about that glistening fresh paint? It looks just great for finger painting. In cold climates, depending on bladder control, the answer is overalls that don't matter if they get oily. (See "Washing: Clothes" in Chapter 6, "Water," for how to get the oil off.) In hot climates try nakedness or near nakedness once the child is acclimatized to the sun. (See "Children" below for removing ingrained grime.)

Food ▪ Your toddler will now be beginning to eat the same food as you but should still avoid salads in the tropics, as well as iced drinks or ice cream if eating ashore in any suspect area. But don't be overfinicky. Brought up in too sterile an environment, children have no chance to build up lusty antibodies and fall prey to every passing bug.

CHILDREN

With babies it was food and diapers; with toddlers it's their mobility; with children it is how to ward off those quite dreadful words "I'm *bored!*" (For long-term cruising families there's also the fraught question of education. I will deal with that later.)

Entertainment ▪ On vacation helping on the boat and exploring ashore combined with the thrills of sailing, windsurfing, and swimming will keep most kids happy until it is time to pack up and go home. If your children do not instantly succumb to the lure of the sea, read on for further ideas. For the long-term family cruise, entertainment needs a little more planning.

Select toys with care. I tried to confine Kate's to small interrelating ones which took up little space. Edward complained that the bits, especially the Lego, were *too* small and got everywhere. I do remember there was a pathetic and much loved tiny teddy who fell in the bilges and was never seen again. There was also a farmyard and farm animals, Matchbox cars by the hundred (that is, once we had learned they had to be the built-up types which couldn't race straight under the toe rail and into the sea). There were Playmobile people and a little village of wooden houses, and a doll's house with electric light. (Katy and I made that together in carpentry class so that it fitted exactly into one of *Johanne*'s lockers.) All these toys could be used in endless combination, and they held their appeal over many years.

I well remember one glorious trip from Seychelles to Kenya. We had a super sixteen-year-old sailing nut crewing for us. One day, as *Johanne* sliced across the Indian Ocean before a fabulous quartering breeze, we stuck numbers onto the bonnets of Kate's huge collection of small cars and then, crouching down, raced them along the deck, furiously betting on whose would win. The "children" engrossed in that particular entertainment ranged in age from nine to sixty-five.

Another on-deck sport is a swing. Better still, sling it under the bowsprit. It needn't be a real one; a bosun's chair, an old tire, and a nice big fat fender all make excellent swings. The rest of the boat, of course, must be allowed to serve as climbing frame, diving board, and adventure playground rolled into one.

Older children delight in rowing, anchoring, or sailing the dinghy ashore to buy stores and explore. They can go fishing, windsurfing, snorkling, make friends with other boat children and adults. The more extroverted among them will also make friends with children ashore. For the more timid, language difficulties often create barriers.

Expeditions • Frequently there are factories, museums, or castles to visit. We have been around a French seaweed factory, an English pottery, and a Sri Lankan batik studio. In Kenya we visited a model farm, a sisal factory, a snake farm, and a coconut plantation. In the Seychelles we toured a tea plantation with its own packing station.

Katy has milked cows, sounded a siren on a fire engine, watched vast ships being unloaded and dry-docked, camped on a desert island and in a jungle, watched red-hot steel being forged, oyster beds dredged, and the Kiel Canal locks opened and shut. She has caught, scaled, and gutted fish, chased baby sharks across the shallows, dived on a glorious coral garden, and learned that to play with German children, it is best to learn German.

She spent many evenings in a French farmhouse playing with some of the farmer's eleven children. A year later she was at school in Bombay learning a little Sanskrit and watching ancient Hindu festivals.

She has known the fear of being caught off Dover in dense fog and being run down by a fishing trawler in the Bay of Biscay, the thrill of watching pelicans dive for fish out of a Caribbean sky and the freedom of jumping off the bowsprit to join them. She has gone swimming in water three thousand fathoms deep before eating smoked shark for lunch and then seeing a giant whale sounding close to the boat before she finally fell asleep on deck out under the stars.

Don't get me wrong, none of this is unusual. I am sure most cruising kids could relate similar experiences. I remember a couple of French children we met in Sri Lanka who had spent a year sleeping on straw in a native hut on the shores of Lake Titicaca before sailing on to a further year at school in Australia. I offer no apologies either to those of you who are reading *The Intricate Art of Living Afloat* before taking a family vacation on the Inland Waterway, fabulous though that will be. You see, I, too, want to play those panpipes; I want to tempt you to stay longer and go farther next time.

I am convinced that this simple life of being and doing is much more satisfying for young people than one of endless having and of watching television. How seldom one actually hears a boat child utter those deadly words "I'm bored." But maybe that's because the poor things are pounced upon by their overenthusiastic parents for daring to utter such sacrilege.

Rainy Days ▪ Rainy days are the most likely times on a boat for children to get bored, and if it rains for a week, you could have a riot on your hands. For such occasions I carry large supplies of art equipment. The back of wallpaper offcuts is excellent for painting on or as a base for collages of shells and scraps scavenged from the beach. For drawing and scrap paper try the backs of used computer paper. Supply powder and poster paints plus felt-tip pens and a pot of Play-Doh, and you are ready to start a young artists' colony.

Paintings which the children want to keep after being duly displayed on the cabin bulkhead can be stored flat under settee squabs. This is also a good place to stow game boards, spare cardboard for making models, even the boat's charts if you are pushed for space.

We carry a box full of card games, plus chess, checkers, Scrabble, backgammon, and various other board games collected over the years; Trivial Pursuit, which comes in both a child's and a boating version, is the latest craze.

Large rolls of Scotch tape, masking tape, and pots of glue, a pair of sharp-edged, blunt-ended scissors, and you are ready for a downpour.

But there! I've omitted the most important thing of all: books. They are our greatest standby. Katy's minute cabin aboard *Johanne* looked like a space capsule for a bookworm; there were so many books and so little bunk. And what a joy when you run into another boat with children aboard and can organize a grand trading session.

Friendship ▪ Boat children get along famously together. Unlike schoolchildren, they have little choice, so they mix well regardless of age and sex. There is however one long-term drawback to this tolerant boating society. They grow accustomed to it. If, later, they have to integrate with their more critical, competitive peers in a large classroom, they are sometimes ill equipped to cope with the gamesmanship and peer pressure to conform. But the conformity of schoolchildren is a fleeting phenomenon, and any difficulty is probably a small price to pay for all the fun and friendship that went before.

One further word of warning: There is a very easy flow of children from boat to boat. Quite often you find yourself inundated with them one day and wonderfully peaceful the next. If you fail to teach your children to respect the sea, boats, and other people, your moments of freedom will rapidly vanish as other parents no longer want the responsibility of having your children aboard.

Discipline ▪ Discipline is the most important extracurricular subject which children on boats have to learn and learn quickly if only for their own safety. Perhaps it is this knowledge of set, strictly enforced boundaries to what is permissible that makes many boat children such pleasant, down-to-earth folk to meet.

At an early age they have greater freedom than most of their contemporaries, swimming, rowing, climbing the rigging, or roaming the beaches and countryside. But they also have stricter limits. They know that in exchange for that freedom a degree of discipline is demanded. Dinghies must be carefully made fast, or you will be stranded. Engines and tools must be treated properly, or they cease to work for you when most needed or when no replacement is available. Chasing about on deck when under way is forbidden because broken legs or heads are not easy to mend at sea, nor are children overboard easy to pull back on deck.

For the vacation child this imposed discipline may come as a shock. At the same time, handled right, she may come to see it as part of the adventure.

Another bonus of a family's living close together is that the children learn young to help out, the way children learned to help out on remote farms in pioneering days. No one is a passenger aboard a cruising boat. The work everyone is, or is not, doing is obvious for all to see. Children soon learn to share chores with their parents and mature quicker for the experience.

But do remember that as children become more able to help with the sailing of the ship, taking the helm, or launching the dinghy, they are still children. Just as a five-year-old may be able to ride a bike but is not safe on the highway, so boat children may know how to haul in the mainsheet but can still get fouled up in a jibe.

Education ▪ For those majority of people who cruise during vacations and work during the semester, education raises no problems. You can sail off with a clear conscience, knowing that every experience during your children's vacation, both good and bad, will be pure gain educationally. But for the long-term cruising family education does raise worrying questions which gloom-mongers love to pick over.

They will tell you that your children will suffer for the rest of their lives if you take them out of school now. Have they ever thought just how much some children suffer *in* school?

There are several ways of coping with the schooling problem. One is to use local schools wherever you are; another is to teach the children yourself; a third is to ignore schooling altogether.

Local schools. If you are planning to stay in one place for a year or more and if the children want to go and the teachers in the school are imaginative and friendly, then attending such a school would seem an ideal entry for your children into local society and, if abroad, into learning a foreign language, too. But when the children move on to another school, do check that they are not handicapped by major educational gaps or confusions. This is especially likely to happen in math and the sciences, where each school is at a different stage and quite possibly teaching by a totally different system as well. Kate actually sampled schools in the Seychelles, U.K., West Indies, France, and India while following a home schooling course in between.

School afloat. The second option is to teach children on board. There are three ways to do this: by yourself without any help, with help from a correspondence course, or with a crew member employed specifically to act as tutor.

Going it alone. If doing it entirely on your own, you would need either to be a teacher by profession or to have very definite ideas on what you want your children to learn and how to go about teaching it. One friend, not a professional teacher, taught all four of her grade-school children at home. Except for the first, she didn't even start formal lessons until they were eight (in the U.K. children start formal schooling at five), yet, when they attended high school, they were well above standard. Mind you, they had one built-in advantage: They were bright kids anyway.

For those who do wish to go it alone, there is a group in the U.K. called Education Otherwise (for address, see Appendix J). It was set up to help parents who want to opt out of formal education but who wish to stay within the letter of British law which states: "Parents have a legal duty to see that their child receives full-time education either in schools or otherwise." They give advice on the "otherwise" part.

By correspondence. If less sure of yourself or your teaching abilities, you may decide, as I did, to enroll in a correspondence course. The course best known in the States is Calvert;* in the U.K., the World-wide Education Service (WES).* Australia, too, has an excellent correspondence course aimed at children living in the outback.

The Calvert* course calls for a frequent exchange of work assignments between pupil and Calvert itself, something which is not always easy when sailing schedules are vague and postal services vaguer. It does mean, however, that the successful pupil remains in step with the U.S. education system, reentering it whenever she wants. The Calvert course also has the great advantage that it demands little active teaching by the parents. Their job is more to supervise and help rather than teach.

The WES system enrolls each child with a qualified tutor at the head office in London. At the beginning of the year the parents receive a booklet stipulating the textbooks needed for the year (which can be ordered from them), which pages to study each semester, and what essays to write, etc.

*For address, see Appendix J.

There is also a booklet on the best approach to teaching and how to make lessons more stimulating. At the end of each semester you have to write an assessment of both pupil and "teacher" (yourself) and send them off along with specimens of completed work.

In some ways this system is better suited to cruising families than Calvert because only one mailing a year is vital, the one with the books and booklets in it, whereas to make a success of Calvert, you must receive all its mail. The major drawback of WES is that the parent is very definitely the teacher.

Teaching one's own children in any formal way is much more difficult than teaching other people's. One has an emotional involvement quite different from that of the ordinary teacher. Just think of the problems a wife faces trying to teach her husband to drive! The child has a similar problem. Any criticism from a parent is more likely to undermine her self-confidence than the criticism of an outsider. Criticism is anyway very unproductive, as everyone knows from his own experience. If someone thinks well of you, you try hard to live up to that image, however ill founded. If people think you incompetent, more than likely you will prove them right.

So, as far as possible, teach only by encouragement.

Whichever system you decide on, don't despair when, from time to time, things go wrong. Do not imagine that you are the only parent who loses his cool when Mildred refuses to cooperate and instead pelts you with putty from her perch on the cross trees. Every home schoolroom has its ups and downs.

I ended up using straight bribery to teach Katy to read. I didn't call it that, of course, I called it the Peanut Method. The problem was she could not or would not concentrate for more than two minutes at a time. So at the beginning of our ten-minute sessions I put out ten peanuts. Each time her mind wandered I ate one peanut. Any that were left over at the end of the session were hers. I love peanuts, and for a couple of days it was great. Then she got the idea, concentrated right the way through, and won the lot.

And that is the part to remember, the ups: the amazing joy when you realize that you alone have given your child one of the greatest gifts on earth, the magical ability to read, to transform black squiggles on white paper into words. You have drawn back the curtain to reveal a whole new world of both knowledge and fantasy, the world of books.

If, however, you have chosen the more cruising-compatible WES system and discover that you really do drive each other up the wall and that little Mildred is in danger of early death by strangulation, then, despite postal problems, a switch to the Calvert course may be the answer to your prayers . . . and hers.

Home schooling. At the end of each semester you have to write an assessment of both pupil and "teacher." *Photograph above by Anon*

Tutor came, too. Another solution is to take a tutor along as crew. This works fine, provided everyone gets along together.

Down with school. So to the final idea, that of ignoring formal education altogether. This depends on several things: how long the cruise is planned for, the ages of the children, and what is meant by "formal education."

If the cruise is expected to last no more than a couple of years, many cruising families and educators alike consider that the children learn far more by cruising than they miss by not being in a classroom.

If it is for longer, then age comes into it and that qualification of "formal" education.

Once a child can read, whether she is self-taught or taught by someone else, then, provided there are enough suitable books available and enough stimulation to native curiosity, she should be able to learn nearly everything she wants to know until her mid-teens.

But what if the child wants to follow a profession later on, go to a university or college? Is it fair, in one's personal search for fulfillment and "freedom" to shackle one's children with an unorthodox education, to force them to be different, possibly denying them their most ardent wish: to be just like everyone else?

When children near the age of high school graduation, parents are thrown into another quandary. Today a high school diploma is an almost

Children learn many things while cruising. Kate aged about ten learning to cut my hair.

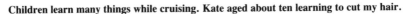

essential first step toward decent job opportunities. It is very hard for teenagers to study for serious exams on a boat. Because of this, there are not that many children of school-leaving age cruising permanently. That means that yours will have even less chance than they did before of socializing with their peers.

The question of education is one which causes much soul-searching among cruising families. I doubt if there is any hard-and-fast rule. Every child is different, and every family. I take comfort from the thought that provided nothing too awful goes wrong, all minor differences and difficulties will come out in the wash. In the end it is character and willpower, not education that decide whether a person fulfills his potential for living. And cruising at least has great potential for building character.

Washing ▪ Despite spending much of their time in the water, boat children still need to wash . . . and still refuse. Here is one good tip if you suddenly notice, to your horror, that a layer of grime has sprouted behind Mildred's ears to join another circle around her neck.

Gently rub the grubby place with baby oil. Leave the oil for a few minutes, and then wash it off with soap and warm water. This use of oil is well known in Asian countries, where babies are massaged every day to keep their skins supple and clean. It is far more effective and less painful than a simple scrub with soap.

Swimming ▪ Once children are able to walk with confidence and are no longer likely to throw the sextant overboard to see if it floats, the first of your worries are over. If the child has not already learned to swim, now is the time.

There are various methods on offer. One way is with a board of polystyrene held out in front. I saw a lovely one the other day with a dolphin's smiling head on it. This method is frequently used by instructors in pools. Another I liked was a large polystyrene "egg" strapped to the child's back, leaving both arms and legs free for swimming.

I myself tried the then-fashionable technique of popping tiny mite, totally unsupported, into the water at age of a few months. Other tiny mites are said to float, even paddle about a bit. Ours didn't. She sank like a stone. As, despite this first foray into an aquatic life, Kate's enthusiasm for the water did not wane, and as she was very strong and wriggly, I bought inflatable armbands with a flat section to place next to the chest. They were marvelous. Too marvelous. We had a real battle to get rid of them once she could swim.

Some children take to the water better than others. I knew one infant, still unable to speak, who used to jump overboard, swim around to the bow, climb up the anchor chain and bobstay, pad down the deck, and jump in again. He swam half submerged like a seal coming up for breath only when he needed to. I have since been told that this is an excellent way to learn and that if I had left Katy alone when she sank, she, too, would have come up eventually for air.

A lot depends on the child. If she is reluctant to make the final effort, try asking an adult friend, another crew member perhaps, to take her in hand. Whatever happens, don't throw a fearful child into the water. Occasionally this does work, and later on in life such pupils boast of their parent's harshness, or is it their own toughness? More often it teaches the child not only to hate water but to distrust the person who threw her in as well.

However, there are times when children become overconfident in the water. They start playing the fool or, worse still, that very dangerous game "Help! I'm drowning!"

I once witnessed a cure for that particular game which made a deep impression on me.

I was visiting a retired naval officer whose sturdy physique was topped by a huge and intimidating beard. A group of young teens were playing in his pool. He had already spelled out the rules: no screaming, no water bombs, and no crying wolf. In their excitement the children soon forgot the warnings, and inevitably one lad shouted out, "Help! Help! I'm drowning!" while struggling suitably in the water.

In a flash the commander dived into the pool. A couple of powerful strokes brought him to the "drowning" child. He turned him smartly on his back and gave him a proper lifesaver's rescue. The other kids watched in complete silence as the boy was pulled from the pool and given artificial respiration before being made to sit in a chair until he had "recovered" enough to walk home. I am quite certain neither he nor any of the other children played that particular game again.

Because a child swims competently off the beach or the boat, it does not necessary mean she will react well if she falls overboard, so continue to watch over her discreetly.

No doubt you will also have to watch children swinging about the rigging like monkeys. Your heart may miss a beat or two, but it can rejoice in the knowledge that they are growing up with physical self-confidence, freedom, health, and strength.

14. Health and Illness

Serious illness afloat is one of my greatest fears. My solution is to live as healthy a life as possible while being prepared when sickness strikes. There are several good medical guidebooks now available written by qualified doctors and designed specifically for people living on boats.

For years I've relied on *The Ship Captain's Medical Guide*. A British government publication (for address, see Appendix J) for merchant sea captains, it is intended primarily for merchant ships which carry no doctor. It deals very thoroughly and in graphic detail (almost too graphic; some of the photos are enough to make you sick before you start) with most of the ordinary and alarming medical problems which arise at sea. Very occasionally, with particularly nasty illnesses and accidents, it tells readers to radio for advice or to go quickly to the nearest port, not always that easy for a small boat armed only with VHF. If, however, I could have only one medical book, this is the one I would choose. And that despite the fact that my copy is printed on that shiny type of paper which, if it gets wet, goes into a single solid mass. Since the book is meant specifically for ships, one would have thought . . .

Suggestions for the ship's medical kit.

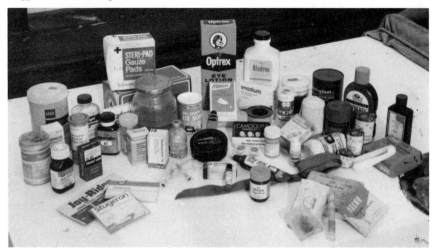

For obvious reasons this book does not cover such childhood problems as diaper rash, but the ship's captain is told exactly how to cope with childbirth, miscarriage, and spontaneous abortion as well as all infectious diseases. As a further boost to my morale I have, on the one hand, a family medical encyclopedia and, on the other, *The Complete Book of Body Maintenance,* which covers the most important and positive aspect of health: preserving it.

A properly balanced diet and enough exercise are two good foundations on which to build. There are a few other things which it is particularly well to recall on boats.

Keep finger- and toenails cut short. A flying jib sheet or a barefoot stumble in the dark will rip nails off in a flash, leaving an ugly, painful mess behind.

When lifting heavy objects, bend your knees rather than your back. Then the straightening leg muscles take the strain instead of the far more vulnerable spine. "Anchor chain back" is the complaint of yachtsmen who failed to follow this rule.

Always have a block and tackle handy on a boat. And don't be ashamed to use it. Great he-man stuff is fine until the rest of the crew has to nurse you flat on your back for a slipped disk or a hernia.

In hot climates a lot of water and salt are lost through sweat. They must be replaced, so step up fluid and salt intake. In the tropics, according to both my medical guides, you ought to drink approximately eight pints of fluid a day and add two teaspoons of salt to your food or drink. If you decide to take it in the latter, disguise the salt in a glass of fresh citrus juice, adding a couple of pinches to each glassful.

HEALTH HAZARDS

Treat all endemic diseases such as malaria and yellow fever with respect. Don't kid yourself it will never happen to you. As an outsider, with no built-in immunity, you are probably even more susceptible.

Malaria ▪ Before leaving for a malarial country, ask your home doctor for some antimalarial tablets. For proper protection most antimalarial drugs must be taken both two weeks before arrival and two weeks after departure.

Once arrived in a malarial country, however, go straight to the local pharmacist and see what pills he recommends. Every area is different, and each country's mosquitoes have built up their immunity to different drugs. And don't believe those tourist brochures which confidently announce that malaria has now been wiped out in their country. It may come back and all the more virulently.

You must also try to avoid being bitten by mosquitoes in the first place.

(See Chapter 21, "Pests," for further enlightenment. Look in your medical guide for malaria treatment.)

Yellow Fever ▪ While malaria is probably the most common disease to attack the unwary sea wanderer, yellow fever, or yellow jack, as it was known on the old African trade routes, can be much more dangerous.

Found mainly in tropical East and West Africa, it, too, is spread by mosquitoes. In its severe form it kills some 90 percent of its victims. Luckily there is a powerful and very effective immunization on hand. The injection has much to recommend it. Although there is a delay of ten days after the injection before you are protected, the protection then lasts for an amazing ten years. However, before you rush off to get one "just in case" (it is administered only at specially designated centers), a word of warning: In a very few susceptible people the anti yellow fever injection has serious side effects on the heart. Also, it is sometimes not advised for children under nine months old.

Cholera ▪ The anticholera injection is another immunity commonly offered via a needle. But this one is, at least to my mind, far less satisfactory. Although it is said to give protection for six months, a doctor I met in Africa reckoned it worked for only six weeks at the most. His advice was to up anchor and leave any place we knew to have cholera around.

Cholera is caught from drinking infected water and from eating raw fruit and vegetables which are already contaminated.

Typhoid and Paratyphoid ▪ TAB is an inoculation to be considered seriously if you are heading for the more unhygienic corners of the earth. It gives immunity for about one year to two waterborne infections: typhoid and paratyphoid A and B. Again, the immunity injection should be given some time before departure. TAB consists of two injections administered four to six weeks apart. Toward the end of the year it can be topped up by another injection, which will then last you twelve months more. At the same time you can also have a tetanus shot.

Incidentally, if you ever cut yourself ashore on your travels, check with a doctor whether you need a booster to your tetanus protection.

With the continuing spread of AIDS it is wise in poorer areas to offer the doctor a disposable syringe and needle from the ship's medical kit for any jab. Needles not properly sterilized can transmit the AIDS virus.

One of the great miracles of our time is the complete eradication of smallpox from the world. If you are ever tempted to curse the sometimes ugly, materialistic age we live in, think about that—and also about how horrible it must have been to go to the dentist a couple of centuries ago.

Fish Poison ▪ In certain parts of the world fish are poisonous. These are often ones which in other places are perfectly edible. So ask first and eat later. On one island, Mooréa, in the Pacific, the local people feed the fish's liver to stray cats. If the cats are okay at lunchtime, then the fishermen eat the fish.

Manchineel ▪ In the tropical Americas and the West Indies there is a tree called the manchineel. If you stand under it in the rain, acid may drip on your skin, badly burning it. If you follow the temptation of Eve and eat its little green apples, they will burn the whole of your gullet and possibly your gut as well. So be warned. Don't be tempted by unknown fruits until you have asked a local person if they are safe to eat.

Poisonous Shells and Stonefish ▪ Some shells have very poisonous stings, and stonefish, so called because they look like stones, must be avoided at all costs. Their spines stick up and, if one treads barefoot on them, they go right into one's flesh, injecting a paralyzing liquid which can be so painful that the victim falls unconscious and drowns or is killed by shock. The antidote to these two dangers is to leave nature alone. Don't pick up shells or shift coral. As for stonefish, wear tough-soled shoes when walking on reefs.

Hookworm ▪ Hookworms have two great loves: bare feet and damp soil around insanitary buildings. To avoid worm infestation, always wear shoes when visiting such areas. The worms enter through cracks in the skin, then go on to thrive and multiply in the walls of the intestine. Hookworms are easily recognized as they are excreted in feces. If they are left untreated, small children can actually die from them. That is a tragedy, for the cure, just one dose of deworming medicine, is simple and immediate.

Drugs ▪ Most medical guides list the basic medicines and ointments you will need aboard. Your friendly family doctor is the one to help you get them. With luck s / he will also be a seafaring type, well able to write up the drugs necessary for a ship's medical kit. But watch it! Some doctors become so enthusiastic about the project that they want to load you up with drugs for every conceivable, and inconceivable, eventuality.

My advice on drugs is to try to avoid taking them altogether. We carry no sleeping pills or tranquilizers aboard. Sleeping pills could turn you dopey at the very moment when you want to be most alert. Pep pills, on the other hand, may produce weird and wonderful hallucinations. Even aspirin is, in some people, an enemy of the body, contentedly eating away at susceptible stomach linings. Far better to live a natural, healthy life with a good balanced diet and, when possible, manipulating that diet to cure your ills.

That said, we carry a small number of ampules of morphine plus syringe and needles for serious emergencies such as major injury or coronary thrombosis.

On top of this we have a variety of antibiotics. Be very cautious when taking them. First, quite a number of people are allergic to them, especially those based on penicillin. Edward had been prescribed penicillin from time to time with no ill effects. Then one day he was given a penicillin injection and his heart stopped. (An immediate injection of adrenaline brought him back to life.) We also carry tetracycline and Septra.

Always take antibiotics for a full course even if you feel better halfway through. The bugs of the world are slowly becoming immune to antibiotics partly because they are being only half killed by people taking only half a course. The more often a person employs antibiotics, the more chance he has of becoming resistant to them and the less effective they may become. So resort to them only in time of serious need, not with every sore throat or cut thumb.

This is not to deny that antibiotics are lifesavers in a case of pneumonia or appendicitis at sea. Taken as instructed on the bottle or in your medical guide, antibiotics have been known to hold appendicitis at bay for two weeks or more, long enough to reach professional help. By the way, more people die from amateur appendix operations than from burst appendixes. So don't cut up the skipper, however strong the temptation.

Septra is an alternative drug to deploy against bacterial infections particularly if a person is allergic to penicillin. Wash every dose down with at least a pint of water to prevent kidney damage. A little bicarbonate of soda added to the water also helps.

Have a range of pain-killers available. Morphine is a dangerous, addictive drug to be pressed into service only in dire emergency. Carry a few pain-killers to deal with medium to severe pain plus something mild for bad headaches etc.

Some sort of medicine for diarrhea and another for constipation can be included although diet alone is a great regulator of bowels. (See "Diarrhea and Constipation" on page 123.)

Minor Burns ▪ There are two main schools of thought on the treatment of minor burns—namely, the wet and the dry.

During the Second World War it was noticed that airmen shot down over the sea suffered far less severe burn scars than those shot down over land. I therefore always plunge the burned part in salt water as soon as possible. When no clean salt water is available, dissolve two tablespoons of bicarbonate of soda in a quart of water. Fashion a compress out of clean cloth, soak it in the mixture, and put it on the burned area. When the pain eases, remove the compress and put on Vaseline gauze, then lint, then a bandage.

With minor burns Vaseline gauze can stay put until the burn has healed. Some experts prefer a totally dry dressing, claiming it is less likely to lead to infection.

Severe Burns ▪ The first treatment in severe burns is for shock rather than wound dressing. (See "Shock" on page 130 or check in your own medical guide.)

If there is no immediate hope of medical help, which must in any case be sought as quickly as possible, pay special attention to fluid replacement. When skin is badly burned, a lot of body fluid and salts are lost and, to avoid shock, must be replaced.

Mix one pint of water with a half teaspoon of salt and a half teaspoon of bicarbonate of soda. Give this in small amounts over a twenty-minute period as follows: For every burned skin area on the body equal to the area of skin on one arm, give two ounces of the fluid. For instance, the skin on one leg equals approximately double the area of skin on one arm. So, if the whole leg is burned, give double the fluid, or four ounces (one-half cup), during the first twenty minutes. (The whole of one side of the trunk also counts as twice the arm area. The whole of the back and the front of the trunk together equal four times the arm area.)

Go on giving the same dose of salty water every twenty minutes for the first eight hours, after which the amount can be reduced to one ounce per arm area every twenty minutes for the next sixteen hours. The aim is to have the patient pass two pints of urine in the first twenty-four hours. If he passes less than that, then continue the one-ounce treatment until he does pass two pints in twenty-four hours.

The greatest danger with burns dressings is infection. See what your medical guide recommends because opinions vary widely on the best course to follow. But severe burns are one case in which every effort must be made to get the patient to a hospital as quickly as possible. Stop a passing supertanker if necessary.

Corrosive Burns ▪ If the corrosive is known to be acid, wash the area in large quantities of mildly alkaline water (two tablespoons of bicarbonate of soda to a quart of water), and then apply a wet dressing of the same solution. Alkaline corrosives, on the other hand, should be neutralized with a mildly acid liquid such as vinegar and water, approximately half and half.

Eye Burns ▪ These can be very serious. On boats they are often caused by incautious splashes of paint stripper or battery acid. Wash the eye out at once. Don't wait a moment. Fill a bowl with either mildly acid or alkaline solution as above (with alkaline burns use only one tablespoon of vinegar to a pint of water). Totally submerge the affected eye, and have the victim blink again and again to wash the eyeball clean. Put a drop of olive or castor oil in the eye before covering it completely with a bandage. Have a doctor look at it as soon as possible.

Sunburn ▪ If you are susceptible to sunburn, there are now many ex-

An all-over covering and a big hat is the kindest protection for your skin *(taken in the sweltering heat of the Red Sea).*

cellent barrier creams which filter out the harmful rays of the sun. However, an all-over covering of very thin, loose-fitting clothes plus a floppy hat is the kindest protection for your skin. Unfortunately the hat will blow off in any wind.

Once you are sunburned, cool tea, vinegar, and bicarbonate of soda dissolved in water are all recommended palliatives. Dab on the liquid of your choice, and allow it to dry off naturally. I swear by cool tea.

Severe sunburn is as serious as any other type of burn and may require hospitalization especially if it coincides with sunstroke.

If flying out for a bare-boat charter in the sun, do be sensible. Okay, you may feel a bit of a Charlie snorkeling around in a long-sleeved shirt, but if you allow your skin time to adjust, with gradually longer exposure each day, you will end up having a far more comfortable vacation and a suntan, rather than unsightly peel, as a memento to take home with you.

If you are a long-term tropical sailor, that is no reason to abuse your skin. In Australia, as the result of long days spent out in the sun, the commonest form of cancer is skin cancer. We ourselves returned from the tropics partly because Edward's skin could no longer take strong sunlight.

Whatever you do, never forget to care for your lips. I've seen burned lips swell to twice their normal size, cracking and bleeding, making both eating and drinking extremely painful. Even when you sit under an awning, the glare from the water is enough to burn delicate lip tissue. Tote a lip salve with you, and apply it often, especially after meals. I stash one permanently near the helm so that anyone on watch may use it.

Cuts ▪ Though our ship's medical kit includes a suturing set, I've never had the courage to sew anyone up. Instead I rely on butterfly clips to hold nasty gashes together. You'll also need plenty of adhesive bandages for cuts and grazes, though I prefer to make up my own with a roll of adhesive tape plus Vaseline gauze and lint.

If there is a chance of keeping a cut clean yet exposed (easier at sea than on land), try washing it in warm, soapy water twice a day, drying it in the sun, and then leaving it uncovered and free from clothing. I have sometimes found this treatment works when creams and bandages have failed. This is especially true in the tropics.

Tropical cuts often cause serious problems particularly if they are coral cuts. Try dusting them with Neomycin powder.

If every slightest scratch is turning septic, try taking an additional daily one gram dose of vitamin C. This is a totally unscientific recommendation; as far as I know, no tests have been done on it. But while we were in the Seychelles, several people we knew were apparently cured of chronic septic cuts by large doses of vitamin C.

While we are on the subject of homely cures, pawpaw ointment also works well with particularly stubborn sores, and neat pawpaw skin applied to the sore is said to speed up healing dramatically. But since pawpaw also tenderizes meat, I'd keep a frequent check on what's going on underneath!

Diarrhea and Constipation ▪ If you are suffering from the runs, but with no other signs of illness such as fever, try cutting down on solid foods for the first day. Instead, drink lots of rice water (salted water in which rice has been boiled for a long time), alternating with glasses of fruit juice and honey. On day two add some solid rice, plus carrots or beets. Always drink lots of fluids when you have diarrhea to prevent dehydration. (For serious diarrhea, see also "Rehydration Therapy" on page 125.)

If you are constipated, again drink extra fluids. This time add handfuls of dried fruits, and eat lots of vegetables which have roughage. Strenuous exercise also helps get bowels moving.

Eye Strain ▪ Glare from the water, dust in the wind, or plain tired eyes after a long night watch can produce dry, strained eyes. Bathe them in Dacriose irrigation solution or Sulamydophthalmic solution 10 percent; then rest them in the shade.

On a boat, contact lenses have several advantages over eyeglasses. Spray on glasses is a constant irritation, as is rain. There is also the danger of knocking them overboard or, worse still, of some flicking block or shackle smashing the lens into your eye.

Whichever you choose, carry spares. If wearing contact lenses, try not to wear them for more than twelve hours at a stretch and, if possible, remove them sometime during the day to let the eyeballs "breathe." Recent research has shown that long-term lens wearers are developing "wrinkled eyeballs" thought to be due to reduced oxygen reaching the surface of the eye.

Object in Eye ▪ If you have something in your eye, *don't* rub it. Lift the top lid well out over the bottom one and close it down onto the lower edge of the eye-socket bone, outside the bottom eyelid. Now, still holding the upper lid, gently push it with your fingers along the edge of the socket toward the nose. This should generate tears under the lid and wash any grit or eyelash toward the corner of the eye without grating on the surface of the eyeball.

If this doesn't work, get someone to roll the affected eyelid outward over a matchstick or pencil to expose the foreign body. It can then be removed with the moistened corner of a clean handkerchief. (See also "Eye Burns" on page 120.)

Insomnia ▪ Insomnia tends to feed on itself. Some people worry excessively about not sleeping, and then that very worry keeps them awake. Sleep is very important for sick people as it helps their bodies to recover, but healthy human beings might profit from a more positive attitude. After all, no one has ever died of sleeplessness. One pope is said to have done no more than catnap for sixty years, and many high-powered people such as Prime Minister Margaret Thatcher sleep for only four or five hours a night. So instead of worrying about sleeplessness, why not see it as a wonderful bonus, giving you all those extra hours in your life? If you do miss out on sleep completely for a few nights and your body really wants more, it will make up for it in its own good time.

If insomnia does bother you, there are various things you can try to induce sleep without resorting to drugs. Avoid stimulants such as tea or coffee in the evenings. Try a warm milky drink instead. Have either a very light book or, better still, a very boring book beside the bunk. Try a dictionary, for instance; frightfully educational and a surefire inducement to doze off. Alternatively put on your earphones, plug in your radio to some program in a foreign language, and try to understand it. Finally, make sure you are really comfortable. In the tropics you may find it better to sleep on deck.

Jellyfish and Sea Urchins ▪ I have as yet to come across an infallible cure for the pain of a jellyfish sting though all the following are worth trying. Calamine lotion dabbed on sometimes soothes it, while Thor Heyerdahl in his *Ra Expeditions* suggests ammonia poured on the sting. If none is available, urine has exactly the same effect. Oddly enough, this is the same treatment advised for relieving the pain of sea urchin spines . . . useful stuff urine.

If you do get sea urchin spines stuck in your foot, don't try to fish them out. They are very brittle and will only snap off. Instead, cover them with pawpaw skin. The results are said to be excellent with the spines dissolving in about half an hour.

Chapped Hands and Chilblains ▪ Any lanolin-based lotion is good for chapped hands, though it is better used regularly before hands become chapped at all. Chilblains are more difficult customers to deal with, as evinced by the number of "cures" on offer. Chief among these is ultraviolet treatment for long-term sufferers while some people paint on iodine or alcohol. Yet others swear by bathing them in urine. . . .

Prickly Heat ▪ This is a rash which, in the worst cases, covers the whole body. In milder forms it often appears on the backs of the hands. It itches and consists of tiny spots giving a pinkish tinge to the skin as one spot merges into the next. Prickly heat is caused by excessive heat and sweating. Stay in a breeze when possible, and wash frequently with freshwater, not salt. Very careful drying and powdering of the skin should help, though I have found most proprietary powders for prickly heat ineffectual. However, in the Far East I bought some Chinese Agnesia powder which

worked extremely well. Heaven only knows what was in it. Both cornstarch and calamine lotion are also said to help.

Rehydration Therapy ▪ Prolonged vomiting and diarrhea can cause
severe dehydration, which in turn causes millions of infant deaths around
the world each year.

To avoid such a tragedy, the lost liquids and electrolytes must be
replaced. But in order to absorb the liquids and salts, glucose must also be
present. So, in mild cases of diarrhea or vomiting, a diet of clear salty
broth plus carbonated drinks (which contain both glucose and bicarbonate
of soda) is good.

In more severe cases you can alternate (1a) and (1b) below or mix up a
quantity of drink (2).

(1a) One cup (eight ounces) of water mixed with one-quarter teaspoon of
bicarbonate of soda, alternated with

(1b) One cup (eight ounces) fruit juice in which one-half teaspoon of corn
syrup or honey plus a pinch of salt has been dissolved.

(2) This is a simpler drink but lacks the potassium found in the fruit juice
above. So, if you have it, add one-half teaspoon of potassium chloride to
the basic drink of one quart of water to which one teaspoon of table salt,
one teaspoon of bicarbonate of soda, and four teaspoons of sugar have
been added.

Green coconut water contains both glucose and potassium. If it is
diluted with an equal part of water and then one-half teaspoon of salt is
added to each pint, it also makes a good rehydration liquid.

One glass of rehydration fluid should be given after each bout of vomiting or diarrhea. If the patient still feels thirsty, more liquid can be given,
but remember to alternate the drinks if using (1a) and (1b). With vomiting
try giving the liquid in frequent small sips rather than a single drink.

Babies should have one glass (or bottle) of plain water for every two
glasses of rehydration fluid.

After about six hours of this treatment restart light meals or, for babies,
breast-feeding, because stimulation of the gut is said to speed recovery
from diarrhea. This rehydration therapy is now used worldwide for most
cases of cholera as well as ordinary bouts of diarrhea.

Seasickness ▪ There is a cheerful old saying that seasickness has two
stages: the first, when you are afraid you may die and the second, later
stage, when you are afraid you may not.

Some people still believe that seasickness is "all in the mind," that you
only have to be firm with yourself for all to be right. Our daughter, Katy,

was first seasick at six months old and continued to suffer for the next ten years, despite every effort and every medicine we could find on the market. She was also swingsick, carsick, trainsick, and oxcartsick. Obviously in her case it was not "all in the mind."

There is an almost endless procession of proprietary drugs on the market designed to combat seasickness. If you suffer from the problem, you will probably have tried some of them already.

There is a case to be made out against most of them. I remember a rare time when I decided to take one. We were setting out on a thousand-mile trip after being in port for some months, it was rough outside, and I was the cook. In the end we didn't leave that day, yet I felt foul—giddy and nauseated for several hours. I could only think it was the side effects of the antiseasick pills.

Another problem is that antiseasick pills often make people dozy and so useless as watch keepers. However, someone in the debilitating throws of seasickness is equally useless and, poor thing, feels far worse.

If you suffer from severe and chronic seasickness and have so far found no cure, then pack your kit bag and jump ship. New "cures" are coming out all the time. Something one day will turn up to suit you. The astronauts use a combination (available by prescription) of twenty-five milligrams of Phenergen and twenty-five milligrams of Ephedrine. Two recent developments have been the Transderm Scop ear patch, which you can stick behind the ear, and Dea Bands. These latter are based on principles of Chinese acupuncture and consist of two elasticated wrist bands each with a large bead sewn onto the inside. With the bead properly positioned over the correct pressure point on the wrist this ancient / modern treatment is said to work remarkably well. And without taking drugs.

One further comfort for seasick sufferers is the knowledge that most people do find their sea legs after a few days continuously at sea. Also, if you were travelsick as a child, the problem often diminishes as you get older.

Keeping in the fresh air, away from diesel fumes, and gazing at the steady horizon help. Stay busy even if only by singing complicated songs. Seasickness is not all in the mind, but thinking about it certainly makes it worse. Avoid close eyework. I also strongly believe in regular, easily digested food since the feeling of hunger is frequently confused with that of nausea.

Different people fancy different things: a hot drink of glucose or something savory. Dry crackers or dissolved soup cubes, glucose candy or pickles—all are things I've been asked for.

Sometimes the feeling of nausea actually comes from air trapped in the stomach. Try drinking half a glass of water with one-half teaspoon of bicarbonate of soda dissolved in it. Often a good burp makes a world of difference. On the other hand, it may actually make you sick. Others enlist fizzy drinks for the same purpose.

Or maybe you prefer to think positively, to lie back like the women of the Seychelles and enjoy it. Just as Victorian ladies thought it delicate to faint, there it is considered refined to be seasick. The women arrive to board the government ferry armed with beautiful lacy handkerchiefs and fresh-cut orange peels. Even before the boat leaves the dock, they lie down as best they can with the handkerchiefs over their eyes, the orange peels pressed fervently to their nostrils and bright plastic bowls, supplied in large numbers free of charge by the management, clasped to their bosoms, hoping against hope that they won't disgrace themselves by not being sick. Frankly, if you tend to feel a bit queazy yourself, it is better not to watch but to close your eyes and once again conjure up those beautiful thoughts.

The chief hazard of persistent seasickness is dehydration, which, in very small children, can be dangerous. (See "Rehydration Therapy".) Frequent drinks are important in prolonged seasickness. Quite often the sickness settles down to a pattern whereby a person is sick and then feels better for a while. In this case give sips of liquids immediately after vomiting and at frequent intervals after that until, with perseverance, the amount drunk will be more than that brought back. Your doctor may provide you with a couple of antiemetic injections for very serious cases.

Sore Throat ▪ This is greatly eased by dissolving an aspirin in a glass of water and gargling with it. If you are at all feverish, the gargle may be swallowed as well, making sure, however, that you do not exceed the stated dose. Saltwater gargles are also soothing. For really bad sore throats, there are excellent tablets on the market which, if sucked, will relieve the pain or irritation.

Teeth and Toothache ▪ If you ever seek dental treatment abroad, ask around before taking the plunge.

I have received excellent treatment from an Indian in Malaysia, a Chinese in Singapore, and a Vietnamese in Andorra. When in Turkey, however, we asked a Turkish friend if he could recommend a dentist. He immediately enthused about his own dentist . . . who had recently extracted seventeen of his teeth. When I tentatively asked if the man was any good at other things, such as fillings, our friend looked quite bewildered. He didn't know any other treatment existed.

Toothache can be temporarily relieved by oil of cloves on Q-Tips applied carefully to the affected tooth. If you have all-over gum / toothache, try the toothpastes specially made for sensitive teeth.

MEDICAL EMERGENCIES' FIRST AID

Although I consider it a mistake to go to sea without a reliable medical guide, here are a few treatments which may help in an emergency.

Everyone who is interested in sailing should know both how to swim and how to resuscitate others who cannot.

Artificial Respiration ▪ It is *vital* that the patient breathes as soon as possible so as to get essential oxygen to the brain. If necessary, start mouth-to-mouth resuscitation while you are still in the water. Then drag the patient to some firm platform (dinghy, beach, or deck), and lay him on his back. Now extend his neck as far back as it will go so that his tongue cannot fall down and obstruct his airway. Do this by lifting the lower jaw upward with one hand and pushing the forehead backward with the other. Keep the patient's mouth open with the hand holding the jaw, while that holding the forehead pinches the nostrils shut.

Draw a good breath; then exhale it forcefully into the patient's mouth. Repeat this eight times, checking that his chest rises with each respiration.

If, after the first eight sharp breaths, the patient's chest still has not filled despite the neck's being fully extended, feel rapidly around inside his mouth and throat for any debris or obstruction. If necessary, turn him on his side, mouth sloping down toward the ground, and hit him hard several times between the shoulders to dislodge anything caught farther back. Again clean around inside his mouth and throat. If the patient is a child, lay him across your thigh, head down, and slap him hard between the shoulder blades.

Once the airway is free and the first eight breaths have been delivered, check the patient for a pulse at his neck or wrist or by listening to his heart.

If his heart is beating, continue to give mouth-to-mouth resuscitation at the rate of ten every minute, or one every six seconds, until he starts breathing normally.

If the patient is very cold from long immersion in water, cover him with warm blankets.

If there is no trace of a heartbeat after the first eight successful respirations, start external cardiac massage at once.

External Cardiac Massage ▪ Because this can lead to broken ribs, administer it only when no heartbeat is present. If possible, have one person respirating while another gives external cardiac massage. If, however, you are alone, then alternate, giving six massages, then one respiration, followed by another six massages and so on.

To give external cardiac massage, the patient must have at least his back on a firm surface. Kneel beside him.

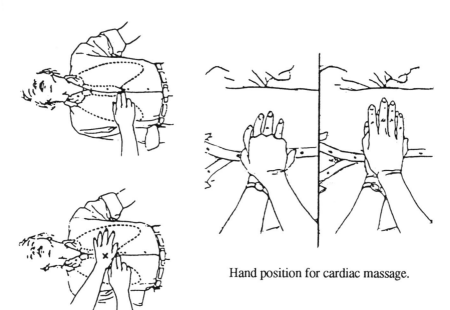

Hand position for cardiac massage.

Head position for mouth to mouth resuscitation.

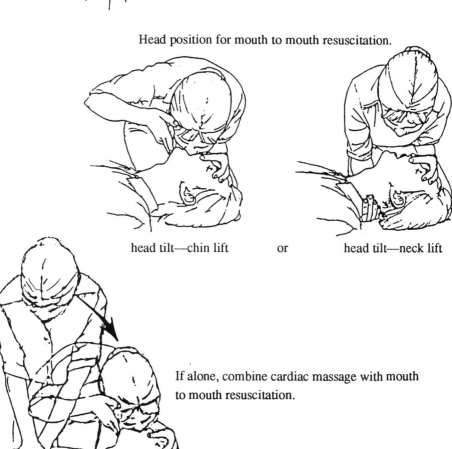

head tilt—chin lift   or   head tilt—neck lift

If alone, combine cardiac massage with mouth to mouth resuscitation.

Locate the lower end of the flat breastbone which runs down the center front of the chest. Place the palm of one hand an inch or two from the end of the breastbone and a little toward the left hand side. Place the palm of the other hand on top and at right angles to the first.

Now press down with sudden force on the breastbone. It should depress approximately one inch, thus massaging, or stimulating, the heart muscle underneath. If you press too hard, ribs can be broken; not hard enough, and it will be ineffectual. Sorry!

If one person is respirating and another giving cardiac massage, then the respirator should locate the pulse and feel one beat for each downward pressure of the masseur. The person applying massage gives one sharp depression every second for six seconds, then pauses while the respirator inflates the patient's lungs.

Continue external cardiac massage until the heart starts beating on its own. After that check the pulse frequently to make sure the heart does not stop again.

As the patient recovers, his color will become a more natural white or pink.

Employ external cardiac massage and artificial respiration in any case of heart stoppage, not only in drowning.

Shock • Clinical shock can arise from several totally different causes. One is loss of body fluids. This can be due to external or internal bleeding, severe vomiting, or burns. Pain, exposure, extreme emotional crisis, and fear also cause shock or make it worse.

Symptoms. The patient's skin is very white and clammy to touch. His breathing is rapid and shallow interspersed with an occasional long, drawn-out sigh. When detected, his pulse is rapid and faint. He seems hardly aware of his surroundings, and if left untreated, he may fall unconscious or even die.

Treatment. The first treatment in shock is, if possible, to find and halt the cause, particularly if it is fluid loss. Bandage thick wads of clean cloth firmly over any external wounds to stop bleeding, adding layers on top if necessary (see "Bleeding" below). For exposure, see "hypothermia" below, and for severe seasickness, try two antiallergy pills or an injection.

Move a patient in shock as little as possible, remembering particularly that pain can both cause and increase shock. Normally the patient should be laid flat with his feet raised about a foot in the air to encourage blood to flow to the brain. Exceptions are as follows: If he has trouble breathing or has possible brain injury, prop him up; if he is liable to choke on inhaled blood or vomit, the former usually with face injuries, lay him on his side.

Moving him as little as possible, make the patient comfortable. If he is cold, wrap him in warm blankets and, if you've got them, put hot-water bottles at his feet, between his thighs, and under his arms. If he is hot, open the patient's shirt, but again don't move him to remove it. Loosen tight clothing at neck, waist, and feet.

Provided the patient is conscious and has no abdominal injuries and especially if shock is due to loss of body fluid from burns or external bleeding, help the patient to drink, in sips only, several glasses of liquid within the first hour. (See also "Severe Burns" above.) With external bleeding this can be warm sweet tea or fruit juice. If neither is available, then water is best. Do not give alcohol.

If despite first aid to his injuries, the patient is still in severe pain, then an injection of morphine may be given, provided he is conscious, has no head injuries, is breathing without difficulty, and has no acute abdominal pain which might need to be operated on within twenty-four hours.

As important as all the rest is to reassure the patient. He is bound to be frightened. Be cheerful yet soothing. Loud voices and strong lights only disturb.

Heart Attack ▪ This can take one of two forms, either what is called angina pectoris or the better-known coronary thrombosis.

Angina pectoris. This starts with a sudden sharp pain in the chest which frequently spreads out along the jaw and/or left arm. The pain is short-lived and very severe, with the chest often feeling tight. It generally comes on during exercise and lasts only a few minutes.

During the attack the patient stands as if petrified, or turned to stone, holding whatever position the pain caught him in, leaning forward slightly and often saying afterward he was convinced that he would die. He usually turns a ghastly pallid gray and breaks out in a cold sweat.

Treatment. It is vital during the few minutes of the attack not to frighten him or encourage him to move. Let him hold whatever position his body has taken up. Any further shock or alarm might kill him.

If it is available, break a capsule of amyl nitrate into a handkerchief and hold it to his nose.

Once the attack has passed, take him somewhere cool and quiet to rest. A tot of brandy may calm him. After an attack of angina pectoris the patient must avoid all mental and physical strain and see a doctor as soon as possible. Smoking in particular should be avoided.

Coronary thrombosis. This produces a similar pain to angina though usually without the pain down the left arm. It is distinguished by the fact that it lasts much longer and amyl nitrate does not relieve it. If the patient continues to feel severe pain for ten minutes or more, you can assume that he's having a coronary. This type of heart attack is not necessarily caused by exertion and is as likely to come on when the patient is asleep as when he is hauling a heavy dinghy on board.

Treatment. If he is not already in bed, carry the patient there. If you cannot lift him, bring a mattress for him to lie on.

Once he is lying down, give him an injection of fifteen milligrams of morphine at once to relieve the pain and shock. Another injection of fifteen milligrams of morphine may be given half an hour later if the pain is still severe and the patient fretful.

Coronary patients are best nursed flat unless they have difficulty breathing, when they should be given enough pillows to support them in a semiupright position.

As with angina, the coronary patient should rest until seen by a doctor.

Bleeding ▪ Generally, when a patient is suffering from severe bleeding, you want to lay him flat with the injured part raised so that it is above the height of the heart to try to slow the bleeding. If the injury is to the mouth or nose, lay him so that the blood cannot run down the back of his throat and choke him.

Now stop the bleeding, or the patient will end up in shock as well.

If bright red blood is spurting from the wound, then you know an artery has been cut. Use fingers and thumb to press down directly on top of the place where the blood is spurting out. Keep up the pressure until you can apply a pressure bandage. For this you will need a large pad of sterile or at least clean cloth and a roll of bandage.

First clean away any clothing around the wound. Next cover the whole wound and a little of the healthy skin around it with the wad of clean cloth or dressing pad. Now hold this in place with a *firm* bandage. Watch the pad. If it slowly becomes stained with blood, this is normal.

If, however, the blood comes through quickly, then apply another pad, larger than the first, and bandage it on *top* of the first. Do *not* remove the first bandage. Again tie the bandage firmly but not too tightly. It is the steady pressure which will stop the flow of blood. If the blood still comes through fast, then a third pressure bandage must be applied.

Only after all this has been tried and has failed should a tourniquet be considered. Tourniquets are *dangerous.* They can cause gangrene if forgotten and, if tied too tightly, may damage nerves, to say nothing of hurting the poor patient. A strip of cloth, a piece of cord, a rubber hose, or even a large handkerchief can be used. Tie it loosely around the limb a few inches from the wound and between the wound and the heart—i.e., top of leg for a thigh wound; top of arm for an arm one. Then tighten it up just enough to stop the bleeding and no more. *Release a tourniquet every fifteen minutes.*

If after fifteen minutes the bleeding has not stopped, release the tourniquet, allowing a little blood to circulate through the lower part of the damaged limb. Then tighten the tourniquet for another fifteen minutes.

This may be repeated until the bleeding is under control, but the tourniquet must never be left for more than fifteen minutes at any one time. And it must never be hidden or put on under clothing. If the patient is suddenly whisked off to the hospital, the people who transport him may not realize the tourniquet is there and he could loose a limb. While you keep the rest of the patient warm to ward off shock, a limb with a tourniquet should be left exposed.

Hypothermia ▪ Hypothermia arises when the body loses more heat than it generates so that the body temperature drops below normal. If you fall into the waters around Cape Horn, you have approximately seven minutes to get out before exposure kills you off. This is partly due to the well-known chill factor, the effect that wind or moving water has on body temperature. The stronger the wind or current, the more quickly your body will cool down as the warmth you generate is snatched away.

The answer when on board is to insulate yourself with layers of warm air as described in the section on cold-weather clothing in Chapter 15. Clothes must be dry, or their insulating effect is lost. If you fall into extremely cold water, then obviously your only hope is to swim like mad to get out. But never despair. There was an incredible guy who fell overboard off a fishing boat some miles off Iceland in midwinter. Not only did he swim to the distant shore, but he then scaled a vertical rock face no one had ever climbed before. Such is some people's fantastic and unconquerable lust for life. Presumably what Darwin meant by the survival of the fittest. (For further information about man overboard, see Chapter 24.)

Treatment. Avoid too rapid rewarming. If the person has fallen overboard, strip off all his wet clothes and dry him with warm towels. Regardless of whether or not the patient has fallen overboard, next wrap him in warm blankets or curl up with him yourself, sharing with him your own body heat. If he is cold, rather than frozen, ply him with hot-water bottles. Place the bottles, wrapped in covers, at his feet and on his body. Hot-water bottles may be improvised from empty glass bottles which have secure screw tops. Never fill one with very hot water, and always wrap it in a towel first to protect the patient. As soon as he can drink, give him hot chocolate or tea, not alcohol, which is not as warming and simply makes the heart beat faster.

Heatstroke and Exhaustion ▪ The human body is fussy about temperature. Just as it doesn't like to be too cold, so it does not like to be too hot either. This is because in the heat one sweats a lot, losing body fluids and salts.

Heatstroke or sunstroke is caused by the failure of the body's sweating mechanism. It can come on after only a few hours of intense heat or may start after a few days. As well as dry, burning skin, the patient usually complains of a headache, nausea and vomiting, and restlessness. In later stages he may suffer delirium, collapse, convulsions, even coma and death.

Don't get heatstroke.

To avoid this, keep away from heat as much as possible especially in the middle of the day; only mad dogs and Englishmen etc. . . . Make an effort to drink eight pints of fluid a day and to add two extra teaspoons of salt to your diet. Wrapping a wet towel around one's head like a turban helps reduce body temperature, as do wet cloths around the neck and wrists. Frequent bucket baths of seawater also help keep one cool. Afterward cover yourself in very thin clothing to slow down evaporation.

Heatstroke is diagnosed by dry, burning skin and rapidly rising temperature. This can range from over 103°F up to 110°F, when death occurs.

Treatment. Immediate cooling of the patient is the number one priority; the aim is to reduce the body temperature as quickly as possible to a reasonable level.

Remove the patient to a cool place, preferably under an awning on deck. Strip him and cover him with wet sheets dipped in the sea. If you are becalmed, fan him. If you have a refrigerator on board, then rub his body with ice cubes or ice water, not forgetting to wipe his face and head as well. If using sheets, redip them frequently so as to be as cool as possible. Watch the patient's temperature. Once it reaches about 100°F, he should start sweating again.

As soon as possible encourage him to take frequent drinks. Add a teaspoon of salt to a pint of water unless he is vomiting. People with severe salt deficiency seem not to notice the salty taste of the water. The aim is to get eight pints of fluid into the patient in twenty-four hours. To avoid a relapse, he should stay out of the sun for a week.

Heat Exhaustion ▪ This is less dramatic but arises from the same causes as heatstroke: too great a loss of body fluid and salts. The sufferer becomes very tired, often with a headache and nausea and sometimes muscle cramps as well. Sweating does *not* cease, and the skin is cool and clammy.

Treatment. To treat heat exhaustion, put the patient in the shade in a breeze, and give him water containing salt as for heatstroke. If he prefers he can take salt tablets downed with at least a pint of water; otherwise he may feel even more nauseated. Again, eight pints of fluid, preferably saline water, should be drunk in a day. In fact, if you ever feel inexplicably exhausted and washed out in the tropics, take extra salt. It can make an amazing difference.

SHIP'S MEDICAL KIT

Store all medicines and bandages in cool, dark, airtight containers out of reach of children. Check medicines for expiration dates, and throw them away once those dates have been reached. Your own medical handbook will tell you what medicines to buy. But as a general guide I have listed below the sort of things carried in our own ship's medical kit.

DRESSINGS

Ace bandages for sprains.
Butterfly clips for open wounds.
Catgut for sewing open wounds.
Cotton.
Gauze.
Lint.
Narrow cotton bandages.
Wide cotton bandages.
Needles for stitching.

Plaster of paris bandages for broken limbs (use as directed, with *caution;* too tight, it can cause gangrene).
Steri-strip for open wounds.
Tube gauze for finger and toe injuries.
Vaseline gauze for open wounds and burns.
Zinc oxide adhesive plaster.

OINTMENTS

Bactroban for tropical sores.
Betadine antiseptic ointment.
Desitin and Sulfamylon for minor burns.
Desitin for inflamed skin and babies' bottoms.

Furacin for septic spots and boils.
Neosporin or Garamycin antibiotic ointment.
Pawpaw ointment for infected cuts and stubborn sores.

POWDERS

Bicarbonate of soda for indigestion, rehydration therapy, and burns.
Neomycin for infected cuts.
Potassium chloride for rehydration.

Potassium permanganate for washing vegetables and sterilizing drinking water.

LOTIONS

Chap Stick lip balm.
Dacriose irrigation solution for eyes.
Iodine disinfectant for minor cuts and grazes.

PhisoHex or Hibiclens for general disinfectant.
Sulamydophthalmic solution 10 percent.
Sunscreen cream.

PAIN-KILLERS

Morphine, 15 milligram ampules, for intramuscular injection in very severe pain. *Not* to be used in head injuries or before possible surgery.

Other mild and moderate pain-killers such as Tylenol for use in less severe pain. Aspirin helps reduce certain fevers.

OTHER

Acute infections: for those prone to allergy, try Bactrim; or Septra (sulfamethoxazole-trimethoprim). Take one pint of water with each dose.

Acute infections: Antibiotic for those less prone to allergy, try Terramycin.

Anesthetic (local): For suturing, Xylocaine by injection.

Angina pectoris: Dissolve glyceryl trinitrate under tongue.

Antihemetic (antivomit): Phenergan, twenty-five milligrams.

Antiseasickness: Dramamine, fifty milligrams.

Constipation: mineral oil *or* milk of magnesia.

Diarrhea: Lomotil.

Eardrops: For infected ears, Otobiotic Otic Solution.

Eyedrops: To ease pain when removing difficult object from eye, Pontocaine. Afterward keep eye covered for several hours.

Indigestion: Amphojel *or* Maalox.

Malaria: Aralen.

Needles and syringes for injections.

Salt Tablets: For salt deficiency. Take with lots of water.

Sterilizing tablets: For water.

Thermometer.

Throat lozenges: For sore throat—e.g., Cēpastat.

Toothache: Oil of cloves applied to aching cavity or tooth.

Vitamin C, one gram: Try one a day if suffering from recurrent septic cuts in the tropics.

Some people, of course, don't believe in all this modern medical rubbish. Just give them a bottle of brandy and a revolver and let them decide on the treatment.

15. Clothing

IN CHAPTER 6 I talked about various ways of washing clothes. Now, before I discuss which clothes to trundle on board and which to leave behind, let us glance quickly at steps to dry, iron, and stow that laundry.

Caring for Clothing • *Drying.* No matter which system you used for the washing, that for drying is the same. The important thing, particularly in winter, is to wring everything out as best you possibly can. I'm a pathetic wringer myself, or at least I was until one chilly November day in Brittany when I was faced with eight pairs of sodden pants and an overcast sky. Obviously what I needed was an entirely new approach. Here it is.

Wrap all heavy garments, such as jeans and towels, around any clean, fixed tubular piece of metal; a stanchion, for instance, is ideal.

Hold the material so that both ends are in your hands while the middle is around the metal. Now twist and twist until every drop of water squeezes out.

Do be careful, though, with that precious pair of ancient jeans, the ones you've lovingly patched for the past ten years. Twist too hard and they'll disintegrate in your hands.

This technique for wringing clothes cuts down dramatically on drying times, especially in winter.

After wringing, pull the clothes into shape. If you do not intend to iron them (see page 138), don't wring smart clothes at all. Instead, let them drip dry.

And so to hanging clothes out on the line.

If a shirt is pinned up badly ashore, it blows off the line and falls in the nearest puddle. Pin it up badly on a boat and you lose the shirt.

When there is a really strong wind blowing, it may even be worth the fiddle of threading the line *through* as many clothes as possible, via arms of shirts and legs of shorts and pants.

Generally I loop one leg of underpants over the top of the line, then pull the body of the underpants through the loop which is hanging down on the far side. I do the same with bras and bikinis. Tights I tie in a reef knot. The rest I pin on with as many clothespins as can be spared.

A good policy is to drape towels and sheets from their centers either side of the line as their flapping weight makes them particularly susceptible to winged flight. It I can rustle up four clothespins for each item, then I am pretty confident they are safe.

Check that none of the washing flaps against the boat or the rigging, causing oil stains or chafe.

In the tropics hang clothes inside out and for as short a time as possible. The powerful sun not only fades the colors but also rots the fabric fibers.

If you are lucky, everything will be dry in a day, a good reason for starting early in colder climates. If not, the cabin will end up looking like a back street in Chinatown, but never mind. Back streets in Chinatown are rather fun, and at least the clothes are clean.

Ironing. Once clothes are washed, dried, and aired, what about ironing? My advice is quite simple: Don't. When living ashore, you may deem it necessary to be pressed and polished. On boats it is better to look for easy, drip-dry fabrics. However, sometimes the odd thing really does need ironing, in which case there are several alternatives.

Twist and twist until every drop of water is squeezed out.

If you and your neighbors can stand the noise of the engine, an electric iron is definitely the most efficient. There are also gas irons, but they have to be recharged, and that is often impossible. There are handsome great charcoal irons on sale in antique shops. You just have to track down the charcoal. I've even heard tell of kerosene pressure irons, though I've never seen one.

We have two small flatirons, which we heat up on the stove. A flatiron is ready when spit sizzles on the bottom before it evaporates. But even so, give a quick test to a hidden corner before applying it to man-made fibers. If the iron is too hot, you'll get an iron-shaped hole in your shirt and a nasty, gooey mess on the iron. Yes, I learned that from experience, too.

The reason for our brace of flatirons is time and motion study: while one is ironing, the other is heating up. I use them mainly for pressing the seams of newly made clothes run up on our Reads Sailmaker sewing machine.

More stubborn creases press out when a damp cloth is laid over them so that the iron works as a steam iron.

If you have no iron at all, try very hot water in a square-sided scotch bottle (be careful the water doesn't break the bottle and scald you). Alternatively, lay clothes flat under the mattress overnight, as impoverished young men have done for centuries.

In the absence of an ironing board a thick towel folded on the table or the cabin sole does a passable job.

Clothes stowage. At this point mildew raises its ugly head. I hang most of my clothes in a locker near the engine and have had no problems with them except the odd rust spot which appears from nowhere.

Clothes lockers need plenty of through ventilation to stop condensation from building up. Holes drilled in locker doors help. Also, lockers under the bunk are less likely to suffer from drips than those directly under the deck.

Clothes not in everyday use can be carefully folded away into airtight plastic bags, but again there's a chance of a condensation buildup inside the bag, in which case everything could be ruined.

Whichever you plump for, a good airing on a sunny day wards off mildew. Also, natural fibers are much more prone to mildew than man-made ones. Don't forget to turn out leather shoes, handbags, and even suitcases, particularly if they have zippers.

Zip fasteners. For years I assumed that nylon zippers were better for boats then metal ones. Wrong! The trouble with nearly all nylon zips is that they have aluminum zipper feet. If left any length of time, the aluminum forms aluminum oxide, eats into the cloth of the zip, and the whole thing solidifies. On the other hand, I've fished out clothes not worn for years and discovered the plain metal zipper still in perfect order. (To help prevent jamming, always leave the zipper foot halfway up the zip when putting clothes away.)

For outer garments like oilskins and parkas I still look for a big-toothed nylon zipper but with a plastic-coated zipper foot. For dresses and pants I am back to the old-fashioned all-metal fasteners when I can find them.

Suitcases ▪ Anything that folds flat will do. A diver's waterproof kit bag is one idea while many boat people take advantage of rucksacks, not only for traveling but for toting supplies home on their backs, leaving both hands free for either children or more shopping. Children, too, are much happier about humping the groceries if offered an adventurous rucksack rather than a boring old plastic bag.

Your Wardrobe ▪ What clothes you take sailing hinges on where you plan to go and for how long. The worst is when, like us, you meander about from temperate to tropical zone and back again, carting two sets of clothes around wherever you go.

Boats suffer universally from drips and humidity. They also have greased blocks and oiled chains (if they don't, they should have).

So easy-to-wash, noniron fabrics in bright and dark colors are the order of the day. White is definitely out.

I do apologize to all those who dream of sauntering ashore wearing their natty white yachting pants, but unless you plan to scrub them each evening, you'd be wiser to leave them at home, along with any other good clothes you don't want ruined. Plain, peaked caps are good protection for both eyes and nose when you are out in the sun's fierce glare.

I try to reserve some clothes for going ashore and others for the boat. Then, as the shore gear turns shabby, it converts to boat gear, which slowly disintegrates into engine room rags.

What is wanted for boat gear are clothes that are hard-wearing and practical. No flapping sleeves or billowing skirts. Still, there's no need to be dowdy. Bright pants and sweaters, particularly if patterned so as to hide the rust/oil marks, do wonders for morale.

COLD-CLIMATE CLOTHING

Long Term ▪ How much you invest in your cold-weather wardrobe depends on how long you expect to fight off the frostbite and, to a certain extent, on your pocket. In the event that you intend sailing in the cold for some months or years, then consider buying specially designed thermal clothing.

The theory behind thermal clothing is that warm air trapped between the tufts or holes in cloth will insulate your body from the cold. Good thermal underwear really does make a difference, and if, on top of that, you pull on a thermal suit, you will be not only as snug as a bug in a rug but wonderfully comfortable, too. Thermal suits are light to wear and easy to wash. Unless it is pouring rain, they should dry within twenty-four hours.

Check with sailing friends and stores on the top brands to buy, for they do vary in both quality and price.

For thermal clothing to work it is vital that the whole outfit stays dry. Wet clothing loses 90 percent of its insulation.

Short Term ▪ If your cold-water cruise is expected to be short—either a vacation trip or a means to get to the tropics—or if you decide that what with the cost of slipping and antifouling, to say nothing of buying a new mainsail, this is not the moment to throw money away on new clothes, then be practical about the clothes you do wear.

The principles of keeping warm are the same. Trapping warm air between layers of clothing is the thing. But in building up the layers, be sure they are neither too tight nor too bulky. You want to feel free and comfortable as well as warm.

Cellular or thermal underwear has holes. If, over this, you put on a fleecy-lined track suit top, you have your layer of warm air trapped.

Sweaters should be of wool, but avoid finishing off your outfit with one of those fancy cable knits. Icy blasts will whistle straight through the holes. Worn underneath, though, they provide excellent air pockets. I like a roll-neck sweater on top, but Edward prefers a traditional fisherman's straight line at the neck plus replaceable toweling scarves (see "Toweling" below). On fine days a quilted parka completes the torso coverings.

Waterproof gloves may not be approved by the skipper (they tend to catch in winches and lines), but they are a great comfort to the poor old crew, especially when steering.

A hat is a must as one's head is a major source of heat loss. A large woolen pompon hat is a perennial favorite. It can be pulled down well over the ears yet still leave a few inches at the nape of the neck for you to judge the wind direction when running. When we are close-hauled, I like a scarf pulled up over my chin as well. But tuck the scarf ends in, or they'll tangle in the blocks and flywheels and end up strangling you.

Now on to your bottom half. After your thermal underpants a pair of woolen tights are excellent. No, men, don't flee in terror. Your masculinity won't desert you because of a pair of wooly tights . . . at least I hope not. Henry VIII managed to survive quite well in them.

Next pull on your thermal long johns and a pair of long, water-repellent socks. Finally tuck a pair of warm, windproof long pants into your sea boots, and you are almost ready to go on deck. Phew!

If the weather is fine, I finish off with a pair of those very light nylon wet-weather pants, which are wonderful for keeping the wind out without being heavy or restrictive. If it is raining, you will, of course, need your regular heavy-duty oilskins (see "Wet-Weather Gear" below).

Hypothermia is dealt with in Chapter 14. It can be a killer, so do take it seriously. Once again, bear in mind that the two most important factors for maintaining body heat are trapped air which is warmed by the body and dry clothes.

Wet-Weather Gear ▪ Before we sail into summer weather and tropical clothing, let us look at wet-weather gear. There are three main types: very lightweight nylon, neoprene- and polyurethane-impregnated cloth, and polyvinyl chloride (PVC) cloth.

I hang on to an old set of the nylon type since they are good for windproofing over long pants in cold climates and at night in the tropics. They are not robust enough for serious wet-weather protection.

Good wet-weather gear is essential even in the tropics.

Not that the others are anywhere near perfect either. Good-quality impregnated-cloth oilskins are probably the wisest investment, especially in the tropics. But do keep them out of the tropical sun because the backing tends to collapse. Also, check the seams before you buy impregnated oilskins. Unless they are double-stitched and then reinforced on the inside with heat-bonded urethane tape, they can potentially leak at every stitch. Seams daubed with glue are not good enough.

On the whole, though, the cloth is very tough and comfortable to wear. As with nearly all waterproof fabrics, it does build up condensation inside, which is only partly relieved by a lining.

PVC (polyvinyl chloride) oilskins with machine-welded seams do not leak, but they tend to tear right alongside the seams. That said, I have one Line-7 smock which I bought in New Zealand eighteen years ago and which is still in perfect condition. (Sadly a rat ate a hole in the pants.) Such long life for oilskins is quite remarkable nowadays though it used to be the norm. Such is progress and built-in obsolescence.

PVC is a little less "giving" as a material than the impregnated cloth and so less comfortable to wear.

A recent breakthrough in fabric construction heralds a new era in oilskins. The latest cloth transfer-coated polyurethane fabric stops water from getting in but allows condensation to pass out, thus preventing that horrible buildup of cold humidity inside waterproof materials. This cloth should never be folded up when wet but is wonderfully soft and supple to wear.

Whatever fabric you decide on, here are a few general points to watch for when you buy any wet-weather gear:

1. Make sure there is lots of room across the shoulders and backside. When trying them on, bear in mind that you may be wearing more clothes in cold weather.

2. Look for few seams. For instance, there is no need for a seam around the armholes, where oilskins often give way.

3. Don't have gear overlong in arms or legs.

4. There should be room at the neck for a towel, yet it must close well, both at neck and where the hood comes under the chin.

5. Choose a cutaway hood with a stiff peak. Turn your head to see if the hood blocks your view to the side.

6. Sleeves should preferably have inside and outside cuffs. The outer cuff should close near the lower edge with wide Velcro strips. The inner cuff can either close with Velcro or be elasticized.

7. Oilskin jackets either pull over your head (smocks) or do up down the front. The smock type has less to go wrong with its weatherproofing and fewer cracks for drafts. On the other hand, it is exhausting to drag on

and off and cannot be opened out to let air circulate between showers. I personally prefer a smock for cold-water sailing and the ordinary jacket for variegated stints.

8. Have zippers of heavy-duty nylon with nylon-coated zipper foots and a strip of cloth held in place by Velcro to protect the zip. Avoid metal snaps. They always rust up in the end and often pull out of the cloth, too.

9. Pockets should have double flaps at the top and small vents at the bottom to let any water that gets in drain out. Some oilskins have two sets of pockets. One is as I describe above and is used for putting things like personal flares in. The others, more to the side, are lined with beautiful fleecy polypropylene lining to keep your hands warm. If only Captain Ahab could see us now!

10. Check that the oilskin pants are roomy. Holding them up is a problem. Elasticized suspenders lose their elasticity and fall off the shoulders, cords threaded through the waist eventually rot and break. I hold mine up with a piece of string attached to a button at the back and tied firmly around the bunched-up material at the front. Not very elegant, but it hasn't given way yet.

11. Have the legs wide so they fit easily over sea boots, and then have wide Velcro strips at the bottom to draw them in tight. The fly is best closed with a zipper and then a Velcroed overstrip. Reinforced knees and backside are an excellent feature. Look particularly at the crotch seam, a common weakness in oilskin pants.

12. Some oilskin jackets come complete with lifeline harness built in and even an inflatable vest so that they serve as a life jacket as well.

Sea Boots ▪ There are now many types of sea boot on the market. Look for ones which have a good, deep grip on the soles plus a long leg. Short sea boots look great—until you have to wade ashore with the dinghy.

The very soft type have a built-in weakness. When not in use, the tops flop down and form a crease near the heel and ankle. After a time this cracks and leaks.

Check that there is room enough inside for several pairs of socks to be worn in comfort and that, in the case of an unexpected plunge overboard, the boots can easily be kicked off.

Edward and I have always worn ordinary heavy-duty farmers' boots, but then our decks are wood with very little camber. For durability, though, I would defy any yachting boot to beat them. Edward's have lasted him fifteen-odd years and are still going strong.

Toweling ▪ A dry towel around the neck is a great comfort in the rain. It stops those icy drips from trickling straight down your chest. I sewed up half a dozen toweling scarves which worked fine. Ordinary towels are too bulky and take too long to dry out.

TROPICAL CLOTHING

The ideal is nothing at all, but sadly, bare flesh is more frowned upon in hot countries than it is in cold.

For going ashore, chose clothes which are airy without offending local people. Long pants are usually too hot. Shorts are the answer in countries where local custom permits them. For women a very loose, waistless, wide-sleeved dress is probably the coolest garment of all, with cotton or a cotton-and-polyester mix the coolest fabric.

Needless to say, when going ashore in a foreign country, never forget that you are a visitor wanting to see and to learn about other people's cultures. Don't offend with unacceptable Western modes and standards.

The Sarong ▪ All you need to make this most universal and practical tropical garment is one and a half to two yards of bright fabric. The width is governed by the length from waist to floor. I buy forty-five-inch-wide cloth, hem it, and wear it.

There are several ways to tie a sarong. Wrap it tightly around yourself, and fix it in place by twisting the top two corners around each other, then rolling the "knot" thus formed outward and underneath the top edge of the fall of cloth, either at the waist or above the bust.

Alternatively, wrap one end as far around to the right as it will go, pull the other end tightly to the left, and tuck it inside the cloth at the top. Tied this way, sarongs worn above the bust fall off much more often than with the first method.

Again alternatively, sew the material up the side so that you have a tube. Climb in, and pull the extra material out in front. Now divide the fabric into two handfuls so that the cloth is tight around waist or armpits with all the extra shared equally between your hands. Tie these two "ends" together, or better, twist them around each other and tuck them outward and under the main material at center front, as above. You now have a large pleat down the front, allowing you to walk and sit in comfort.

If your knots come undone with embarrassing regularity, you can always thread some elastic through the top of the "tube." This arrangement is particularly good if you want to bathe in public, for instance, in a river. You can get at all parts of your body without upsetting the local sense of propriety or worrying about the whole thing's crashing around your ankles.

That said, it is basically much more practical to leave the sarong as a simple piece of straight material. Then it has innumerable other uses as well. Coiled wet around the head, it wards off the sun. Covering you completely at night, like a very thin sheet, it keeps off mosquitoes and dew. Underneath you on the beach, it protects against coarse sand, or, with the corners gathered up, it instantly transforms into a holdall.

Shoes ▪ I personally live in flip-flops in the tropics. Although aesthetically unappealing, they are ideal for boats. They don't mind salt water, they float if you drop one in the oggin by mistake, they can be replaced anywhere for next to nothing, and once you get used to them, they are very comfortable to wear.

For serious coral wading where there is danger of stonefish, I wear even uglier shoes in the form of those plastic sandals with a buckle and strap made popular by the French.

If you expect to cruise the tropics for some time, make sure that any good leather shoes are not too pointed whatever the dictates of fashion at the time. It takes only a few months of going barefoot for one's feet to try to spread into their natural shape. They then rebel strongly against being squeezed back into the unnatural confines of fashionable leather.

Finally, don't forget that the nights can be cool in the tropics and that temperatures drop fifteen degrees in a rainsquall. Pack proper oilskins plus some warm clothes for cold-night watches. I often wear long pants and windproof overpants plus a sweater and parka when on tropical night watch, but then I do feel the cold more than most.

16. Bedding

CHOOSING BEDDING follows the same general rules as clothing: drip-dry, quick-dry, no ironing, and bright, strong colors with at least a dash of man-made fibers to keep off the mildew. If you have white sheets at home, dye them before bringing them aboard.

Whether you then turn the sheets into sheet bags is very much up to individual taste and also the temperature. Inside sleeping bags they are ideal. But in the tropics one often doesn't want a top sheet at all, and if used underneath, a sheet bag invariably gets into a terrible tangle.

Sleeping bags themselves are very convenient. They stow neatly, and the modern ones wash and dry well. The zippered types open out into quilts.

Blankets are a pleasant luxury but take up space when not in use. One good place to stow them is flat under the mattress, but watch out for damp.

In really cold winters a tough space blanket is the answer. They are thin yet strong with shiny silver on one side. This is the side that you place toward you. The shiny surface reflects back the body heat and so keeps you warm.

Space blankets have successfully saved lives of people caught out at night on mountainsides, so I include one in my "Grab Bag" (see Chapter 24). But they also offer excellent protection from heavy dew when you sleep out on deck under tropical night skies. Then you want to turn the reflecting side outward.

Settee covers are again a matter of personal preference. Mock leather seems ideal when people come in wet and dripping from a swim or a storm and want to sit down. It is not so ideal when people come in hot and want to sit down. They sweat, and when they stand up, there is a pool of damp on the settee and its embarrassing counterpart emblazoned across the seat of their pants.

Personally I prefer material squab covers which wash easily. I made mine with elasticized corners like a fitted bottom sheet. That way they are easy to remove for washing while calling for less washing water and less fabric in the first place.

Carpets and linoleum can damage wooden and steel decks because they trap moisture underneath them, starting rot or rust. However, if newspaper is laid underneath a carpet and an eye kept on it for signs of dampness, it is certainly a whole lot more inviting to step out onto on a cold morning.

Small scatter mats are more of a danger from skidding than their homely effect warrants.

Heated thick towels are my dream of perfect comfort, but alas, on a boat, it is better they remain a dream. They are the devil to wash, need tons of water to rinse, and absorb salt air to develop mildew.

17. Sailing Etiquette

PERHAPS the piece of naval etiquette which I enjoy most is dipping the ensign.

For this you first have to locate your naval vessel of no matter what nationality. Once it is found, make sure that your ensign is properly hoisted and fluttering bravely in the breeze.

Now sail as close to the aircraft carrier or naval patrol boat as you can, and when you are sure you have been seen, lower, or dip, your ensign.

Aboard the mighty vessel pandemonium often follows as some young rating is detailed off to dip back in reply. Once her ensign has been lowered, you can raise yours again.

Ancient naval tradition and the courtesies of the sea thus observed, there's usually a lot of grinning and waving on all sides before you part company. Unless, that is, you do what Edward did, which was to sail through an entire national fleet while it was in the midst of getting under way. There he was busily dipping to them all just as they were halfway through shifting their ensigns from "at anchor" to "under way" positions. Chaos wasn't in it.

In years gone by all this sailing lore and much more was handed down from captain to cabin boy. Now there are no cabin boys. Still, it would be sad if the courtesies of the sea were lost forever simply because we have all become captains.

Most sailing etiquette is, in fact, a matter of simple good manners, which in themselves are no more than consideration for other people.

When a person is living aboard, the deck of a yacht is frequently the owners' living room and should be approached with the same concern for privacy that you would show for someone's house ashore. Unless you know a person well, you would not dream of marching into their family room without first knocking at the front door.

Yachts do not have front doors, so you cannot knock; instead you hail. To begin with, you may find this a wee bit embarrassing, imagining that everyone for miles around is listening. Don't worry, it's not your imagination; they are. I once let out a stentorian bellow aimed at carrying to

Johanne half a mile across a river. Unfortunately, right beside me, was a yacht manned entirely by the British army.

"Hmm. I could use you for a sergeant major" came the dry comment from the officer in the cockpit. However, you will quickly grow accustomed to hailing. You may even be pleasantly surprised at the volume you can muster when impatiently waiting to be picked up from the beach.

When hailing from the shore, do bear in mind the wind direction. Yelling into the face of the wind gets you nothing more than a sore throat. Whistling to any boat but your own is also fairly ineffectual as there are usually several boats around, every one of which will ignore you, thinking the whistle must be for someone else.

When approaching someone else's yacht in the dinghy, stop a few feet off and hail from there: "*Sea Star* ahoy!" or whatever. This allows time for dirty socks to be hidden under the settee, yesterday's leftovers to be stuffed in the oven, and the finger paints to be wiped off the cabin table.

I have found most sailing people wonderfully welcoming, happy to sit and talk to anyone who comes along. But because of this, it is sometimes difficult to get enough free time aboard to finish off vital maintenance jobs. So, if you intend making a casual call, try to go at the end of the working day. And remember, if a yacht has just arrived in your anchorage, the crew may be dog-tired after sailing all night and want nothing more than a good long sleep.

If you have come by previous invitation, then bring the dinghy gently alongside, removing the oars and oarlocks, if you are rowing, so that they do not damage the yacht's topsides.

If no one appears, first hail the boat. Then hand the painter to your hosts and say, "Permission to come aboard?"

Once it has been given, climb up carefully without putting undue strain on fittings which may bend, such as inadequate stanchions. If the owners suggest a good place for boarding, follow their suggestion. It is their boat, and they know what is least vulnerable. If necessary, remove your shoes. High heels and clogs, in particular, spell death to good decks.

If the owners tie your dinghy up for you, it is likely that they know where it is safest. It is also possible that they don't know a granny from a bowline, so give a surreptitious check. Countless dinks go missing from being incorrectly made fast. (To my perpetual shame I must confess I once lost one that way myself.) Unless the dinghy is an inflatable, never leave it bashing against a yacht's topsides.

Except if you have made prior arrangements with friends or if there is absolutely no alternative (and at times there is none), do not raft up alongside another anchored yacht. Each boat's anchor is designed to hold the weight of that boat, not that boat plus another one. If a squall hits in the night, both boats could drag with very expensive consequences.

Apart from the impracticality of rafting up, once again it is an intrusion of privacy rather like parking your camper in a stranger's backyard. In the tropics in particular, the deck is where one washes, sunbathes, and relieves oneself over the side. Not everyone relishes an audience. The idea is to get away from suburbia, not to form a floating one.

If you have to tie up alongside another boat, usually against a dock, try to get lines from your own boat to the shore. Otherwise the whole strain will come on the inside yacht's mooring lines. Apart from anything else, you have no idea how old they are.

If passing a line to the next boat, hand over only enough to make fast. When it is attached, pull in your end and make it fast too. Never leave a long length of line on the dock. Someone may cut it off and take it home.

If there is no one on the yacht you are going alongside, put out lots of fenders and then think before making fast. Don't tie your lines onto the poor people's chain plates or stanchions. View the problem as if it were your own boat. Then you should not go wrong.

Once you are rafted up, this is the one time when you are allowed to walk across someone's deck without asking permission. Do it as quietly as possible by the route least likely to be intrusive. In either type of rafting up, keep that noise pollution down.

Noise is the curse of our modern age. Let's at least try to confine it to the cities. People who play hi-fi music over deck speakers (believe it or not, there are some who do) should consider returning to the high-rise jungles where they belong. People who start noisy generators after dark and then go ashore for an evening out deserve the potatoes they find thrust up their exhausts. The most beautiful anchorages in the world, and they are out there waiting for you, need only one blaring radio to be utterly ruined.

There are several polite ways of asking people to turn their Muzak down. One of my favorites is when Edward points at the offending machine and says in his most tactful voice, "Do you think you could ask those people to play a bit quieter?" If all else fails, give a prolonged blast at close range on your foghorn. Silence should fall swiftly and heavily.

There is an unwritten law among the cruising fraternity that in an emergency you can borrow a dinghy without permission. The rest of the law says to return the dinghy as soon as possible and in the same condition as when it was borrowed. Ours was once returned leaking and with one oarlock missing.

Cruising people do not care, and would usually rather not know, whether you have sailed fifteen times around the world backward or been president of Citibank except that, if the former, you may have picked up some handy

Caleta Horno, Patagonia.

The most beautiful anchorages in the world are there waiting for you *(La Digue, Seychelles, looking across to Praslin).*

tips on the way. These they will want to discuss at length and, alas, almost ad infinitum.

There's no need, however, for all cruising talk to be about boats and cruising. One of the great joys of cruising is the amazing variety of people one meets, drawn together from every nook and cranny of life by love of independence, adventure, and the sea.

Often they do not volunteer much about their past, not because they have something to hide but because they mistakenly believe that their other lives have become irrelevant. Tread softly, and you will learn many fascinating things about the world that you never knew before. But don't press too hard, for that, too, would be bad etiquette.

Sadly, though, there is now another side to international cruising. It has expanded enormously in recent years, and along with all the ordinary, honest, interesting folk you meet, there are some who might be described euphemistically as "undesirable."

These few, and they are few, with their drugrunning, gunrunning, and thieving, are rapidly eroding cruising yachts' international welcome, making it more and more difficult for the rest of us when "going foreign."

18. Going Foreign

THE ONLY essential documents for a foreign cruise are the ship's papers plus a current passport for each member of the crew.

In highly bureaucratic countries, especially Communist ones, a birth certificate can also prove useful. Why anyone should be so reassured by this proof that one has been born I do not know.

Occasionally you will be asked for your health certificate. This is an internationally recognized booklet in which any immunizations you have had are officially recorded. Before smallpox was eradicated from the world, every country demanded a health certificate showing that you were properly vaccinated against this killer disease. Since its eradication the most common requests are for proof of immunization against yellow fever and cholera. If you are planning to travel to, or have come from, an infected area, the authorities will want to check your vaccination record. (See Chapter 14.)

If visiting certain Communist countries, you must obtain an entry permit or visa before arrival. Most other countries welcome you for a short visit, but in a few you have to buy a visa on entry. For the pleasure of setting foot on Egyptian soil, we were charged, in loaded exchange rates and taxes, a mammoth hundred dollars each. And keep your ear open. International politics is fraught with petty tit-for-tat squabbles, and depending entirely on your nationality, you may find that a traditionally friendly country has turned hostile overnight. One poor German yachtsman was even given a hard time by a Greek official because the German chancellor had recently made a lightning visit of only two hours to Athens, whereas the previous week the French president had stayed in the Greek capital for two days.

Entry stamps on your passport may last as little as two weeks, after which you have to leave the country, while others expire only after three months and can then be renewed.

And then there is the boat. On average, boats can stay in a foreign country for one year. After that governments impose crippling import duties. But some countries allow you only six months, some only two weeks, so check up before embarking on a prolonged stay anywhere, and remember the rules vary depending on the yacht's country of registry.

Harbor and light dues also differ enormously, but smaller yachts, under twenty tons net, are frequently exempt.

On Exit ▪ To get clearance to leave a country, the skipper plus ship's papers, passports, three copies of the crew list, and preferably the crew as well do a tour of the immigration and port offices and occasionally customs, too.

Head the crew list with the yacht's name and port of registry. Underneath, in neat columns, put the name, nationality, and passport number of each crew member. An added touch is to write in their theoretical positions on board: skipper, mate, navigator, or cook.

Have a rubber stamp made up showing the yacht's name and port of registry. Flourish this at every conceivable opportunity. The rubber stamp people will positively purr with pleasure. Without it they may bare their teeth and spit.

Once you have your clearance you must leave the country bound abroad within twenty-four hours. Wait longer and you may have to go through the whole rigmarole again. Getting clearance can take anything from one hour to one day.

Duty Free ▪ If you wish to export goods, such as alcohol or tobacco, duty free, contact a duty free shop or ask customs and you will be told how to proceed.

Generally you buy the duty-free goods, then tell the merchants when you are leaving and where the boat is lying. They will then contact customs, which will deliver the goods to your boat just before you cast off.

Once aboard, the customs agents will want to watch the goods stowed away, preferably in a locker designed for the purpose. They will then seal the locker. These are now bonded stores, and the seal on them must not be broken until you are out of territorial waters. Once outside, you can break the seal and imbibe the contents to your heart's content. I know one elderly couple who regularly sail across the Channel between France and the U.K. in order to liberate their liquor.

If you are buying expensive equipment in Europe, such as engines or cameras, it is sometimes possible to recover the 15 percent VAT (tax) after leaving. As a rule you have to be buying goods worth two hundred dollars or over. Check before buying your equipment (a) if the country operates such a scheme and (b) if that particular firm will help you. It is not obligatory.

In Britain the system works as follows. You buy, say, a generator at the normal price. The seller fills out a special rebate form and receipt, including the purchaser's passport number and permanent address, which must be outside the European Economic Community (EEC). This form will be handed to you along with an envelope bearing the firm's address. Then, just before leaving, maybe along with your duty-free goods, customs agents must come aboard and check that the equipment is there. They will sign and stamp the form and, if asked nicely, may even mail it for you.

The form then goes back to the retailer of the generator, who will eventually send the rebate to your address—a brilliant piece of bureaucracy no less. This rebate can also be obtained if you leave the EEC by air. Sometimes, though, if you are heading for another EEC country, customs will tell you to have the forms stamped and goods inspected at the final EEC country on your itinerary.

On Entry ▪ When entering a country, head for the nearest large town. Fly your national ensign from the stern and a courtesy flag, a small national ensign of the country being visited, from high up on the starboard spreader. Underneath this, hoist the yellow Q, or quarantine, flag, indicating that you wish clearance to go ashore.

Contact the port authorities on the VHF to say you are coming in and ask where to anchor.

What happens next varies from country to country. If you have failed to get instructions over the VHF and the country is a democratic one, the skipper can row ashore in search of the authorities.

In more insecure or corrupt places it is better to sit tight for up to twenty-four hours to see if any customs or health officials come out, meanwhile calling them up on the ship-to-shore-radio. If still nothing happens, the captain should go ashore with the ship's papers, passports, and crew lists in search of the port office. Everyone else must stay on board.

If there are other foreign yachtsmen in the harbor, ask their advice, but stay in the dinghy. Don't go aboard any other yacht until you have been cleared in and your Q flag has been lowered.

Immigration officials will want at least three neat crew lists plus all passports and ship's papers. Sometimes they ask to see your clearance papers from your last port of call, so take them along, too. Finally they may ask how much money you have with you. This is a good reason for taking at least some traveler's checks on the voyage (see Chapter 19). Many minor officials around the world are unfamiliar with credit cards or bank transfers.

On no account lower the yellow flag before permission is given to do so. Once cleared, you may take it down, but the courtesy flag of the country being visited must be left up until you are again outside its territorial waters.

Emerging nations are particularly sensitive that their flags, symbols of their unity and nationhood, are flown correctly. In this respect it is important to stay abreast of international events. One friend sailed into the Seychelles flying the Seychelle courtesy flag . . . or so he thought. Unfortunately the democratically elected government had just been overthrown by a power-hungry man claiming to rule for the "People." The flag had changed. To be flying the old one was tantamount to counterrevolution.

If you do not possess the necessary flag, it is usually on sale near the port. Ask at the port office where to buy one. Many are simple enough to make at home and much cheaper. I made the more complicated Greek flag by painting the white design on a piece of blue cloth. However, do make sure that your homemade flag is absolutely correct; otherwise neurotic, or plain corrupt, officials may cause trouble. Another friend, captain of a small freighter, was dragged from his bed at gunpoint by an irate West African soldier because the freighter's courtesy flag was not flying correctly. Happily it turned out that what the guy really wanted was whiskey.

Both your ensign and courtesy flags should be lowered at sunset and hoisted again at 8:00 A.M. local time. Also, you should never fly the courtesy flag when your own ensign is furled. However, few officials know this, and you are more likely to get into trouble with them for not flying the courtesy flag than for not following the above rule.

Once ashore, you will discover, if you have not done so already, that there is a worldwide conspiracy among immigration officials to be as stoney-faced as possible. Smile. They say your papers are not in order. Smile. They tell you to go to the back of the line and wait. SMILE! SMILE! SMILE! It is all a game, and it needs two players. They want you to lose your cool. Don't. In some places it is a criminal offense to lose your temper with any government employee. You could end up in jail, so be smart: Play dumb and smile.

Pack a book along with you; state what you want clearly and politely; then wait, either reading a book or thinking beautiful thoughts. That way, provided your papers *are* in order, you will win in the end. And don't forget, even the most well-trained and belligerent official is human underneath. If you are nice and friendly to him, if you behave as if you expect him to be friendly in return, he will probably relent after a little and be pleasant in return.

Customs • Customs agents may want to come out to the boat before giving you clearance. Welcome them aboard with a smile, sit them down, and offer them a coffee (but they may prefer scotch, even at nine in the morning). They will want to hear about any bonded stores or other goodies aboard. Declare them. They will probably want to reseal your bonded locker again after allowing you to keep out only the country's normal duty-free allowance.

Some countries also demand a list of all removable valuables aboard, such as the ship's engine (sic!), inflatable dink, windsurfer, and video camera. These countries have high import duties on such luxuries and want to check that when you leave, you take them with you and don't smuggle them ashore and sell them on the side.

You will also be asked about firearms. In some countries declaring firearms leads to an enormous and sometimes expensive bureaucratic performance. Often the arms have to be taken ashore under escort to be locked away in police vaults. Then, when you go to take them away, you can climb into a taxi with them and drive off! On the other hand, if you are found with undeclared firearms, you may face imprisonment or even the death penalty.

Whether to carry firearms or not is a question much argued over by everyone traveling in a small boat and facing increased piracy around the globe. We have been threatened on a good many occasions. Most of the time we have outwitted our attackers. My own preference is to wield a flare pistol at petty thiefs. Nothing short of a grenade launcher is going to deter real pirates from attacking you, especially when, in more corrupt countries, they are often disguised as customs patrol boats. You cannot answer machine guns with a rifle, however trusty.

Once you have declared, or not declared, your firearms and all formalities are complete, you will be told to lower your Q flag. At last you are free to go ashore and meet the real people.

Going Ashore • Have you ever come across a noisy, loudmouthed foreign tourist in your hometown and immediately thought disparagingly of his country, his compatriots, and foreign tourists in general? Sadly it is not too difficult to come across visiting yachtsmen behaving in similar fashion. One such lout can give all cruising people a bad name and, therefore, a hard time.

Clothes • Down below on your own boat you can wear what you like although some countries will jail you for wearing nothing at all on deck. But when you are ashore, it is only right to recall that you are a visitor in a country by courtesy of its people, a courtesy that you can repay with a sensitivity to their social mores. Islamic revival is in part a reaction to the recent rising dominance of alien values.

One of the saddest effects of widespread travel is that the rich, overbearing tourist with his clinking camera and expensive clothes impresses some less prosperous societies with a misguided wish to imitate.

If we are not careful, the day may yet come when everyone wears the same clothes, speaks the same language, and sings the same songs to the same pop music. The world will be greatly impoverished. There will be little point in traveling at all. By accepting and attempting to follow local customs, by trying to speak local languages, one can help reinforce rather than destroy them.

Another aspect of going ashore is thievery. There is only one place where I have felt totally secure from it; that was anchored off a desert island in the middle of the Indian Ocean. To be fair, Islamic countries are also pretty safe, for under Islamic law or Shari'a, a thief has his right hand chopped off for the first offense, his left hand for the second.

Isle Poule, desert island in Chagos Group, Indian Ocean.

When you are in parts of the world notorious for theft, I would strongly advise you stand watch day and night with a powerful light burning on deck after dark. In less pernicious places it is usually safe to leave an anchored boat in daylight, providing nothing of value is left lying around on deck easily to hand. But always have someone on board at night.

On a recent visit to Barcelona would-be thieves boarded *Johanne* six times in twelve nights. But Barcelona is an exception. It ranks with Naples and Marseilles as the thieving meccas of the Med.

If you do have to leave the boat at night, either get a yachting friend to boat-sit for you or go ashore very discreetly, leaving a light on below (though not, of course, a pressure lamp).

Manners ▪ If you are lucky, you may be invited into a local person's house for a meal. Bear in mind that every country has different ideas of good manners.

In France, for instance, you never sit at table with your hands on your lap. In some countries it is considered good manners to leave one's knife and fork together in the middle of the plate, in others they must be neatly left to one side, and again in France you are often expected to hang on to your cutlery from one course to the next.

A tricky point is to decide whether it is thought polite and appreciative to accept and then to finish up every morsel given to you or whether this is, in fact, insulting, indicating that your host has been mean in his helpings and should have given you more. I read of one poor fellow who swallowed seven cups of black and bitter tea before he realized that in that particular society he had to leave the cup half full to signal that he had had enough. The answer is to eat slowly and watch carefully.

In countries where people eat with their fingers, it is totally taboo to use your left hand either for eating or for giving presents. If you are eating a rice dish, the idea is to mix the rice with whatever else is provided, then roll it into a ball and pop it neatly into your mouth. Not easy, especially if the accompaniments are red-hot and greasy. Then they either burn your fingers or, if left to cool, stick to them in a glutinous mess.

Chopsticks just require a bit of practice. We use them quite often on board. Hold the underneath one firmly between right thumb and middle finger while allowing the upper stick to pivot around its position between index finger and higher up on the same thumb. The result should be like jaws opening and shutting. Once the sticks are positioned, align the two tips by standing them up on your plate.

There is one other very Chinese habit which comes in handy when you cannot stand chasing grains of rice around the willow pattern any longer. Pick the bowl up, hold it close to your lips, and shovel everything in.

In many countries it is considered very forward for members of the opposite sex to speak to each other. In Islamic countries a woman may not even have eye contact with a man unless he is her husband or a close relative. Physical contact such as shaking hands is also often taboo. Watch what local people do and follow suit. I particularly like the graceful Indian habit of bowing to each other over hands held as if in prayer.

Now to one final generalization on good manners: In countries where it is polite to burp after meals it is usually impolite to inquire after the host's wife, and vice versa.

19. Finance

~~~~~~

IF YOU FIRST PLAN to test your pioneering spirit on a short vacation cruise or if you have just won a state lottery, then skip the beginning of this chapter and move on to some suggestions on how to lay hands on your money when you are away from home.

If, however, like many sailing people, you are dreaming of a long cruise while at the same time wondering how you will ever make ends meet, then here are a few ideas for you.

With hard work, patience, and luck it is quite possible to save enough to cover the costs of a couple of years of cruising. After that, though, the more extended the voyage, the more ingenious must be your approach to financing it. Money matters do tend to weigh somewhat heavily on the cruising person's mind.

But that is absolutely no excuse for the insidious growth of the idea that no one can sail off around the world without a sponsor. I suspect this illusion has been fed by the fact that at the end of a sponsored trip the sponsored person writes a book in which he naturally pours lavish and grateful praise on his generous benefactor without whom, he implies, he could never have left.

Rubbish! A few years ago in Antigua a party was held exclusively for the crews of transatlantic yachts which had arrived from Europe during the one single month of December. Of the more than forty people who turned up, including several families, not one of them was sponsored.

What is more, one of the most impressive circumnavigations that I know of, sadly not written up, was made by Margaret and Terry Banks, who set out to sail around the world as a very young couple (aged twenty and twenty-one) in a very old boat.

Their ancient engine collapsed completely during their first ocean passage. Nothing daunted, they dumped the thing overboard and completed the rest of their circumnavigation under sail alone. Terry, a highly skilled electrician, found work wherever he could. Margaret, a busy mother, produced their two babies during the five-year trip. (They got married on June 17, 1967, sailed on June 19, 1967, and returned on June 17, 1972.)

Their life was at times precarious, cash often low, but they made it free

Variable sources of finance add flexibility to foreign travel.

from commitments, independently of Big Brother, the result mainly of two great attributes: guts and hard work.

Earning While Traveling ▪ In the story of Terry Banks you have the first and probably best way to make money while cruising: Have a trade. Professions do not export so well. Trades and craftspeople have few language or cultural barriers; their skills are universally in demand.

There are, however, many countries where foreigners are not allowed to work or where work permits are hard to come by. But this still leaves plenty of scope for working on other people's yachts scattered in harbors around the world.

If you know how to fix an engine, refrigerator, or, best of all, electrical or electronic equipment, if you can repair woodwork or fiber glass proficiently, you will have little trouble earning your bread. Or at least something to put on it. One friend received a whole case of peanut butter in exchange for a job well done. If you are paid in money, make sure it is in cash. Checks have a nasty habit of bouncing even on oceans.

If you have no trade to offer, there are sometimes people who want a hand with painting or sanding their boats or doing some repair work ashore. Usually the smarter, more expensive the boat, the better the pay for working on it.

I have chiefly mentioned boat work because it doesn't entail work permits. Obtaining work ashore depends more or less on how useful your particular skills are to the country being visited. One young chap we knew, a well-qualified mineralogist, found excellent, highly paid work in most parts of the world though he had to stay in each place for some months. Another guy got a government job teaching carpentry to local youths, and a woman friend taught an island youth corps to sail dinghies.

Others find jobs as windsurfing instructors, and English teachers are frequently in demand, particularly if they have TEFL (teaching English as a foreign language) qualifications.

Making and mending sails and awnings are a lucrative business, provided you have a sailmaking machine and a bit of know-how.

In English Harbour, Antigua, there were so many small children living on yachts that I was asked to run a day nursery on board our old ex-Baltic trader. Much as I love children I am afraid I declined.

Photography and writing for magazines can also be lucrative, but you must study each magazine's requirements carefully and learn not to give up after the first few rejection slips.

Another basic attribute to working your way around the world is to be flexible, ready to have a go at anything that's legal. Sometimes a few weeks' well-paid work on a charter boat or even a delivery job will come up. There may be a chance to do some chartering yourself.

If, however, you want to become seriously involved in the charter business, plan to be in one place for several years and prepare for a struggle. Generally there are more boats than charterers. Successful chartering depends on building up contented customers over the years. Occasionally there's still an opening to be found for a day charter business in conjunction with a local hotel in some out-of-the-way place. But there are an awful lot of yachts nowadays looking for out-of-the-way hotels.

Charter money is good when it comes but fluctuates so much that to make a go of it requires time, hard work, and high standards. Aim to have all your charterers go home feeling that they have had an even better vacation than your publicity brochure promised. They will tell their friends, and with luck, after a few years, you can forget your brochures and rely on your hard-earned reputation.

One further problem for the cruising charter boat is that each year more and more countries introduce regulations to protect their native-born charter fleets. In Greece any charter boat must be more than half owned by a Greek. In most other countries some sort of expensive license is needed.

For artistically gifted people making money afloat is not so different from making it ashore. After all, they take their most precious asset, their genius, with them. We met one man, a brilliant painter, who cruised throughout the West Indies, painting pictures, before sailing on to sell them in exhibitions in the States and Europe. A writer, too, needs only a typewriter and a mailbox to start work. Recently we met two women making intricate and beautiful jewelry to sell in their next port of call.

Some cruising people try to trade, buying goods that are cheap in one country, then selling them in the next. This can lead to problems with customs and is much easier the second time around when you have learned the markets at both ends and know what's best to buy. One boat motored into Antigua with a hold full of bananas for sale; the results were, alas, rotten in all meanings of the word.

However desperate you are, *never* trade in drugs. Moral issues aside, in a house the narcotics squad seizes the drugs and occupants. On a boat they seize the boat as well, and that is the last the criminal sees of his home. Incidentally, in Malaysia execution by hanging is mandatory for anyone caught dealing in drugs.

Living afloat normally works out much more cheaply than living ashore. As long as you sail, fuel bills are minimal. If you head for the tropics, clothes and heating cease to be expensive. If you stick to local foods, not imported luxuries, the cost of keeping alive is sometimes unbelievably low. Do not rely on catching fish, however. They are never there when wanted.

One increasing expense these days is harbor dues. Once confined to the United States and Europe, harbor dues are now spreading inexorably around the world as more and more governments realize the rich pickings to be harvested from yachts—and at absolutely no expense to themselves. In Kenya ten years ago a yacht of *Johanne*'s size (sixty-nine feet) was charged fifteen dollars a day for the privilege of anchoring in a remote bay which had absolutely no facilities whatsoever.

This leads me to the question of how to carry the money to pay the harbor dues.

Traveler's Checks, Credit Cards or Cash ▪ Is it best to take traveler's checks, international credit cards, cash, or gold bars under the bunk?

One point to bear in mind is that while cruising, you will be living off savings or capital for much of the time. The longer the capital is working for you—e.g., in some sort of savings account—the longer your money will last.

That said, traveler's checks have a lot going for them, not least that you can reclaim the money if they are lost or stolen. Also, they are known and accepted by banks and larger hotels around the world. On the debit side, as mentioned above, the money is dead, earning you nothing, maybe even losing it if the exchange rate drops. Traveler's checks cost more than their face value to buy. Then, when you cash them, there is another charge, in some countries exorbitant. Shop around for the best package of exchange rates plus charges. (Banks often lure you in with highly competitive exchange rates and then make a whopping charge for changing the check.)

If you do buy traveler's checks, order both small and large denominations. There is usually a charge for each check changed, but without some small denominations you will end up having to change a hundred dollars into Turkish lira to pay your final ten-dollar, grocery bill.

Charge cards such as Diner's and American Express are offered only to someone with a steady income or healthy bank balance. Drawing facilities in most third world countries are extremely thin on the ground and if, as happened to one of our crew, you lose your card, you will find yourself wishing you had traveler's checks, cash, or some previous experience at being destitute.

International credit cards such as MasterCard or Visa are more acceptable abroad, particularly in Europe and the more developed world. But even they should not be relied on as your only source of money. All cards are unpopular in third world countries, where competition has already honed profits to a minimum and shopkeepers are understandably reluctant to hand over 4 to 5 percent of what profit is left to first world card suppliers.

Cash is fine until it is stolen. (The same presumably applies to gold bars.) At the time of writing, U.S. dollars are welcomed by banks in most parts of the world and even demanded by Eastern bloc countries, where they give ludicrously low exchange rates. Pounds sterling are also welcome by the Communist bloc and are well known in the forty-nine countries of the Commonwealth. But like traveler's checks, cash is money lying fallow. Unlike traveler's checks, it is uninsured. Exchange rates for cash are normally worse than those for traveler's checks, while the bank charges are equally high and open to rip-off.

Finally, money can be telexed to banks overseas if and when required. In some places it will even arrive within the promised twenty-four hours; in others we have waited more than a month for money to come through. When you ask for small quantities, the actual telexing costs more than the percentage charged on traveler's checks. On top of that, the local bank often insists on converting your money into local currency and then back into dollars, naturally taking its commission on both transactions.

So there's your choice. Confused? Well, it is confusing, because there are so many ifs and buts. If it is any help, our personal solution when in developing countries is to rely mainly on bank transfers if we are staying three months or more, with some cash and traveler's checks in the boat's safe as a backup. Traveler's checks are also useful for showing to immigration on arrival. If passing through, we use traveler's checks alone. In Europe we rely entirely on Eurochecks (unavailable from U.S. banks) and credit cards.

One final word of advice: Once your immediate financial problems are solved and the boat is seaworthy, go. Don't wait for the taxman to send you a check apologizing for overcharging you the last five years or for Grandmama to declare the boat perfect. In either case you will never leave.

We were halfway across the Atlantic before *Johanne* had a sink in the galley, and even today, thirteen years later, we still hand our guests small plywood boards to balance on their knees at mealtimes while we wait for a free moment to rig up a table. But we are sailing.

Have you ever dreamed of drowsing away an afternoon on the white beaches of the Caribbean or glimpsing the high peaks of the Andes, of unraveling the mysteries of Easter Island or studying the coral reefs and rare birds of Indian ocean atolls? With a well-found boat and crew, a fair wind, and determination, they can all be yours. The world is out there waiting for you and the wind is free.

20. Pets

~~~~~~

IF GOING on a vacation cruise and your pet is a carefree, adaptable soul, you may decide to take it, too. But do remember dogs need lots of exercise and cats fall overboard.

For longer trips the decision is even more difficult.

Many countries combine thieves with a local population that is afraid of dogs, so, at first glance, you might think a dog would make a good addition to the crew. But what does the dog think? Unlike cats, dogs must have plenty of exercise to be healthy. I have seen beloved pets who have lost half their hair and all their *joie de vivre* after a long passage because boating is essentially an unhealthy way of life for them. On top of that, the poor things frequently compensate for lack of leg exercise with frustrated, nonstop lung exercise.

In fact, one such wee yachting pooch was actually strangled by a

All pets have their pros and cons.

neighboring yachtsman who couldn't stand the incessant yapping any longer. Another cruising couple, arriving in a Muslim country with a small dog on board, watched in unbelieving horror as a customs official calmly drew out a handgun, and, without a word, shot their pet dead in front of their eyes. His only explanation: "We don't like dogs here."

There are also countries, like Britain, where by law no pet from overseas is allowed ashore. This is an attempt to keep the country free from rabies. Any foreign yacht and any British yacht coming back from abroad have to put their pets into government quarantine kennels for six months. If caught trying to evade the law, owners face a heavy fine. The pet faces death.

If you are coasting in your native land, life is much easier. You can take the dog for a five-mile run every afternoon as usual, although this does mean that your cruise will be ruled by the dog.

Cats are the traditional ship's pet and for good reason. They are far better suited to sea life inasmuch as lack of exercise does not undermine their health. The only worry with cats is that they may fall overboard and drown or go absent without leave when alongside. But I doubt if the risks are actually any greater than those of being run over or straying on land. Some people object to the strong smell of cat on board, but if you are a cat lover, then presumably you won't mind.

All other pets have their pros and cons. We had French friends who carried a parrot with them wherever they went, and we knew an American magician who had tame panthers on board.

As far as I know, only the owl and the pussycat ever went to sea because they chose to. I doubt if animals really enjoy cruising. The continual restriction month after month cannot be healthy. A small, smooth rock complete with its own blanket is still, in my view, the most suitable pet for a boat.

21. Pests

~~~~~~

Rats and Mice ▪ These usually scuttle on board when the boat is tied up to a dock or on a slipway. Here a cat may, or may not, earn its keep, depending on whether it's a keen ratter. If you have no cat, then buy a trap.

The most efficient trap for the rat is the walk-in cage variety. But this leaves you with a live rat on your hands. Traditionally you are supposed to hold the trap plus rat underwater until it drowns. But for the tenderhearted there is an alternative. Take the trap into the countryside and let the rodent go.

Snap-spring rat traps must be big, heavy, and well secured. Otherwise, when the powerful spring whips shut, it propels the trap backward, often maiming the rat instead of instantly killing it. Tie the bait on carefully, wrapping it around many times with thread so the rodent cannot simply grab the cheese and go. I say "cheese," but just like humans, different rodent cultures have different tastes. For instance, West Indian rats and mice prefer their traps baited with fish or bacon.

On no account use poison. The rodent is bound to die in the most ungettable corner it can find and stink the boat out.

Cockroaches ▪ I can tolerate rats and spiders and actually rather like mice. Large, flying cockroaches I detest.

There are two main sorts of cockroaches: the large and the small. The small, whiskery types are the ones that sneak on board as stowaways hidden in cardboard boxes or with their eggs laid behind the labels of cans (see "Cans" under "Storing Up" in Chapter 7).

These whiskery types can, with care, be left ashore. The large, flying cockroaches are another matter. Though their egg sacs are bigger and more visible and so less likely to steal aboard with the supplies, any calm tropical night can reveal huge adults homing in on you through the moonlight accompanied by a revolting whir of wings.

Once you are invaded, there are various extermination techniques available.

Some firms specialize in fumigating boats or sell bombs with which to do it yourself. Roaches breed far too efficiently, their life cycle being two weeks from first laid to just hatched. So, if you are truly infested, it is wise to have two fumigations two weeks apart. Fumigation entails an awful lot of upheaval, packing everything and moving it out on deck, and it isn't guaranteed successful even then. So, if your case is not desperate, try some other remedies first.

When we bought *Johanne,* she was positively buzzing with large roaches. Luckily she had been abandoned for some time, so they were pretty peckish. We collected empty short jam jars, the type with the neck that curves in, dropped a layer of honey in the bottom (jam will do, too), smeared a little honey near the top, placed the jars in tempting corners, and beat a hasty retreat.

Each morning for the next week the jars were black with a seething mass of roaches. At a guess I would say we caught well over five hundred big ones.

Once trapped, the roaches must be killed before they're dumped overboard or you will have them swimming back to you in enthusiastic relays. One way to kill them is to pour enough salt water into the jar to cover them. Add a little squeeze of liquid detergent, and they will die almost instantly. Alternatively, in hot countries they will die if left out in the sun.

Boric acid mixed with a little sweetened condensed milk and dropped into a barely opened matchbox is effective with small roaches.

The best trap we have come across so far is the Japanese Roatel (hotel for roaches?). Japanese scientists discovered that after eating, cockroaches like to move upward. So the ground floor of the "hotel" is entered through a one-way swing door to a central "lobby." Here a delicious, specially designed meal is waiting. Once they've eaten their fill, they go upstairs for a postprandial nap, passing through another one-way door as they go. And there they stay until killed by the trapper either with liquid detergent or sunshine.

There are also aerosol sprays: "Do not inhale the mist. Do not let it alight on your skin. Do not spray on fabrics, plastics, food, children, pets, surfaces used in food preparation. . . ." How is one supposed to chase a lively cockroach around the cabin without the spray alighting on one of the forbidden articles? And the very fact that the smell is revolting proves you've inhaled the beastly stuff. Yet with all these warnings manufacturers are completely silent about the gravest danger from aerosols no matter what their contents: their destruction of the protective ozone layer above our planet Earth.

So if you *have* to use a spray, resort to it only as a final weapon of defense rather than attack, and buy one of the cans with a long direction nozzle for a more accurate and limited blitz.

One final solution, at least for the small roaches, is a lizard. For years we have kept small lizards on board. They do a stalwart job eating up whiskery cockroaches and also ants.

Fleas, Bedbugs, and Head Lice ▪ Other pests likely to bother one are fleas, head lice, and bedbugs. All can be picked up ashore in markets or on public transport. However, the slight risk of their temporary residence is, to my mind, greatly outweighed by the delights of sharing in the vibrant life of local people ashore.

Fleas are tricky beggars to catch. Their bites are easily recognized: small, very hard, itchy lumps, often in lines or groupings where clothing is tight, such as the waist or wrist.

Soak all the clothes and, if you think it is in your bed, your sheets, trying to drown it. If you spot one, grip it tightly between thumb and index finger. *Do not look.*

Get a glass of water, and submerge your fingers, plus the catch. You can then let go—and probably find that all you caught was a bit of bed fluff. But if it is the flea, it now can't jump free as it undoubtedly would have done if you had peeked earlier. Fleas can also be caught on a bar of wet soap. Alternatively, you could resort to flea powder.

Bedbugs are small, slow-moving insects that suck blood. They hide under bunk boards, around the edges of mattresses, and in the hems of sheets.

To get rid of them, wrap all the movable articles in an uncontaminated sheet, and carry the lot to a small, enclosed area, such as the fo'c'sle.

Put a little kerosene in the bottom of a tin can. Place a rag in it so that all free liquid is soaked up. Light the rag, and allow it to smoke for several hours in the closed space. The fumes kill the bugs, but watch out for fire. Go over the remaining bunk structure with an insecticide.

Head lice also succumb to kerosene, though I don't know what a doctor would say to it. Dilute the kerosene well with water, then comb it through the infected hair, taking great care not to get any in the client's eyes. Shampoo thoroughly afterward.

Nuptial Flights ▪ These are a real pest. A great swarm of insects arrives on board, usually at dusk or after dark. Frequently they drop their wings on arrival, and if you are not quick, they get into everything, including your eyes and nostrils. The best thing to do is to shut all the hatches and put a hurricane lamp out, either on deck or, better still, in the dinghy astern. Provided they haven't already dropped their wings, they will fly to the light. Happily, nuptial flights only last about half an hour.

Watch out, though, for the remaining ants. If you have any wood on your boat, they may burrow inside it and gobble it up.

Mosquitoes ▪ These are potentially dangerous in countries where malaria or yellow fever is endemic. Everywhere else they are simply a nuisance. If you are in a malarial country, always take the very latest antimalarial tablets. (See Chapter 14.) On top of that, take what precautions you can to avoid being bitten. Luckily mosquitoes don't like smoke. In this respect mosquito coils are amazingly effective, though they do give some people headaches.

Light a coil before turning in. Place it on a nonplastic saucer on the cabin sole and as close to the bunk as possible, but beware of fire. You won't hear a single buzz, until about four in the morning. Then look over the bunk board, and sure enough the wretched thing will have burned itself out. Why manufacturers can't make coils that last all night I do not know.

In fact, on board a boat anchored out, one is far less bothered by mosquitoes than are the poor souls trapped ashore.

An insect repellent is also effective against mosquitoes but must be used with caution as it is agony if accidentally applied to the more tender parts of one's anatomy, such as the eyes. If the mosquitoes are really bad, use a fine mosquito net. In hot countries a good suntan plus acclimatization works wonders. Mosquitoes make a bee line for new arrivals from cold climates with their rich, tasty blood. After a time in the tropics, as one becomes more and more stringy and yellow, they are less and less tempted to bite, and if they do, the bites don't usually swell up or itch.

Weevils ▪ Once one moves out of range of highly refined cereals, one invariably comes in contact with the weevil. To remove them from foodstuffs requires an assortment of tactics.

The quickest way of deweeviling flour is with an extrafine sieve which holds back both weevils and their little white grubs. (See also flour storage under "Cans" in Chapter 7.)

Weevils are particularly partial to semolina but are easily removed. Just before cooking, put the quantity you want into a bowl; then pour enough freshwater to cover the semolina (the water can later be used in cooking). Stir the semolina briskly, and the weevils will float to the surface. Fish them out with either a small tea strainer or a spoon. Drain the semolina, and cook it as soon as possible.

How wonderful it would be if rice, like semolina, could be cleaned by being immersed in water. But, though I have tried it several times, it doesn't really work. I think the weevils cling to the rice grains and then deliberately hold their breaths. Anyway, in countries where the rice has weevils, it almost certainly has stones, bits of string, even wire as well, so a dry system of cleaning is necessary.

For this you need a measuring cup, two plates, and a trash can. Fill the cup with the required amount of rice. Pour a small quantity on the far end of one of the plates. Then move the grains of rice toward you with your finger, transferring weevils, stones, and other alien bodies to the trash can as you go. Watch very carefuly because teeth can easily be chipped on the treacherous little stones which lurk among the rice; some are even rice-colored, and only sharp eyes will spot them.

Once the rice has been cleaned, empty it onto the second plate, and continue the process until all is ready for cooking.

Lentils are also sold with an inordinate number of foreign bodies thrown in for bad measure. Clean them in the same way as rice.

22. Boredom

~~~~~~~~~~

MANY PEOPLE, setting out on their first long cruise, worry that they are going to be either bored or frightened out of their minds. Ashore there's a job to go to, hobbies to pursue, friends to visit, libraries to browse through, countrysides or parks to walk in, even, God help us, television. On a sailing vacation there is almost the same choice with a whole lot of new excitement thrown in. On the high seas there is not. What is there to do on a small boat bobbing about in the middle of a vast ocean? Lots.

First, though, it is worth remembering that unless you are planning to go around the world nonstop (and what would be the point of that?), most cruising is done at anchor with short forays into offshore sailing in between.

In ports overseas there is almost more to do than at home. There is the country to explore, the shops and markets to unearth, the language to learn, and a new people with a different culture to try to understand. If you have fold-up bicycles aboard, you can go farther afield. Or why not hop on local transport? It is always interesting and often great fun.

If there are other cruising yachts around, then there is a whole new group of sailing people of umpteen nationalities to meet and entertain. And what about all that work which has to be done on the boat?

A boat is quite different from a house. If your house collapses around your ears from neglect, you can always call in the builder while you seek refuge next door. If your boat sinks from neglect, you have to swim for it. So the lady has to be pampered and polished with the same loving care that you would lavish on anything that holds your life in its hands.

Granted, different types of boats call for different amounts of maintenance; to be absolutely sure of never being bored, buy an old wooden one. But no matter what type of boat she is, there is always some job that needs doing, even at sea: blocks and shackles to be greased; sails to mend; whippings to renew; decks to scrub. There is a well-known saying that a boat is a hole in the water into which money is poured. To money add time and energy.

Although with many couples a cruising boat is a glorious joint venture and equal partnership, there is sadly an occasional woman who becomes jealous of what is, in her eyes, her man's mistress, his boat. To see all the free time from the office, which she dreamed of passing in loving tête-à-têtes, squandered while he goes off to the boat to scrape, with apparently equal love, at his beloved's bottom is too much. A boat does become, for some owners, a sort of living thing. Some men seem more comfortable

The author at work. *Celia James photograph*

The author at rest.

loving inanimate objects rather than people; maybe they find them less demanding. Boats become their courtesans . . . and some unhappy feres react to them that way. I met one man who came back to his adored boat to find his wife had filled the cabin with sticks of dynamite.

Why not try a more positive approach? If you can't beat it, join him. If you are not in full partnership and agreement about the boat, at least give it a try. Go down and get stuck in there, join in the pampering. You never know, maybe you'll be bitten too. And after an exhausting day of scraping her bottom or a creative one slapping on new paint, what is more likely than a loving tête-à-tête in the cabin? And if, after giving it a fair trail, you don't like it, that's fine too. Follow your own hobbies, but it may be a waste of effort trying to wean him from his.

Love of boats and the sea is a disease. Like chronic malaria, once a person is "infected" it is recurrent and lifelong. Once bitten by the sea, those that succumb can never leave it. For me the most remarkable and shocking part of the Baileys' ordeal and suffering described in their book *117 Days Adrift*, was not that they survived in a life raft for 117 days after their yacht sank, amazing though that was, but the fact that as soon as they were back on dry land, they started to build another boat!

I personally enjoy the soothing rhythm of painting and the more aggressive satisfaction of chipping rusty metal. Once I get down to it, I don't even object too much to sewing up yards and yards of canvas on the machine.

So what else is there to do besides maintaining and actually sailing the boat? Pretty well anything you like, provided it doesn't require space or electricity. Still, I know one whiz kid who took his computer around the world with him. Mind you, he was only allowed to compute when the wind charger was working full bat with the wind blowing more than Force 4.

On *Johanne* we have had people fashioning beautiful belts, bags and mats out of rope. Others have painted pictures in oils and watercolors. Several have been first-class musicians, bringing their instruments along and giving us all enormous pleasure. You can take up scrimshaw or collage, put ships in bottles or design the perfect dinghy.

We nearly always have someone doing an intensive navigation course, and on one trip we all became besotted with spotting stars and constellations. I like to identify birds as they pass and to keep a log of all the dolphins seen en route. (See Appendix H.)

Many people read, others write. Photography is popular, with some people developing their own film on board. I like to sew when there is a calm, and I collect empty shells off the beach to decorate birthday cards and presents. Carving driftwood is an ancient sailor's craft; making jewelry takes up no room at all.

Then there is chess and Scrabble, solitaire and pencil-and-paper games. In fact, everything people used to do with their leisure hours before the "box" came along to anesthetize us all.

I have known people to fly kites in mid-ocean and go swimming when becalmed. One can even take up thinking, a forgotten art for many in our helter-skelter world.

For a while I tried Yoga, but headstands and heaving decks were a trifle incompatible. Edward has a tiny watchmaker's lathe with a fitting for wood. With it he can turn out belaying pins and parrel beads, to say nothing of small curios for sale ashore. It fits in a box fifteen by twelve by five inches but it does need power to drive it. Still, armed with that lathe plus a set of taps and dyes and a selection of metal rods for making bolts, you could be busy forever and earn a simple living at the same time.

Now, too, is the time to catch up on all the learning you wished you had done earlier. Take along a selection of technical and classical books as well as easy-to-read best sellers.

Edward turns out belaying pins on board.

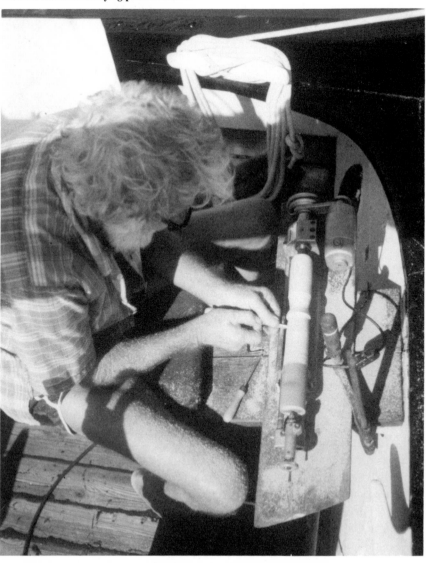

Finally, to what is arguably the most enjoyable occupation of all: "paper sailing." Few things are more stimulating to a wanderer's dreams than spreading out the battered, much-thumbed pilot charts to see where the winds and currents might carry you next. A newfound friend raves about a perfect anchorage thousands of miles away. Look it up on the charts and plot out your route; see which month the winds will take you there.

Once you have a boat, even an old atlas has marvelous dream potential. No, you need never be bored again.

23. Fear

~~~~~~~~~~~~~~~

"Aren't you afraid, crossing oceans like that?" people ask. If humans were logical beings, they would not ask at all. It is demonstrably more dangerous to go for a drive in a car than for a sail in a well-found boat, safer to sail the Atlantic than dash off to visit Aunt Winnie. If we were logical, the open sea would be a pretty fear-free place. But we are not.

I think one fear is of isolation. Once out there, if anything happens, you are thrown entirely on your own resources. In a car accident, if there is any life left, people rush you to a hospital and doctors try to save you. At sea you have to save yourself, rely on your own and your companions' wits, something we are much less used to doing than in centuries past.

There are times when it is natural, even better, to be afraid. If the boat springs a major leak, a healthy dose of fear shoots adrenaline into the bloodstream and has the body working at peak performance in seconds, the fear itself submerged by the demands of the crisis only to reappear when the drama's over.

My cure for chronic fear is to keep busy (with a major leak that is never a problem). And in a gale try singing or chatting, anything to shift your mind away from your fear. If the waves are very large, it is sometimes better to go below, where, with a following sea, you might even persuade yourself it wasn't happening.

On the other hand, a lower sea, but beam-on to the boat, often sounds far worse below, where everything is banging and crashing about, than on deck. I have several times been amazed to come up and discover that all my terrors were quite unfounded.

Oh, yes, I suffer from fear as much as most. Edward calls me "Worry-guts" . . . among other things. Six months after we were run down by a trawler in the Bay of Biscay the sight of an approaching ship turned me so wobbly at the knees I could barely stand. It was only through such sightings without any further mishaps that the fear left me.

Experience quickly lessens fear as one learns just how far over a boat can heel without being turned upside down and how much wind the rigging can stand without everything crashing around one's ears. Only a fool or a psychopath is quite without fear (only a fool claims to be), but as each fear is cut down to size by experience, ocean sailing becomes more and more intoxicating, an exhilarating feast of the senses. As day follows day of glorious sea and skyscapes, sunsets and moonrises, stars and star-dust phosphorescence, you watch, breath-bated, as graceful birds dip their wings to graceful dolphins in the sea below. Fear lurks in the gods, but wonder and joy sit beside you in the front row of the orchestra.

24. Safety at Sea

MORE AND MORE governments are bringing in more and more regulations for yachts because more and more yachtsmen are getting themselves into trouble. Yet safety is mostly just straightforward common sense.

How to Avoid Accidents on Deck and Below ▪ There are four main antiaccident rules aboard ship which have been respected and followed by seafarers from time immemorial:

1. One hand for the boat and one for yourself—that is, always have one hand free to hold on with.

2. Always walk on the windward side of a boat. Then, if you are thrown off your feet by a sudden lurch, you will fall into the boat, not into the oggin.

3. Never run except in dire emergency. Running on board is totally unseamanlike. It gives the appearance of panic in the runner and so can engender panic in everyone else. It also leads to accidents. That leads to rule number 4.

4. Keep decks free from clutter and loose line at all times. They can trip someone up and either injure him or fling him o.b.

Here are a few more suggestions to add to those four basic antiaccident rules:

Cultivate a great respect for booms; they will have none for you. In an accidental jibe a boom can knock you to kingdom come and not even apologize.

Never stand under a person working aloft. He might drop something.

Never make a half hitch to finish off on a belaying pin or cleat (the only exception is with that treacherous springy stuff which Edward calls "polyawfuline"). Instead, make an extra figure-of-eight turn. It will hold the line fast and in an emergency can be whipped off in a second. We once almost destroyed a beautiful little yacht which was trying to sail up alongside us. Someone had made her jib sheet fast with a half hitch, which then pulled so taut that, at the crucial moment, the sail could not be let fly.

When lowering someone in a bosun's chair without the use of a winch, take half a turn round a belaying pin or cleat; then slowly feed the halyard out around the pin, *never* taking your eyes off it. The man coming down will let you know if there is anything amiss aloft, but if you take your eyes off the halyard and it jumps off the pin, he won't even have time to shout "Help!"

Watch that you never have your feet in a coil of rope or chain. "Main-sheet men hop on one leg."

Always carry a knife in a sheath.

When going below, never turn your back on a ladder.

When pouring hot liquids in rough weather, hold both future container and kettle in the air so that they swing in unison. Or put the cups to be filled in a saucepan and pour into that.

Whenever possible, gimbal your stove.

Sharks • Many people have a terror of sharks, and not without reason. Not all sharks, however, are man-eaters. Still, if you do decide to swim off the boat in seas known to be favored by sharks, always have someone on deck standing shark watch. Never swim in such waters at night. It is well known that sharks are attracted by blood, so beware when spearfishing. Not so well known is the fact that sharks are also attracted by white shapes splashing on the surface of the water, possibly mistaking white hands and feet for dying fish. So, if a fin is seen, get out of the water as quickly as possible with a minimum of splashing.

I have been assured by some people that sharks are afraid of loud noises and human aggression. Such people claim that yelling "Boo!" at a shark underwater, followed by a good clout on the head, will send it packing. Happily I have never been in a position to verify these claims.

Fire • Fire is, or at least should be, one of the most dreaded disasters afloat. For despite the sea all around, boats are horribly flammable things and water seldom quenches the flames.

Twenty percent of yacht fires are caused by faulty electrics (when not caused deliberately), the chief danger areas being in the galley or near the engine and fuel tanks. Distribute your dry-powder fire extinguishers (at least three) so they are ready at hand both from below and on deck. Keep a fire blanket near the galley stove.

Gasoline is far more combustible than diesel. Cut its presence on board to a minimum. Store what there is as far from the galley, engine, and hot exhaust pipes as possible.

No yacht should have a gasoline main engine.

A few types of fire, such as wood and alcohol, can be put out with water. All the rest need a dry treatment. Water simply spreads oil or fuel-fed flames farther afield. Aim fire extinguishers at the source of the blaze. If it's a galley fat fire, make sure the gas is off at the bottle, and then try dumping lots of bicarbonate of soda, salt or sand on the flames. This suffocates the fire, which requires oxygen to burn. A proper fire blanket or an ordinary blanket soaked in water will do the same.

If a person's clothing is on fire, immediately push him horizontal. That way you may save his face from the flames. Once he is flat, roll him in a carpet or smother the flames with a blanket or even yourself. With the flames out, treat the person at once for shock and burns. (See "Shock" and "Burns" in Chapter 14.)

Always take extra care when cooking in heavy weather. A sailing friend received third-degree burns and was scarred for life when a saucepan of boiling water accidentally poured down her leg.

Lit cigarettes are in reality smoldering bundles of leaves waiting to ignite. Consider having a No Smoking Below rule on board.

Once they are lit, never leave pressure stoves, lamps, or heaters unattended. One clogged jet and you've got a flare-up on your hands.

Explosions ▪ These are nearly always caused by gasoline fumes or gas. Treat both substances with utmost caution. As mentioned in the preceding section on fire, never have a gasoline main engine on board a boat.

Butane gas is heavier than air and sinks. Never stow gas bottles below or in deck lockers from which the gas can seep down into the cabin and bilge. Gas lockers should have a vent low down to funnel fumes to the outside air. Check all bottles and gas piping for leaks. (See "Gas" in Chapter 1.)

If you do have a gas leak because the wind has blown the flame out or someone has accidentally knocked one of the taps on, pump the bilges out immediately. And continue pumping well after the bilge is dry as the gas lies above any bilge water. Persevere, and eventually all the gas will be sucked out.

A doctor friend of ours had just such an accident aboard a small yacht which boasted no such refinements as mechanical bilge pumps. Quite a crowd gathered to watch this "lunatic" as he solemnly tipped one apparently empty bucket after another over the side of his boat. He steadfastly ignored his audience and, after a couple of hours' hard work, had safely bailed out all the gas.

There are a number of gas sniffers for sale which provide an added safeguard—provided you never rely on them.

Recently natural gas, which is lighter than air and therefore much safer on boats has appeared in bottles.

Collisions ▪ Collisions at sea are becoming ever more likely not only because of the sheer number of yachts and ships around but because too many people on board those yachts do not know the rules of the road. The main ones are as follows:

When navigating in narrow channels or fairways, keep as far to starboard as possible unless an alternative scheme is in operation. Bear in mind that large ships, restricted by size and draft, may be able to navigate only down the center of the channel. It is up to yachts to get out of the way.

In areas where traffic lanes are in operation—i.e. the English Channel, the Gulf of Suez, the Panama Canal, or the Malacca Strait—stick to the correct lane. If you have to cross a lane, cross it as close to right angles as possible. And remember, even if you are under sail, you have lost your right-of-way and must stay clear of all shipping traveling in the main thoroughfare.

In reality, if not in law, small sailboats lost their rights over steam years ago. It is the right of weight which rules today. For it takes some of those huge tankers five or ten miles to stop. Ordinary commercial vessels often cannot afford to alter course to avoid a yacht, and shoal waters are sometimes too shallow or narrow for them to do so. Either way stand by, ready to tack or jibe out of danger at a moment's notice.

Other international collision regulations are these:

WHEN TWO SAILING VESSELS APPROACH EACH OTHER:
1. The one with the wind on the port side gives way.

> When the wind is on your port,
> Then of wisdom be not short.
> Like the ladies of the street,
> You'll avoid them when you meet.

2. If they both have the wind on the same side, the one to windward gives way.

> If you are closer to the wind,
> Of her stay clear and peace you'll find.

3. If one sailboat is overtaking another, the overtaking one must keep clear.

WHEN TWO VESSELS UNDER POWER APPROACH EACH OTHER:
1. If crossing each other's tracks, the one to port keeps clear.
2. If powering head-on toward each other, turn to starboard.

> When both lights you see ahead,
> Starboard turn and show your red.

If yours is the boat which has to adopt the avoiding action, take it in good time and in a positive manner so that the other captain is in absolutely no doubt of your intentions. Check that the altered course won't put you in danger with any other vessel.

> If to your starboard red appear,
> It is your duty to keep clear.
> To act as judgment says is proper
> To port or starboard, back or stop her.

If, on the other hand, you have the right-of-way, maintain your course and speed, but stay alert. The other guy may not know that international collision regulations exist, so be prepared to dodge out of his way at the last minute.

> But if upon your port is seen
> A vessel's starboard light of green,
> There's not so much for you to do,
> For green to port keeps clear of you.

Not only are the international collision regulations frequently unknown to yacht crews, but with the introduction of radar, lookouts in many large vessels are, at best, casual, while since the introduction of automatic pilots in small ones there is often no one at the helm or even on deck.

Mark the progress of other ships vis-à-vis your own. One way to do this is to put your boat on a steady compass course. Then line up the approaching ship against some part of your rigging or hull. After a few minutes check that you are still exactly on the selected course. Then see if the ship has altered against the chosen spot on the rigging.

If she hasn't and neither of you subsequently alters course, collision is inevitable. (Unless, that is, you are running exactly parallel to each other at identical speeds. It has happened to me once in eighteen years.)

Alternatively, take a compass bearing on the vessel, or line the vessel up against a conspicuous landmark, a stationary cloud, or a star. If the ship moves in relation to the fixed land / star / cloud / or compass bearing / bit of rigging, this means that collision is not inevitable, though still possible.

If the ship advances against your fixed point, it means she will probably pass your bow. If she goes backward against it, she should cross your stern.

Be particularly careful at night. Yacht's navigation lights are often so low down that they are totally invisible from the bridge of a ship, especially if there is any sea running.

Navigation Lights ▪ A yacht under sail alone shows a port and starboard light (red and green) with a white light in the stern.

> Steamers have white lights on the mast.
> A sailor no such light will cast,
> But if she shows red over green,
> Then a sailor you have seen.

The "red over green" here refers to sailboats over forty feet. Your white masthead light is meant to be used only if you are proceeding under power. If, however, your yacht is under forty feet, you are now allowed to carry a tricolor masthead light which shows red, green, and white, the white being in the stern sector. Although it is not essential, I would still carry a single white masthead light above the tricolor for use both when under power and in emergencies. Because of this latter use, have the white masthead light as powerful as possible.

If you are becalmed and a great monster appears bearing down on you out of the darkness, try flashing your white masthead light on and off several times. With luck someone on the bridge will spot your tiny signal way below him and alter course. Another idea which works well is to shine a searchlight or powerful flashlight on your sails so it reflects back at the oncoming ship.

Do remember, after throwing the navigation light switch, to go around and check that all your lights are working. And be sure you can reach the masthead to change a blown bulb.

When converging with a ship in the dark, remember that ships are technically schooner-rigged. In other words, the forward mast sports a lower white light than that of the after mainmast. These two white lights separating from each other one way or the other are the best guide to which way the ship is swinging.

Your other important piece of anticollision equipment is a good radar reflector, properly angled and fixed high up the mast. It's no good attaching it discreetly low down. In any big sea the waves would obscure it. Ours flies like an unsightly pennant from the top of the mizzen. One day I'll get one of those more attractive white "sausages," but for the present we appear on a radar screen as a 150-foot cargo boat. Even the most purse-pinched commercial ship might think twice before slicing into that.

Man Overboard ▪ *Avoiding it.* This nearly always happens in the worst possible conditions for swift recovery: bad weather or a dark night. Those, afterall, are precisely the moments when you are most likely to miss a foot or handhold.

So good handholds along with stout guardrails, lifelines, and stanchions are essential to safety at sea.

Some skippers insist on everyone's wearing a harness and lifeline at all times when on deck; others only in bad weather or at night. Yet others, some of them very experienced sailors, think that lifelines actually add danger on board a stable cruising boat (as opposed to a tender racing machine). They say lifelines lure one into a false sense of security so that one becomes careless, relying too much on one factory-made hook. Also, lifelines sometimes get so much in the way that they actually help one to fall overboard.

Still, for the average small yacht and its crew setting out on their first long cruise, a strong harness and line *clipped on* with a reliable clip and attached to a single jackstay running along the deck from cockpit to pulpit is a sensible precaution in foul weather and on dark nights. Always clip on to the windward jackstay, and if necessary, crawl forward rather than walk, giving the wind and waves less to grip on to while you keep you own center of gravity low.

Where harness and lifeline spell "prevention," life jackets are meant as a "cure." However, some are very bulky and hinder movement, so most crews favor harnesses. Best of all, to my mind, is an oilskin jacket which incorporates both harness and inflatable life jacket.

Man Overboard ▪ *The reality.*Once someone has fallen overboard and is still attached by his harness, slow the boat and haul him back on board. This is often more easily said than done.

If someone falls overboard and is unattached by his harness or if the clip fails, the first thing to do is yell, "MAN OVERBOARD!" to bring everyone else on deck. (If it is you that has fallen in, change that to "Help!") At the same time throw over the dan buoy, life buoy, and, if at night, a light marker as well. If you are close enough, try throwing a lifeline from a flick stick. Stow all this equipment near the helm.

If possible, have one person constantly watching the man overboard. One small head bobbing in an ocean is easily lost.

Meanwhile, check the course so that you can turn around and return on the reciprocal track.

When once more near your man overboard, go to windward of him so that you gently drift down toward him, not away from him. This will also mean that the lee, or lower side of the boat, is next to him, sometimes a vital factor in dragging him back aboard. If using a motor, put it into neutral when close so that he's not in danger from the propeller.

Now comes the tricky bit, getting him back aboard. With luck he can still climb up the boarding ladder. But if he is injured or in a state of shock, you will have to winch him aboard. For this either hook the halyard onto his harness or life jacket or slip a noose under his arms and winch him up that way.

Whatever happens, speed is of the essence. A man can survive for approximately seven minutes in the icy waters off Cape Horn. (See "Hypothermia" in Chapter 14.)

If it is you yourself who has fallen overboard, then give thanks that you took the first and most important precaution for self-preservation before leaving port: learning how to swim. We met one couple, a man and his nine-year-old son, who sailed the whole way across the Pacific while neither one of them could swim. I kept wondering what would have happened if either had fallen overboard.

Once in the water *shout*. Make sure they know you've gone.

If a dan buoy, lifeline, or life buoy is thrown to you, swim to it and stay there. It will greatly increase your chances of being picked up.

If you have a life jacket on, curl up around it in a fetal position, arms clasped across your chest, knees drawn up. This is the optimum position for conserving body heat.

If no buoyancy aid is thrown to you and you have no life jacket, then the next best way of preserving energy and heat while waiting to be picked up is to imitate the seals, which, like us, breathe through lungs yet can float for hours with their faces beneath water, just coming up for air.

The idea is to draw in a calm, steady breath, then place your face under the surface of the water so that your whole body hangs relaxed. When ready for a new breath, and this should be at regular intervals, causing no panic or strain, compress your lips, snort the air out through your nostrils, and then gently raise your head so your mouth is clear of the water. Draw another breath, and slowly subside again.

This is the position of natural buoyancy. If you try to keep your head above water, you are holding up an extra fifteen pounds' weight, which is much more exhausting and so liable to lead to panic.

The great thing is to relax and to stay as motionless as possible so as to retain warm water around you. The more you move, the more your body loses its heat and the more you are likely to suffer from exposure (hypothermia).

This position, however, is only a "waiting" position. Naturally there are occasions when it is better to swim for it. If your yacht is visible and it is daylight, then concentrate on letting the others see you. Maybe wave a pair of bright swim trunks to catch their attention.

Abandoning Ship ▪ The loss of one's boat is the one disaster dreaded by all. Maybe you think only great gales, seas, collisions, or attacks by power-crazed killer whales can sink your boat.

You are wrong. More boats sink in port through failed sea cocks and leaking heads than through any other cause. At sea it is often open hatches or portholes which do the damage. (Open portholes can sink a yacht in port, too, if you are alongside a dock during a gale.) The more through-hull fittings there are on your boat, the greater the danger. One faulty plate of steel, one particularly voracious teredo worm in the wood, one spilled bottle of nail polish remover on the fiber glass or crack in the cement—any of these little accidents may jeopardize a boat.

So thorough maintenance and sensible precautions are an important part of keeping afloat.

Of course, damage does occur. If it is at sea, do all you possibly can to save the boat for there lies your best chance of survival. Remember the Fastnet Race where fifteen men lost their lives? Twenty-four yachts were abandoned in mountainous seas, yet, after the storm, nineteen of them were found to be still afloat (of the five that were lost, one was holed by a rescue vessel and a second sank while under tow.) In the meantime fifteen yachtsmen had died. So stay with your yacht until she is absolutely certain to sink. Now there are devices on the market which can be attached to the deck head of the cabin and then inflated when foundering is possible. With this bladder of air inside the hull the vessel should never sink, and though it will be uncomfortable, it might help in your ultimate rescue.

If you have no such device but your boat is wooden, try nailing canvas or plywood over the outside, or inside, of the damaged area. Then stuff it with mattresses and pillows.

Alternatively, with any boat, you can try wrapping a sail around the hull to act as a sort of bandage.

If the sea is fairly calm and the damage is near the waterline, try shifting the booms and ballast to the opposite side in an attempt to heel her over enough to raise the damaged part above the water.

If, after trying everything your imagination and determination can dream up, and there really is no hope, then you need a decent lifeboat. That brings us to a subject, or object, which raises a whole host of arguments and recriminations among cruising folk: the government approved life raft.

Life Raft • This is a circular, inflatable object ideally suited to the purpose for which it was designed.

If a ship founders, the radio officer sends out a distress call. The message is received. The crew members calmly abandon ship for their government-approved floating circular object which is specially designed to stay in one place near the shipping lane in which the sinking vessel was abandoned. It, and they, will sit there until the next passing ship comes to their rescue.

Cruising people often do not have single-side-band radios to send out powerful Mayday signals. (A VHF transmits over a maximum of sixty miles, with its best performance at night.) Even if they do have a powerful ship-to-shore radio, their signal may not be picked up. When we were being shot up by a South Yemeni gunboat only a few hundred yards from a whole convoy of large ships, not one responded to our Mayday call. (By the way, the word "Mayday" comes from the French *m'aidez* ["help me"].)

Apart from that, whenever possible, cruising yachts stay clear of shipping lanes to avoid being mowed down by the blundering dinosaurs of modern ocean transport. Some supertankers are actually launched with two red lights permanently showing "I am out of control."

So, when a cruising boat sinks, the chances are that the occupants will be on their own, fending for themselves as best they can. It is more difficult to do this if your lifeboat is a circular floating object specifically designed to keep people in one place. Inflatable life rafts are not meant to get you anywhere.

If you read the literature on those who survived such terrible sinkings (and without wanting to be pessimistic, I advise that you do, if for no other reason than to admire the amazing courage and determination of all the people involved), if you read about the Robertsons in their family ordeal *Survive the Savage Sea,* Simon Callahan in his beautifully written book *Adrift,* and, most impressive of all, the Baileys in *117 Days Adrift,* one thing stands out very clearly: They all wished that their life raft could *go* somewhere.

The Baileys were only 250 miles from land when their yacht foundered. Yet their efforts to row there, or anywhere else, were constantly foiled by their life raft. In the end they were to drift 1,500 miles before being rescued.

Another objection often voiced against the inflatable life raft is that it is packed away in its neat little case unable to be opened except in an emergency. How does one know that the thing will work, that the bottle will fill the tubes with air? One doesn't. And if your experiences of modern products are anything like ours, your confidence in this one's working without major modifications on your part will be low. And then there's the yearly maintenance overhaul. Who is going to do that on some beautiful coral atoll a thousand miles from nowhere?

What is needed is a life*boat* which can be maneuvered. One only has to read Bombard's amazing story of crossing the Atlantic in an inflatable dinghy to know that it can be done. Already the Tinker Tramp inflatable dinghy / lifeboats are trying to fill the cruising people's demand. This is a sailing / rowing / outboarding dinghy which can have an inflatable canopy attached to turn it into a proper lifeboat. The Seven Seas Cruising Association recently nominated the Tinker Tramp not only the best inflatable yacht tender but also the best yacht lifeboat or raft. (For Seven Seas and Tinker addresses, see Appendix J.)

If you cannot afford the Tinker, consider keeping some other first-class, seaworthy, unsinkable dinghy on deck ready to be launched. It must have oars and oarlocks, a jerry can of water, a bailer, a sea anchor, and, if inflatable, a pump permanently attached inside. Ideally it should have floorboards to hold survivors clear of bilge water and enable them to stand

and stretch their legs. Don't fill the jerry can to the very top, or it may sink on launching.

Undoubtedly a dinghy on deck on a small boat is inconvenient, but it may save your life. (It is no good having an inflatable lifeboat deflated and rolled up in the fo'c'sle.) Quite often owners of small boats construct their own dinghies in wood or fiber glass to fit a specific place on deck. If the dinghy is also a sailing one, so much the better.

Near at hand but well protected should be a "grab bag," preferably an airtight wide-necked plastic container with the necessary equipment for survival stowed inside it.

The contents of the grab bag are up to each boat, but after reading various books on survival at sea, I would like to find the following in mine.

Grab Bag ▪ *For protection against the elements:* Giant plastic bags, plastic sheet, and robust space blanket.

One thing that a life raft provides and an unsinkable dinghy lacks is proper protection against the elements. A good space blanket should have one side shiny and one mat. Turn the shiny side toward your body and you conserve body heat against the cold. Turn it shiny side out, and it deflects

Some suggested contents for the "grab-bag" which should preferably be an airtight, wide-necked plastic container.

the rays of the sun and helps keep you cool. Buy a stout one with eyelets punched in the corners for hoisting like an awning. Large strong plastic bags provided for each crew member to climb into will also protect against hypothermia.

For water: Airtight empty containers, fruit press, small plastic medicine glass, and solar still.

The small plastic medicine glass is intended as a ration measure. The solar still, if good and working, may produce several pints of freshwater a day. The theory of a still is based on evaporation. Salt water placed under a tent-shaped clear plastic cover and left in the sun will heat up and evaporate, leaving the salt behind. When the evaporated moisture hits the plastic, it cools, condenses, and runs down the sides as droplets of freshwater. The plastic sheeting can be used not only as protection from the elements but also as a rain-catchment, funneling the water into the empty containers which should have watertight lids. The courageous Frenchman Bombard, in his inflatable dinghy, used a fruit press to squeeze freshwater out of the fish he caught. If possible, I would also grab an empty bucket or two, and of course the jerry can of fresh water should already by attached to the lifeboat.

For food: Glucose powder, many fishhooks, mung beans, plankton net, raisins, spear gun, tiny glucose candies, twenty-five-milligram vitamin C tablets, and wire traces and stout line.

Raisins, tiny candies, and glucose are easy to ration and give energy. Mung beans contain a wide range of nutrients, and the freshwater needed for rinsing them can later be drunk. The plankton net can be fine muslin or panty hose. Plankton is edible.

For physical health: Bandages and adhesives, and basic medicines for cuts, sore eyes, and sores.

Be wary of taking any pills when you are dehydrated. It could intensify their side effects, especially on the kidneys. Mrs. Robertson gave all her family seawater enemas in the hope that the liquid would be absorbed by the gut while bypassing the sensitive kidneys.

For mental health: Cards and pencils and paper.

High morale is the one most important requirement for survival.

For navigation and self-rescue: Compass, lots of line, oars plus spare for jury mast, Rude star chart, and world chart.

In case you forget to grab the in-use chart as you abandon your ship, mark a world chart with any permanent (not seasonal) winds and currents. Keep the chart in the grab bag. This, combined with the Rude star chart and compass, will help you to work out a course. The line will be needed to improvise a rig, unless of course, you are in a Tinker lifeboat, which doubles as a sailing dinghy.

For signaling: EPIRB, flares, flashlight, hand mirrors, and radar-reflecting balloon.

An EPIRB (emergency position-indicating radio beacon) has a range of 150 to 250 miles. It puts out signals on a frequency monitored by aircraft, so set it going if you see or hear one. The batteries last for thirty-six to ninety-six hours of continuous use. If you see a ship, try smoke flares for daytime and preferably rocket flares at night. A hand mirror, so angled as to flash light toward the bridge of a ship, may attract attention. A radar-reflecting balloon tied to your dinghy might be picked up on a ship's radar. But do note the "might." All survivors report terrible despair as ships pass without seeing them. Look on this as a self-survival / self-rescue exercise with help from a ship being a chance in a million.

For repairs: Glue, inflatable repair kit (for inflatable lifeboat), knives, nonsetting putty (for wood or fiber glass boat), pump, sail needles, spare canvas, and strong twine.

Think positive; you are going to survive this however long it takes, so you may want to do a few running repairs on the way.

On top of all this, include strong line for lashing everything down and for improvising. Grab as much clothing and bedding as possible. It could prove useful later on. When you launch the lifeboat, keep it fast to the yacht until the last moment, and then cut it adrift. As long as you stay fast to your yacht, you've a chance of salvaging more equipment. Use every opportunity. If you are shipwrecked, don't despair. Remember people have sailed the inhospitable Atlantic in six-footers. Bombard crossed it in a rubber dinghy, and he had no jerry can of freshwater either. What he did have was the most important thing of all: sheer determination to survive. He was convinced, and the more one reads, the more he appears to be right, that it is the mind which gives up before the body.

The body can go for several days without a drop of water and for thirty days or more without any food, but if one is convinced there is no hope, one will most certainly die.

On reading the stories of the Baileys and the Robertsons, one sees that it was basically the incredible force for survival of one person in each case which brought them all home alive. With Simon Callahan, adrift all alone, it was his own indomitable spirit which saved him.

Radio ▪ This seems as good a moment as any to bring up the difficult question of radioing for help. If the skipper has gone to the trouble of installing a ship-to-shore radio, it may be with this in mind; on the other hand, it may be that he just wants to keep in touch with his pals every day.

Before tuning in your radio to summon help, however, do consider for a moment the people who will have to turn out to rescue you. You are in a howling gale off Cape Cod. The boat is actually okay, but you are afraid of what may happen next. Is it right, in such conditions, to risk other people's lives by asking them to fly out helicopters or launch lifeboats to rescue you?

No one has asked you to go sailing. It was your own independent decision. Gales are one of the hazards. Because of hundreds of unnecessary calls every year, governments are threatening to curtail individual freedom by inspecting vessels before they go to sea and, in some countries, demanding that all skippers be qualified. We cannot have it both ways.

So, though I wouldn't go to the extreme and say never ask for help in a gale, do at least think twice before calling out other people. Cases of serious injury or illness are different. In fair weather help can often be given with virtually no risk to the helper.

There are two main types of ship-to-shore radio; very high frequency (VHF) and single side band (SSB). VHF frequencies travel in straight lines and so will only carry really well for fifty miles or less. SSB radios work by throwing angled radio waves up at the ionosphere from which they are thrown back at the earth again, allowing the single sideband radio to transmit much farther. But there are two drawbacks to SSB. One is cost and the other is that nearly all coastal vessels and yachts listen only on VHF so that often you cannot communicate with them, despite plumping for the more powerful transmitter.

For this reason many cruising yachts now carry ham radios aboard. Ham radio is not supposed to be used for everyday conversations, and the examination to obtain an operator's license is much more stringent than the exams for the other two ship-to-shore radios. However, most people seem able to surmount these difficulties, and the advantages offered are enormous. Ham radio fanatics are to be found in every corner of the globe where there are humans with enough freedom to be allowed to transmit. The isolated estancias of southern Patagonia nearly all have their ham radios. Any message sent out is likely to be picked up. On top of that they are cheap to buy.

All this said, does one need a ship-to-shore radio at all? Edward spent many years sailing around the world on his own with nothing more than a pocket-sized transistor receiver to give him the time signals. When he was off sailing on his own and I was waiting for him in a strange country with a small baby for company, I often wondered where he was, but because I was expecting no news until he arrived in person, I was not unduly worried.

That brings us to the other side of ship-to-shore radios: unreliability and the inevitable clash between electrics and salt-laden air. Time and again you read of trips which have been turned into a misery of guilt because sailors promised to radio their families and then something went wrong with the radios. It throws the people at home not only into great anxiety but also into a quandary. Should they call out the rescue service or not? But their anxiety is hardly greater than the concern felt by those on board who realize all the trouble they are causing.

We have now installed a ship-to-shore radio, on my insistence and against Edward's better judgment, because I am afraid one of us may develop appendicitis or have a heart attack. Whether we would use it if *Johanne* was foundering in a gale I don't know. What we never use it for is telephoning the family.

After all these years they have, I hope, learned not to worry unduly. For until now, even if a thirty-day trip takes us seventy-five days to complete, we have always turned up sooner or later . . . most often later.

25. Dinghies

ONCE you have cast marinas adrift and ventured on to gunkholing, a good dinghy is a must.

Design ▪ Dinghies, or dinks, come in all shapes and sizes—blunt, round, sleek, and pointed—but as far as I know, the ideal dinghy for a small cruising yacht has yet to be designed (though see Tinker Tramp under "Life Raft" in Chapter 24).

When it is, it will be small enough to stow on the cabin top; light enough for two people to carry, and one person to drag, up the beach; strong enough to take the knocks of cruising; unsinkable; and stable enough to double as a life boat.

It will seat five adults, have two rowing positions and be able to be sailed, rowed, sculled, and outboarded. It will transport stores without getting them soaked and Granny and Grandpa with their five suitcases.

It will not have a bluff bow which charges into all the waves, sending up sheets of spray nor a large chunk eaten out of the stern, ostensibly to mount the outboard but in fact designed so that surf can pour in on the picnic fixings as the dink is beached.

The mast, spars, and oars all will fit inside the dinghy. Oarlocks will be strong and bow and stern painters at least double the normal length, thirty feet being about right. There will be lifting eyes for pulling it aboard, a secure lid for the centerboard casing, and secure bottom boards as well. The painter's bow fitting will be very robust, and if it's fiber glass or wood, the gunwale will be protected by an all-around rubber fender.

If anyone stumbles across this paragon hidden away among the myriad different designs stacked up in every yacht club around the globe, do let me know.

Till then go for the best you can find. The bare minimum is that it is unsinkable and will row easily, preferably with two rowing positions for light and laden work. Many a time have I had to ferry people ashore because the wind was too strong for their own inflatable dinghies to cope.

Oars and Oarlocks ▪ Have oars long enough to reach well into the water with ample leather or plastic protection pieces where they chafe in the oarlocks.

Never buy oarlocks which have one arm longer than the other. They are both impractical and dangerous—impractical because the oars jump out of them when you back down (maybe the designers don't know about backing down); dangerous because on a dark night, when you are trying to pull off a beach in a heavy surf, they can get the wrong way around. Then, as you heave mightily, an oar jumps out, and you go flying over backward.

Because of that mighty heave, oarlocks must also be strong, preferably made of galvanized steel. One dinghy we bought had plastic oarlocks. They snapped in two on their first outing. If given the choice, buy turnover oarlocks in captive sockets. These allow you to unship the oarlock in a second while it still remains neatly attached to the boat, out of the way of passengers and thieves alike.

Another oarlock or semicircle scooped out of the stern of the dinghy provides for sculling when an oar or oarlock is broken or lost o.b. Don't forget that a tholepin or peg of wood stuck in the oarlock hole and fitted with a loop of string or even a handkerchief serves as a temporary replacement for a lost oarlock.

Outboards ▪ *Never* go in a dinghy with just the outboard. Outboards take a perverse delight in breaking down as far from home as possible with wind and tide carrying you out to sea. Always take oars as well. When they are not in use, tie them in tightly.

That is not to say I am against outboards. When they work, they make life a breeze. Unless planning to water-ski, consider a fairly small one that is not too difficult to lift in and out of a bouncing dink or too heavy to drag up the beach on the stern of the dinghy. Tip an outboard up when not in use or it will grow weeds and barnacles.

Before stowing an outboard away after a summer vacation, run it through with freshwater to prevent corrosion. If possible, when going on an ocean passage, do the same.

Using a Dinghy ▪ Particularly if you are using an outboard, check that your dinghy is carrying the minimum requirements for safety: oars and oarlocks, a bailer, and a long painter. A small anchor is a sensible extra precaution.

Getting in and out. Like everything else afloat, there is a right and a wrong way for clambering into a dinghy. To do it gracefully is something which takes a little practice, the ultimate aim being to get in and out without the other occupants knowing you've moved.

When climbing in from a jetty or yacht, face toward said jetty / yacht, and gently lower one leg until your foot touches either the dinghy's bottom or a thwart. If it is an inflatable dinghy, the best place to tread is on the tubular sides. However, never stand on the gunwale of a hard dinghy. Not only will the other occupants know that you've arrived, but they'll probably end up swimming around in the water beside you.

Once you have both feet in the dinghy, move smoothly to a vacant seat and sit down. Avoid having more than one person standing in a dinghy at a time.

To climb on board, reverse the procedure. Catch hold of something firm on the yacht or jetty; thin stanchions bend, so watch out. Once you are ready to pull up, place a foot or knee aboard, then use that foot plus your arms to heave yourself up. Do *not* push off with the foot that is still in the dinghy or again you will rock the boat.

If loading a baby or small child, let someone else hold the child until you are on board or in the dinghy. Then hand it over. Once in, spend as little time as possible standing up with it.

The above instructions for getting in and out of dinghies do not apply so strictly to inflatables with bottom boards in them because they are much more stable. (Climbing into an inflatable without bottom boards is an art in itself!)

When everyone is in, make sure that the dinghy is well balanced, particularly if you are rowing. There is nothing worse than trying to row a lopsided dinghy. With an outboard see that there is not too much weight forward or the bow will dig in, and everything will be soaked. For the best performance with an outboard you want the hull to ride as horizontal as possible. Then, provided you've a powerful enough engine and a well-designed hull, there's a chance you may plane, which is akin to flying over the water and quite as thrilling.

Under way. Unless you are creeping along searching for a safe passage through the reef, *never* stand up in a dinghy powering under outboard. It is dangerous.

Captains of old sailing ships were permitted to stand up in the rowboat when going ashore or visiting other captains at sea for a gam. In very heavy weather they were even allowed to grab on to an oarsman's hair.

A motor-powered dinghy is very different. An upright passenger not only slows the dingy down through extra wind resistance but also blocks the helmsman's view, preventing him from spotting obstacles ahead. But most of all it only needs the dinghy to hit one submerged bit of driftwood or for one plastic bag to foul the propeller and the standing guy can be catapulted headfirst into the water.

So what? you say. So what if the outboard recovers before the helmsman, as it sometimes does? It can roar on, momentarily out of control, chewing ugly great holes in the swimmer's back. A cruising friend, who was an ex-ambulance driver, told me of one man chewed up by a propeller who was held together only by his wet suit. When they took it off, he fell apart.

Yet there seems to be no end to the number of people willing to risk life and limb for the sake of some sort of macho ego trip. (Sorry, but when did you last see a woman standing up in a fast-moving dinghy?)

If people refuse to sit down in our dinghy, Edward throttles back just hard enough to show them the possibilities. They sit down.

That said, you can have good fun standing up in a dinghy which is without an outboard. Why not turn yourselves into human masts, hoist your beach towels, and, with "towels'ls" billowing before a following breeze, head for home? Once, in the West Indies, we navigated past two islets like that.

Getting ashore. When you row ashore, bear in mind that the current usually decreases near the beach. With any strong current head slightly up and across it, making some effort to stem it but not worrying too much about any drift downstream. Once you are close inshore, you can work your way back up.

Going out to the boat, do the opposite. Row yourself as far upstream as you judge necessary and then a bit more, before heading out into the stronger current and aiming a little upstream of your destination. Head directly for your target only when you are very close; otherwise you could be swept right past. Follow the same tactics but to a lesser degree when you use an outboard. You never known when it will break down, leaving you to row for it.

When you land on a beach with breakers, everyone should jump out as soon as possible and rush the dinghy up the beach before the next wave hits. If there is no time, then point the bow around into the surf; otherwise the dinghy and outboard will be swamped.

Dinghy ashore. Once ashore with your dinghy, *make it fast.* No matter how quick you plan to be, never leave a dinghy unless it is either tied up or anchored, the only exception being in tideless waters such as the Med. Even then the dink is less likely to be stolen if it is secured before being left.

If you are not certain of the tides, look them up before going ashore, and moor the dink accordingly. If the tide is going to be farther down when you come back, then either leave the dinghy where she is and make fast to a stake, ring, rock, or anchor or else push her out and leave her floating at anchor. If tying up to a jetty, remember to leave enough free scope of painter for the dinghy to drop down with the tide. In some parts of the world this can mean twenty feet or more.

If the tide is going to be higher, then pull the dinghy well up the beach, and then either anchor or moor her with the painter at full stretch away from the sea. On a jetty find a place where the dinghy cannot get caught underneath and sunk by the rising tide.

If landing at steps, don't tie up across them. Other people want to land there, too. It is often a good idea to drop a small anchor over the stern of the dinghy as you approach the steps. Then, when you tie your painter to a ring, railing, or bollard on the dock, the anchor will hold the dink out from the jetty.

In towns hunt for a jetty out of the way of commercial craft where the dinghy is less likely to be in the way and also less likely to get crushed. In the country look for a gently shelving beach that is kind underfoot. Rocks and coral play havoc not only with feet but with dinghy bottoms as well. Mud has rather obvious disadvantages, too.

In many parts of the world it is unsafe to leave anything loose in a dinghy. Padlock the outboard, and chain the fuel tank to it. Tie in the oars. On the whole thieves will only pinch loose things in broad daylight. At night it may only be safe to leave your dinghy tied up to a yacht club pier or marina where there's a guardian to watch it.

Getting out again. To leave a beach, first make sure the oars are free. Have the dinghy just floating, bows out. As the passengers pile in and sit down, be sure the dinghy continues to float. When everyone is in, give a mighty shove and hop in over the stern. If outboarding, you may find yourself already in deep enough water to start up. If not, punt or paddle out to deeper water. If rowing, take up your position and heave ho!

When going out through breakers, don't rush it. Wait for a lull, even if the wait is ten minutes. Be quite certain that people know what they are doing: one person rowing, one giving the final push off, and, if you are using an outboard, someone standing by to start it.

If you are on your own, either row into deep water and then pray the motor starts at first go or just keep rowing until you are clear.

Take breakers bow, not beam, on, and distribute most of the load very slightly forward of amidships. I've seen two inflatables in succession flip head over stern in heavy breakers. At the same time, if the bow is too weighted down, it won't rise to the waves. If I've put you off completely, you could always camp on the beach and wait for the waves to go down.

Coming alongside. When coming alongside a yacht, point the dinghy into the strongest force—i.e., wind or current. If the yacht is swinging to her anchor, there is no problem as she will also be pointing that way, so you just need to have your bow heading the same way as hers.

With an outboard the operation is pretty simple—provided, that is, you know how to stop the thing. With oars it is best to practice on your own boat first, especially if it is a hard dinghy.

If the yacht is swinging free, approach from the quarter, pointing the dinghy's bow at about forty-five degrees to the yacht and aiming for a spot amidships.

When you are only one stroke from being alongside, quickly ship (lift out) the oar nearest to the yacht. Remove the oarlock, and with the other oar, ease the dinghy alongside. Hold on with one hand, and ship the remaining oar and oarlock with the other.

As I say, it takes a bit of practice, but how satisfying when you can at last do it without even a hint of a crunch. Once you've mastered the basic principles of the thing, it is more seamanlike to ship the oars with the blades forward to prevent wetting the passengers.

Never leave oarlocks in position. They catch on topsides and lines and can easily be lost, bent, or broken, to say nothing of causing nasty gouges and scratches to the yacht's hull.

Remember that if you tow your dinghy for long distances, you will one day break either the painter or the towing eye and possibly loose the dinghy into the bargain.

If towing a dinghy while maneuvering in port, don't forget that, when you go astern, the dinghy painter will do its best to tangle around the propeller.

26. Painting and Varnishing

PAINTING and varnishing are two jobs which anyone with more than a theoretical interest in boats ends up doing sooner or later. Even if you start off as a complete novice, after a season or two, your painting skills can equal any professional's.

PAINTING WOOD

Tools to Remove Old Paint ▪ Blowtorch, paint stripper, sander, and scraper.

Paint Supplies ▪ Gloss, old newspapers or bed sheets plus old canvas, paintbrush, paint bucket, rags, screwdriver, stirring stick, thinners, undercoat, and wood primer.

Preparing the Surface ▪ For a first-class job every trace of old paint must be removed. There are various tools for doing this.

Liquid paint stripper is most effective, but being both powerful and caustic, it should be treated with care. Protect your eyes and skin. Follow the instructions closely. After painting on the stripper, wait until the old paint bubbles; then scrape it off. If there is a buildup of old paint, you may need to repeat the process several times. Be careful to sweep up all the paint flakes as you go along; otherwise the stripper on them will blister any new paint they land on. Ensure that all traces of stripper are thoroughly washed off with either freshwater or thinners before you apply paint. If you don't, the new paint won't stick.

A blowtorch, powered by kerosene or gas, sends out a potent flame. Use it with caution, or you will scorch and injure the wood even if you don't set the whole boat ablaze. An electric heat gun paint stripper is much safer but requires mains electricity or a generator.

To bare-wood a large surface with an electric disk sander calls for both skill and considerable effort. Dust scatters everywhere, so one needs a mask and goggles. On top of that it is all too easy to cut ridges into the wood with the sanding disk. Frankly not for novices.

For soft, peeling paint try a hand scraper. There are several different types, triangular, Scarsten and Stanley, to name a few. Their main drawback is the elbow grease needed to power them. However, if you start off with a really sharp blade, plus strong determination, you will finish the job in the end.

If the boat is old and the layers of paint are thick, you may decide to opt for second best and remove only loose paint, leaving the rest.

With a hand scraper always scrape *with* the grain of the wood to avoid damaging the surface.

If painting from the dinghy, tie the scraper to your wrist with a long length of string. If you don't, one day it will catch on something, tear from your nerveless grasp, and fall in the oggin.

I personally would *never, ever* use an electric tool from the dinghy. Several people have been killed when the power tools they were using accidentally fell in the water and they instinctively reached out and grabbed them.

Once the surface has been cleaned off to your satisfaction, sandpaper the wood and any remaining paint until it is completely smooth to the touch. Wet and dry sandpaper is best for this job. If you are not removing all the old paint, carry a scraper around with you while sanding. Invariably loose bits of paint which you missed the first time around show up. If they are left, the new paint will soon flake off with the old.

Choosing Paint ▪ There are many paints on sale in ship chandlers' specifically created for yachts . . . or so they say. For years we bought nothing but the best. Then, one day, we met the owner of a magnificent charter boat who said he never used anything but house paint above the water and could detect no difference at all. Since then we've done the same with equally satisfactory results. I've even been told by someone in the business that the only difference between most yacht paints and house paints is the wording on the can—oh, yes, and the price.

Unless you're about to use large quantities, go for quart cans. Gallon ones dry up before you've had time to finish them.

Primer. Bare wood must first be protected with some sort of primer. Again there are many fancy names on the market. After trying several of them, I have decided a slow-drying red lead is as good as anything, provided it isn't used below the water. (See "Antifouling" under "Underwater Treatment" below.) Alternatively, a mixture of varnish and kerosene feeds the wood well and prevents rot. A gallon can of normal primer covers approximately forty-eight square yards of boat.

Undercoat. If possible, track down an undercoat to match the color of the top coat. Unfortunately this is often impossible, particularly in developing countries. In this case buy white undercoat and mix in some gloss to produce a pastel shade of what is wanted.

Apply undercoat thinly, up and down and then across. Paint on two coats. In between, lightly sand each coat, leaving plenty of time for each coat to dry out. Brush any dust off with a dry soft brush.

One gallon of undercoat covers approximately forty-four square yards.

Gloss. Gloss does not cover in the same way as undercoat, the reason why it is so much better for the undercoat to match. If using a lighter undercoat, try to find a gloss with a higher than normal obscuring quality. One gallon of gloss covers approximately forty-four square yards. Apply it liberally with all the brushstrokes ending in the same direction.

Preparing the Paint • Properly preparing the actual paint is an important part of the process. If you trust the lids of the cans, it is an idea to store paint upside down. Then, when you open the can, all the goodness is at the top and easier to mix in. Normally, though, it lies in a thick sludge at the bottom.

For a quick job hold the can with one hand firmly over the lid and then shake. Stop when you can feel the liquid slopping both the top and the bottom of the can. Sometimes the paint is so thick or old that this doesn't happen. Stop anyway.

Top professionals do not approve of shaking paint to mix it, saying it fills the paint with tiny air bubbles. So, for a perfect job, stir as below.

Before opening the can, choose the brush you intend using (see "Brushes" below), and find a piece of old canvas or thick newspaper to protect the work surface.

You also need a screwdriver with a very sharp end. Some paint manufacturers provide such small gaps between the can and the lip of the lid that it is almost impossible to open the can without damaging the lid, thus ruining any chance of sealing it properly later.

Once you have managed to force the screwdriver under the lip, lever gently upward, giving a slight twist at the same time. Repeat this all the way around the lid if necessary rather than put too much pressure on one place.

An alternative is to get the screwdriver under the lip and then turn it parallel (rather than at right angles) to the rim with the wedge end of the screwdriver vertical rather than horizontal. Slide it along under as much of the lip as you can while gently levering up and down. This technique works particularly well when an internal vacuum is holding the lid shut.

Once the lid is free, brush any paint on it back into the pot.

If it is a new, full pot and you plan to stir it properly rather than shake it, find a clean, empty can. Put both full and empty cans on the old canvas. Standing with your body between the paint and the wind, quickly pour the top third of the paint into the empty pot. Brush up any drips down the side.

Now it is easy to stir up all the thick goodies from the bottom of the can without spilling the liquid out of the top.

A flat, spatula-shaped stick makes the best stirrer. The most efficient way to mix paint is with a circular movement from bottom to top and down again rather than around and around horizontally. Once all the thickness has gone, return the liquid from the second pot, either blend it in carefully or replace the lid, and give the lot a final shake.

Rather than paint from a full pot, pour off what you require into a spare one. Murphy's Law states that any full pot of paint is bound to be knocked over. Better still, always put the pot in a bucket. Then, if you kick the bucket, the paint will only slop inside. If you kick the pot, you'll have paint all over the deck.

To close a lid, press it down evenly all around. Never clobber it around the edges with a hammer. If necessary, place a good heavy piece of wood right across the lid, and hammer down on that so as not to distort the lid.

How to Paint ▪ For those who have never wielded a paintbrush in their lives, here's what to do.

Dip the bristles of your brush no more than one-third into the paint. Give them a gentle wipe on the inside rim of the pot to remove excess paint; then paint it on in long, smooth strokes. Quick, flappy ones splatter paint everywhere, including your nose and chin.

If painting above your head, cover your hair with a cap or scarf and the deck with an old sheet or newspaper. Then either wrap a folded sheet of paper towel around the neck of the brush, holding it in place with a rubber band, or cut out a circle of old foam rubber, make a small slit in the middle, and force the brush handle through the hole. Both techniques stop your fingers from gunging up with dripping paint. When working overhead dip even less of the brush in the paint than usual.

So that's it, folks! The painting is done. Unless, of course, it rains just as you finish, in which case the gloss will be a mass of raindrop pits and you'll have to sand and paint all over again.

Varnishing ▪ When it comes to varnishing aboard, there is both a prevention and a cure technique. The owners of *Noa Noa,* one of the smartest-looking charter yachts I've seen, lightly sanded and revarnished all their external brightwork every month. That way it never had a chance to deteriorate. A frequent wash down with freshwater also helps save the varnish. Fragile stuff, varnish; it is particularly allergic to salt.

Ordinary mortals, however, usually end up with the cure method. This means that every three months in the tropics, longer in cooler climes, all the varnish work has to be taken down to the bare wood (here an electric heat gun is ideal), then built up again. And it is no good removing only the flaky bits because the places newly sanded come out lighter than the other parts with their extra layers of varnish.

If there are black metal stains around fastenings in the wood, try dabbing on oxalic acid (on sale in pharmacies). Alternatively, something like Teak Brite contains the same acid. It works by "bleaching" out the stain.

Once sanded, mahogany can be given several coats of raw linseed oil to help preserve its rich color. Next comes the enjoyable part of building up the new coats of varnish. Dilute the first two layers with 50 percent kerosene or thinners to make a penetrating preservative primer. After that use undiluted varnish. Leave each layer to dry and harden. Once it is hard, sand the surface thoroughly with very fine wet and dry sandpaper to get an even color. This also gives the next coat something to key to. Carefully brush away every speck of dust before giving another coat; otherwise the next layer will feel rough.

Varnish does look beautiful, but the price for that beauty is high. Many cruising people decide early on that the best place for pots of varnish is on the jetty.

If you do go ahead with varnishing, then apply at least five coats of varnish. Eight coats are about average while Her Majesty's coaches in London are given twenty-seven coats of varnish each.

One gallon of marine varnish covers approximately fifty-six square yards while the same amount of polyurethane varnish does only forty-four square yards. But then it usually lasts longer.

PAINTING METAL

Tools to Remove Old Paint ▪ Chipping hammer, protective goggles, and wire brush.

Paint Supplies ▪ Gloss, primer, rust inhibitor, and undercoat.

Preparing the Surface. ▪ Steel calls for a slightly different approach from wood. Surfaces should look smooth. If bulges appear under the paint, then you know there is rust forming. Soon there will also be nasty rust streaks to prove it.

To remove lumps of rust, use a sharp chipping hammer. Again, attach this to your wrist by string if you are leaning over the side, doing steel chain plates or hull.

Hold the chipping hammer some distance from the hammerhead; then let it swing and bounce off the metal at a slight angle. This helps prevent the sharpened end from making nicks in the metal.

As you chip, rusty metal will fly off in all directions, so wear some sort of protective goggles or spectacles. This applies even to the smallest job. One crew member spent a nerve-racking hour in a deserted anchorage while we tried to fish a bit of metal out of her eye. She had refused to wear protective sunglasses.

After a little practice you will become expert at judging just the right angle from which to attack each rusty lump and at knowing whether you have got to the very bottom of the corroded places. I personally find chipping one of the most satisfying jobs aboard, watching the old rust shoot off to reveal smooth, shining steel underneath. Edward even gave me a chipping hammer as a birthday present, but then, he hates chipping.

When the metal looks free from loose corrosion, go over it all with a wire brush. Treat a wire brush with care, and it will last for ages. Don't scrub it around and around in corners or over bolt heads. This twists the wires in all directions until the thing looks like a pensioned-off toothbrush. (By the way, never throw away old toothbrushes; they have a hundred different uses aboard.)

Wire brushing will probably reveal new patches of corrosion which were missed the first time around, so tote your chipping hammer and spectacles along, too.

Do not chip galvanized metal unless the galvanizing is really flaking right off.

Painting ▪ Once all the metal has been wire-brushed and the rust stains removed you may like to paint on a rust inhibitor such as Rust-Oleum. I am not convinced it works, but I still put it on just in case.

Next you want a good metal primer. It is worth here considering some of the new primers developed by industry to protect metal. In Malaysia people were coating the steel decks of vessels used in the tin industry with a rubber compound which I was told lasted eight years or more. It is, of course, far more expensive than normal paints and needs very careful application. But it is worth looking into for owners of steel boats.

If however, you choose to follow the traditional methods, your next need is a traditional primer. On areas out of the water I still think red lead is hard to beat, though recently, in Turkey, we discovered some absolutely marvelous antirust paint ("antipas" is the word to use) which gives a thick, tightly clinging coat and lasts better than anything else we have tried.

Again, apply two coats with a good drying space in between. Follow this with two layers of normal undercoat and then one or more final layers of gloss. (See instructions on painting wood above for details.) If using more than one layer of gloss, you will want to sand the previous layers before applying a new one to make sure the new paint sticks. We met one guy who had twenty-five coats of paint on the topsides of his immaculate new steel hull. Maybe he too had heard about the Queen's coaches.

If you have any new galvanized fittings do not paint them right away, but leave them to weather for a while first; otherwise they will throw off the paint. All galvanizing should be hot-dipped, never sprayed. If well done, galvanizing lasts years without rusting and comes at half the price of stainless steel. Right now *Johanne* has a massive mast band put on twelve years, and many thousands of sea miles, ago. It has never received a spot of paint nor does it show a speck of rust.

PAINTING FIBER GLASS

To ward off the dreaded day, give the hull a regular cleaning with fiber glass cleaner and polish, particularly near the waterline.

When the day does come, any major job should be left to professionals working in a specially controlled environment with special equipment.

If you have to do it yourself, first sand the area with fine sandpaper until the surface looks mat and water thrown at it spreads rather than falls straight off as it does from the gloss surface.

Then, using a two-part epoxy, paint it on with rapid strokes, first up and down and then across, doing a small patch at a time.

In the tropics two-part epoxy dries very quickly, so only mix up small amounts at a time. The paint in the brush also dries up, so have plenty of solvent or spare brushes handy. And lots of patience, too.

One gallon of two-part epoxy covers approximately forty-eight square yards but depends enormously on the climate and the skill of the painter.

PAINTING THE BOTTOM

Preparing the Surface ▪ When you haul out your yacht covered in weeds and barnacles, try cleaning it off with a hand hoe, one with a foot-long handle. It is ideal. You have complete control, can remove large areas at a time, and still keep the skin on your knuckles. We sharpen ours (bought in a gardening shop) for better effect and often lend it out to covetous friends.

For scrubbing off weeds, we use a stiff, long-handled deck brush. One with a hose running down the center is particularly good, provided there's a faucet nearby.

I have always found it best to clean off while everything is wet and fresh from the sea. Once weeds and encrustations dry out, they are much tougher to remove.

Once you are down to the old antifouling, you may decide to sand off any loose bits. If so, cover up well. Wear goggles and a face mask to protect yourself from all the poisons still lurking in the paint.

Painting ▪ The proper care and treatment of the underwater hull are essential for the boat's ultimate survival . . . and yours. For this special paint *is* needed.

Primer. Depending on your hull, you will first want some sort of primer to paint over the raw material. Red lead should never be used for this.

Don't be vain; cover yourself up before you paint.

While it is superb abovewater, underwater the salty liquid softens, and gets behind, red lead and attacks the very material you are supposed to be protecting. Instead, look for a commercial underwater primer.

Once the surface has been primed, apply a coat of good antifouling undercoat, for contrary to common belief, very few antifoulings are waterproof, while antifouling undercoats are.

One gallon of antifouling undercoat covers approximately forty-four square yards of hull.

Antifouling. When it comes to the actual antifouling, don't be vain; cover yourself from head to foot with old clothes: scarf, long-sleeved shirt buttoned up, and jeans. Otherwise your skin will end up antifouled as well. If any paint does fall on your skin, wash it off at once, using lots of water. I recently ignored a drip on my wrist. The blister was less easy to ignore. On the other hand, the antifouling was first-rate.

Antifouling is, arguably, the most important job of all on a boat. How often you do it depends on (a) what your boat is built of, with wood demanding the most frequent attention, and (b) the temperature of the water you sail in. In the tropics we have to antifoul *Johanne*'s wooden bottom twice a year, in the Med, once, while in the cold seas of the Baltic traders are left in the water for two years at a stretch.

Antifouling paint is horribly expensive, some more so than others. The self-cleaning paints are best suited to fast racing hulls because these paints need speed to work efficiently. Copper-based antifouling, though excellent, should be used with caution as it can set up electrolytic action between itself and steel, aluminum, or ferrocement hulls or even iron fastenings in wood. The same applies to copper sheathing, which should be applied only to copper or bronze-fastened wooden boats.

Read the can carefully before you buy antifouling. Some antifoulings are incompatible with others, so if you plan to change brands, check first.

Antifoulings also have different drying requirements. Some have to be in the water within a few hours of application; others can stay out indefinitely. Yet others must not dry out again once they've been in the water (no good, for instance, if your mooring dries out at low tide).

All antifoulings contain poison, their point being to deter the growth of weeds, barnacles, crabs, and worms on (or in) the hull. The poisons are nonspecific, equally dangerous to humans and everything else, so take care not only of yourself but also of the environment. The British government has recently brought in legislation banning the use of organo tin (TBT), antifoulings on yachts. Sadly the legislation lacks one thing, logic. For while yachts are banned from using it, commercial vessels are not. One yachtsman worked out that a single supertanker painted with the stuff caused as much pollution as would 14,500 yachts using the same paint.

Could it be that the voice of "special interest" was heard when drawing up this superficially sound, but ultimately absurd, document?

One gallon of normal antifouling covers approximately forty-four square yards while one gallon of heavy antifouling does only twenty-eight square yards.

Prepare your antifouling with as much care as yourself. In the olden days boatyards detailed off one small boy to stir the paint continuously while the men slapped it on the hull. The "goodies" in antifouling quickly sink to the bottom, so for optimum results they must be constantly returned to the top. If you ever come across an almost empty pot of antifouling, grab it (provided it is compatible with your own). What remains is almost certainly the cream of the whole can.

Most people use rollers rather than brushes for applying antifouling. It is very much quicker and also much more fun. If you have an old boat, however, whatever its material, you would do better to go over it afterward with a brush, looking for holidays which the roller missed because of the rougher surface. If planning to put on two coats, nearly always better than one, leave the roller in water overnight to stop its drying out. If you cannot afford two coats, at least try to give a second covering to the most vulnerable first couple of feet below the waterline.

PAINTING THE WATERLINE

If your hull is very fair, use masking tape when painting the waterline. It doesn't work nearly so well, however, on older boats, be they wood, metal, ferro cement, or fiber glass; the slightest dip or bump in the hull and the paint oozes in behind the tape, ruining everything.

If you want to put on a new waterline—maybe your boat is floating six inches below her marks because of all the junk you've collected on board— here's what to do. Firmly attach a straight piece of wood (or metal) at right angles to the stem and stern so that it sticks out, absolutely horizontal, on both sides and past the widest part of the beam. Have the top edge of each piece of wood at the desired level for the new line, and check that the two pieces are exactly the same height. Now, starting with the port side, stretch a thin bit of string from one piece of wood to the other, slowly sliding it in until it is just touching the hull and dead straight. Secure the string at this point, near amidships, with tape and thumbtack. Next, carefully slide the string in along the wood, keeping it taut until it touches the hull from bow to stern. Secure the string at intervals all the way along.

Repeat this process on the other side, and then mark the line on the hull. You will have a perfect waterline.

With a wooden boat you can then cut in the waterline if you want. To do this, make straight, shallow chisel cuts right along the line with a second cut from above coming down at forty-five degrees to form a V about one-sixteenth of an inch deep. Once this is done, you will never need masking tape again. To paint it, first paint the topsides down into the V. Then simply antifoul up to the bottom of the cut-in waterline.

Preparing Old Paint ▪ If the paint forms a skin in the pot, go carefully around the edge, cutting the skin free with a screwdriver. The aim is to remove the circle of skin in one piece. Using screwdriver and stirring stick, pick it up, let the paint drip off, then put the skin in the garbage. If the paint does become bitty, strain it through an old pair of panty hose.

BRUSHES

Choosing Brushes ▪ When buying paintbrushes, choose thick heads. Thin ones are useless because they carry so little paint. Inspect the brush carefully before buying it. Remove its pretty cellophane wrapper, and ease the bristles gently apart to examine the center. At least one firm fills the center of its brush with a wedge of plastic to make it look thicker.

If you prefer a brush to a roller for antifouling, try the big, round-headed ones. They hold lots of paint and are excellent for getting into nooks and crannies. The Chinese have a long-handled brush with the head set at an angle; much better for odd corners, it also stops the paint from running down your arms.

For delicate work I prefer small-headed brushes with fairly short bristles. Long ones are less easy to control.

I also like to keep a thinners-soaked rag handy to wipe away all evidence of shaky hands and untoward splashes.

Care of Brushes ▪ Always clean brushes before putting them away. Pour the appropriate thinner into a container; an old jam jar or large empty fruit can will do. Plunge the brush up and down in the thinner (kerosene usually works perfectly well) until all the paint, especially that lodged at the base of the bristles, has come out.

Once the brush is clean, wipe it on old canvas; then wash it thoroughly in warm, soapy water. I pour a bit of detergent in the palm of my hand, then twirl the wet brush around and around until there is no further sign of paint. Dry brushes away from direct sunlight. Once they are dry, we string ours on a "necklace," actually an old piece of three-stranded rope, through which we push the handles of the brushes up to the neck. This way they are stored out of the way in perfect condition with no pressure on the bristles.

If you are lazy, like me, and plan to use a brush again the next day, leave it in thinners overnight, thoroughly wiping off all the excess before painting (otherwise you will end up with painty thinners all over your hand). Do not change colors, however, without first giving the brush a good cleaning and drying. If, also like me, you sometimes forget the brush in the kerosene altogether and it dries out completely, all is not lost. A short soak in either very strong thinners or paint stripper will quickly clean it—and any other good, dried-out brushes you find thrown out by more profligate yachties.

If paint has clogged at the base of the bristles, try pushing a wire brush from the base to the tip of the hairs. Do this ashore or the whole deck will become measled with spots of flicked paint. Never throw dirty thinners or remnants of paint over the side. Seal the can and put it in the garbage ashore.

Lamb's-wool rollers can also be cleaned in thinners, but it never seems very satisfactory and uses buckets of thinners. (Foam rubber rollers often dissolve in antifouling thinners.) I am afraid to say I now throw ours away once we have finished antifouling. If you plan to use a roller the following day, put it in water overnight, and squeeze it out well the next morning.

CLEANING PAINTWORK

When washing down paintwork, avoid both abrasive cloths and powders. They remove the gloss finish from the surface, which then quickly picks up more dirt. Liquid detergent mixed with warm water and a dash of antiseptic plus either a very soft brush or cloth brings up paintwork with ease and helps keep mildew at bay.

27. Leaks

~~~~~~~~~~~~~~~~~~~~~~~~~~~~~~~~~~~~

EVEN THE best-regulated boats leak. One friend, cooking aboard a famous fiber glass racing yacht, had to don sea boots in the galley every time the boat heeled over during a transatlantic crossing. So although wooden boats are the most prone to leaks, none is totally exempt.

An underwater leak is serious, perhaps even disastrous, while deck leaks are more often just a pain in the neck. How to deal with the former is beyond the scope of this book, but the latter frequently succumb to minor ministrations.

The first thing to do is to track down the source of the leak. This may be some distance from where the water actually drips into your coffee or down your back.

Once you've tracked down the point of entry, often a join, seam, or skylight edge, try filling it with putty or rubberized filler. Before applying the putty, paint the seam or crack; it will help the putty to key. Leave the putty till it forms a skin; then sand it smooth. Now paint it again before it has time to dry out and pull away at the edges.

Because putty does dry out, I much prefer Plumber's Mait, a nonsetting putty. Designed for plumbers, it can be used both above and below the water, yet always remains malleable. On a recent trip across the Indian Ocean, some of our antifouling flaked off and worms ate away at the garboard. We dived down and smeared nonsetting putty over the holes. It was still in place four thousand sea miles and one beaching later. To get a smooth finish with Plumber's Mait or its equivalent, rub a wet / licked finger along it. Since it is always malleable, it cannot be sanded, but it takes paint as well as ordinary putty and, unlike putty, allows the underlying cracks to move without breaking the seal.

Silicone rubber compound, applied from a gun, is more expensive but also very effective at stopping small leaks. However, in the tropics, it sometimes remains too gooey for use where people walk or sit.

28. Boatwise

~~~~~~~~~~~~~~~~~~~

THIS CHAPTER is a ragbag of techniques and ideas which, over the years, I have found useful. Maybe you will, too.

1. Most yachts carry either a masthead wind sock or telltale ribbons fluttering from the shrouds. Both show the helmsman the apparent wind direction. Neither is much good on dark, starless nights. That's when knowing how to find the wind direction pays off.

The ultimate aim of all dedicated sailors is for the elements to become so much a part of themselves that their subconsciouses know instinctively, at all times, where the wind is coming from, even where it will come from next.

Such surpassing skill is reserved only for your genuine sea salt. For ordinary mortals, the step prior to that is knowing where the wind is by consciously searching for it on your skin.

When the boat is running before the wind, feel it playing on the nape of your neck. When she is beating, sense it on your face. (I have at last pinpointed the exact bit of my leeward cheek which the wind should brush for *Johanne* to be sailing full and by.)

To find the wind, turn your face toward where you think it is; then search out its exact direction with your nose. As you slowly turn your head back and forth, you will notice that one ear has more sound rushing past it than the other, that one cheek is more ruffled by the wind. When both ears sound the same and both cheeks feel equally caressed, your nose is pointing straight into the wind.

If there's a panic on and your nose still isn't too sure of itself, then check that no one's watching and take a leaf from the Boy Scouts' book. Lick a finger, and stick it up in the air. The cold bit is where the breeze is coming from.

One further aid to finding wind direction in light airs which are too feeble even to lift the wind sock is to study the ripples on the water. They will be running before the true wind. (The wind you feel on your face and see from the telltale is the apparent wind, distorted by the boat's progress and backdrafts off the sails.)

2. There's more to filling a deck bucket than you might imagine. First, if it is not already provided, tie a loose loop at the free end of the bucket lanyard, and always put your wrist through it before attempting to draw up water. One poor guest lost two buckets o.b. in one afternoon simply by ignoring that loop.

Once the lanyard is loosely around your wrist, you have a choice of ways to fill the actual bucket.

One is to hold the bucket upside down, mouth pointing toward the sea, then to drop it straight into the water. The bucket should right itself, filling up with water as it does so. This system is easier to learn but not guaranteed to work in strong winds or rough seas.

For method number two, dangle the bucket just above the surface of the water. Then, with a practiced flip of the wrist and lanyard, topple the bucket over so the lower rim plunges underwater and the bucket fills. Once mastered, this technique is more reliable and as such is the one favored by professional seamen around the world.

When you are under way, wedge yourself firmly against a solid bit of boat. Then throw the bucket well forward, trying to snatch it up again as soon as it's abreast of you. If you wait until it has passed and is being dragged behind you by the forward momentum of the boat, you may lose the bucket or jerk your arm half out of its socket.

3. Think of a boat as a Thoroughbred horse. You treat her right and respect every part of her, and she'll do her best for you. If you become negligent, she is liable to kick. Watch out especially for anchor chain, mainsheets, booms, and blocks. (See also "Accidents on Deck and Below" in Chapter 24.)

4. *To take a star sight,* turn the sextant upside down. Now find the star through the eyepiece, and bring the horizon *up* to meet it. When it is almost correct, lock the sextant arm in position and turn it the right way up. *Voilà!* You've got the right star in the right place—near the horizon—and all those hours of frustrated cursing are a thing of the past. It needs only a small final adjustment to take the sight.

5. *To calculate a boat's speed* through the water, watch the bubbles passing the hull. If there is no one experienced enough on board to guide you, then check what speed the mechanical log gives and watch just how fast the bubbles are going past.

We reckon it takes novice crews less than a week to learn to judge *Johanne*'s bubble speed so accurately that over a twenty-four-hour period, our dead-reckoning log is often only a mile or so different from our final sextant position. (Obviously this system does not take current or leeway into account.)

6. Leave when you are seaworthy. One is never "ready."

7. Close all hatches when going ashore however fine the weather looks. In many climates, including the sunny West Indies, that rainsquall is lurking just below the horizon.

8. Six-foot lengths of oilcloth or thick plastic sheeting have innumerable uses aboard. They cover bunks when decks leak, serve as spray shields for people and stores in the dinghy, protect things left out on deck, and act as groundsheets for putting the washing on when rinsing clothes ashore.

9. Carry a large magnet on board. It is invaluable for rescuing tools; both those dropped overboard and those that fall into the bilge under the engine.

10. Small sheets of canvas, approximately eight by five feet, with lines to each corner, make excellent temporary awnings when you are working on deck in the tropics and temporary catchment areas in rainsqualls at sea.

11. When stowing for sea, imagine the boat turned upside down, and stow accordingly. This applies in particular to batteries. The last thing you want in a knockdown is to have a great battery careering across the cabin toward you.

12. Be able to reach the top of the mast at all times and without help.

13. Scrub wooden decks across the planks. This stops the wood from wearing into ridges. In hot countries scrub and sluice down those decks with *salt* water every evening. The salt helps retain the moisture in the planks overnight and keeps them swollen and tight.

14. If you opt to live aboard while on the slip, invest in a bucket with a lid (a diaper bucket is fine). Many slipways have totally inadequate washroom facilities.

15. Save old nylon windbreakers and long-sleeved shirts and pants for protection when antifouling.

16. If sailing a boat in which the crew actually steers, arrange for the evening meal to be ready ten minutes before the change of watch. This allows the person going on watch to grab a hasty meal and the person coming off to eat a warm one when he arrives below.

17. Always come on watch punctually.

Keep a large magnet on board—you never know your luck.

Scrub wooden decks across the planks.

18. When handing over the helm, state clearly the desired course to the next helmsman and have him repeat the course back to you. In this way no confusion can arise.

19. On *Johanne* we have no self-steering gear and the steering position is completely open to sun and rain. After much trial and error we now organize watches as follows. Putting Christian names in alphabetical order and with a crew of four, we divide the night into five watches:

2000 hours–2300 hours
2300 hours–0200 hours
0200 hours–0500 hours
0500 hours–0800 hours
0800 hours–1000 hours

These watches are not so long that the helmsman falls asleep at the wheel yet are long enough to allow everyone below to get a decent rest.

The first and last watches are taken by the same person, after which we continue in our alphabetical order and, in the tropics, steer for only one-hour stints during the day.

With that extra two-hour watch from 0800 to 1000 we all automatically switch times the following night. This way everyone has a chance to steer during the popular hours and takes a turn at the unpopular ones too. I should add that our bunk is five feet from the helm and Edward is on call at all times.

20. At the end of your night watch, take a flashlight and go around all the sheets and halyards, checking for chafe. It needs only a couple of hours of chafe to wear right through a soft plaited line.

21. Unless the oilskin locker is next to the cockpit, always bring your wet-weather gear with you when coming on night watch.

22. In port, tie halyards away from the mast with shock cord to stop chafe and also that infernal tapping noise.

23. On long passages think twice before motoring during a calm. You may actually be keeping yourself in the calm system, whereas if you wait, the calm will normally pass and a new wind follow it. Relax and enjoy yourself. There's no commuter train to catch now.

24. Polaroid sunglasses show up coral heads and reefs in a quite re-markable way.

25. Finally, here is an invaluable navigational tip from my skipper. If you lose the compass and want to know where north is, tie a string to your sextant, twirl it several times around your head, and let fly. Watch where it goes 'cause that's the sextant gone west. The rest is easy. . . . Sorry!

29. Weather

~~~~~~~~~~~~~~~~~

ARE YOU one of those people afraid to set sail without a daily weather forecast to guide you? Don't be. While weather forecasts are certainly helpful, they are by no means indispensable. What they do tell, with considerable accuracy, is what the large weather systems, the depressions and anticyclones, are doing. But there is no call for panic once you are out of reach of a reliable, or sometimes unreliable, forecast.

Weather and wind shifts are not total mysteries brought down on defenseless mariners by a vengeful Neptune. There is a lot more rhyme and reason to it than that. Buy a good book on weather, study it carefully, and you will be able to make your own fairly accurate forecasts. (The sea will always retain the right to be capricious.) Here I want only to whet your appetite for more knowledge.

There are no less than three major weather indicators ready to help us: the barometer (mainly for temperate zones), the sky, and the sea itself.

Barometer ▪ Barometric pressure at sea level is normally around 29.92 inches of mercury (or 1013.2 millibars). If the barometer drops one-tenth of an inch or more, then variable or deteriorating weather can be expected. The faster the fall—"The barometer is crashing down!"—the worse the weather is likely to be.

Let's look at an example. You notice the barometer is suddenly dropping rapidly. A low-pressure system, or depression, is approaching. Quickly you reduce sail and batten down for a gale. The wind blows hard until it is screeching at you through the rigging. There is a lull. Your taut nerves ease. You breathe out for what seems like the first time in hours.

But the barometer remains low. It doesn't budge.

The barometer is warning you that the gale is not over yet. You are in fact in the center of the depression. It is passing directly overhead. You are in the famous quiet, in the very eye of the storm. The initiated will leave their sails reefed, waiting. For they know that when the barometer starts to rise again rapidly, the second half of the depression will pass overhead. And this time the wind may blow even stronger.

> First rise after low
> Foretells a stronger blow.

With the help of wind direction, much of this could be predicted.

In the Northern Hemispheres winds in a depression *always* go counter-clockwise around their centers. (In the Southern Hemisphere it is the exact opposite: like the bath water down the drain, depressions always go clockwise around their centers.)

If, in the Northern Hemisphere, the center of a depression passes to the northeast of you (as it often does), a preliminary blow from the southwest will veer sharply to the northwest as the depression moves on. Such knowledge is invaluable when you are looking for a truly, as opposed to a deceptively, sheltered anchorage. Many yachts have been lost because their skippers lacked knowledge of such basic wind-shift patterns. (If you are still not sure you understand it, try holding your right finger, representing the yacht, stationary, while turning your left index finger, representing the depression, around and around counterclockwise so that it approaches, and then hits, your right finger [the yacht] first from the southwest and then [as the depression moves past to the northeast of the yacht] from the northwest.)

In the tropics there are no real depressions, so here the barometer is less effective, staying almost stationary most of the time. Only with the approach of a tropical storm or hurricane will it drop dramatically. So in the tropics look to the sky and the sea for your weather guide.

Sky • The sky is a good pointer to future weather wherever you are in the world. Note the color of the sunsets. Though this varies from place to place, as a rule an angry-looking purple sunset foretells bad weather while a quiet red or yellow one means settled weather to come.

Note also the direction of the clouds and wind high up. It is often different from the local wind at sea level. The higher wind may foretell a wind shift.

High cirrus clouds, the wispy ones, in strong, harsh streaks across the sky show there's a lot of wind up there which may become a lot of wind down here later.

> If clouds look as if scratched by a hen,
> Get ready to reef your topsails then.

If the contrail from a jet aircraft lingers thickly before falling slowly apart, there is high humidity and unsettled weather around.

A large halo circling the moon also shows high humidity, as does a scaly "mackeral sky" (or "seeds of rain," as they are picturesquely called in the West Indies).

Often, in the tropics, squalls gather at around sunset and dawn. If you see a hard line of dark, unbroken cloud on the horizon, watch it closely. It is a line squall.

If, instead of a straight, horizontal bottom line, the clouds form an arch with a bruised-purple underbelly, then it is an arch squall, often even more potent than a line one. The main strength and direction of the wind are pent up under the highest point of the arch. Don't be fooled into relaxing because it is downwind of you. Line and arch squalls can work their way up against the wind, as can thunder squalls. Sometimes I almost feel they are deliberately altering course to catch us.

One way to gauge whether a tropical squall is coming toward you is to hold your arm at full length in front of your eyes with your index finger turned horizontally across your line of vision. Lay that finger along the horizon below the line squall. Use one, two, or three fingers to fill the gap between horizon and the bottom of the solid line of clouds. If, a few minutes later, you need more fingers to fill the gap, then the squall is lifting toward you. If you need fewer, it is with any luck chasing after some other hapless mariner.

When a tropical squall is imminent, there's a sharp drop in temperature, often as much as fifteen degrees. Moments later the water on the horizon may be churned into a white and frenzied froth. That's the rain beating up the water. Alternatively, the water may simply turn a deeper shade of blue-black; that's the wind. There's another old sailor's ditty which goes:

> If the rain's before the wind,
> Then your sheets and halyards tend,
> But if the wind's before the rain,
> All will soon be fine again.

The wind nearly always changes direction during a squall, so stand by the helm when it hits, ready to bear away sharply as soon as it arrives. Often you will have to keep bearing away for anything up to 180 degrees or even more. I actually find rainsqualls incredibly exciting, testing as they do one's skill at the helm while all around the rain and wind rage unchecked. Gales are another matter. They last much longer and have time to build up high seas, which scare the wits out of me!

Sea ▪ That brings us to our third diagnostic tool, the sea. Both wave direction and swell direction are excellent harbingers of weather to come. On a recent trip from the Far East to Europe the sea gave us twenty-four hours' warning of an approaching humdinger of a gale. A large, inexplicable swell appeared from the southwest, in an area where for months the northeast monsoon had been blowing. The swell length got shorter and shorter as the wind approached. Later, when the wind finally eased, the swells first lengthened out, then died away.

In the tropics and, to a certain extent, in temperate zones as well, wind and weather are influenced in a daily cycle by the heating and cooling of landmasses.

Tropical fair-weather puff clouds *(taken off Malacca).*

Squalls gather around sunset and dawn *(Galle, Sri Lanka).*

This sunset would fortell the end of the world in Northern Europe; in Malaysia it was simply magnificent. *R. K. Thompson photograph*

A line squall is a hard line of dark, unbroken cloud.

A distant thunder head off Africa.

Seeds of rain indicate high humidity.

In settled tropical climates the land warms up during the day, heating the air above it. This hot air rises, drawing in cooler air off the sea to fill the vacuum. This produces the famous sea breeze which blows across the sea and onto the land with varying strength (anything from a mere zephyr to Force 6 or 7).

At night the land cools off more quickly than does the ocean. Then the cooler land air is sucked out over the sea, giving an offshore land or night breeze. Other weather systems may intervene and upset this basic pattern, but it is, on the whole, very helpful to yachts sailing in coastal waters.

The usual strategy is to allow the daily breeze to carry you into the coast so that you are fairly, though not dangerously, close inshore by nightfall. Then you are ready to take advantage of the first whisper of the night breeze as it creeps out from the land and onto the sea.

In many parts of the world there are very distinctive local weather patterns. Maybe there is a calm in the morning, and then, come midday, a strong wind blows for four hours from the north and dies away at sunset. These local weather patterns are well known to coastal fishermen, but their secrets are also open to any visitor who cares to study the barometer, the sky, and the sea. Keeping such a weather eye is one of the most distinctive marks of the true seafarer.

Appendices

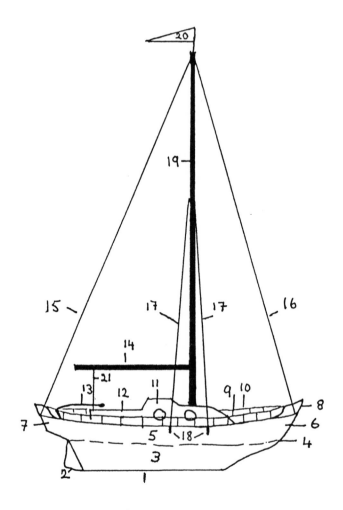

PARTS OF THE BOAT EXTERIOR

1. keel
2. rudder
3. bottom
4. waterline
5. topsides
6. bow
7. stern

8. pulpit
9. stanchions
10. lifeline
11. cabin top
12. cockpit
13. tiller
14. boom

15. backstay
16. forestay
17. shrouds
18. chain plates
19. mast
20. burgee
21. boom crutch

APPENDIX A

Beginner's Glossary

BELOW ARE some of the nautical terms which will fill your ears and possibly baffle your brain when you first join the sailing world.

To begin with you may think, as I did, that to sit down and learn a whole new vocabulary, and an obscure one at that, is a chore dreary in the extreme. Actually it's not nearly as hard as you think, and in no time your efforts will pay off, not least when the skipper snaps out precise commands on a black night in a howling gale. For the whole point of nautical terminology is that it is precise.

The frustrated searcher who cries out, "Where the heck have you hidden my socks?" will know exactly where to lay hands on them when given the reply "Oh, I put them outboard and aft in the starboard galley locker."

And what about those delightful cockpit evenings when sailors softly spin their yarns beneath the stars? Without some nautical vocabulary they might as well be talking Mandarin for all you'll understand. I know. I would have spared myself all the agonies of jealousy mixed up with fury had I not originally insisted that plain English was good enough for me.

One day I overheard my brand-new husband evidently discussing with a sailing friend the physical attributes of a female they both fancied.

"She's maybe a bit long in the leg, but wow, what a shape!"

"Yeah, and what about her bottom, eh?"

"Hmm, not so sure about that. Buttocks a bit heavy for my taste."

If only I'd realized it was a boat they were raving about.

ABEAM   At right angles to the length of the boat.

AFT   Toward the stern.

ALOFT   Up in the rigging.

ANEMOMETER   An electrical gadget for measuring wind speed. It has spelled death to many a sailor's yarn.

ANTIFOULING   Highly poisonous paint used to prevent weed, barnacles, and shipworms from taking up residence on a boat's bottom and making it "foul."

ASTERN   To go backward, as in "going astern." Also, behind the boat, as in "Astern lay a fantastic blaze of phosphorescence."

ATHWARTSHIPS   From side to side across the ship.

AUTOPILOT   An electrical device for keeping a boat on course.

BACK   A verb used to describe the wind changing direction anticlockwise, e.g.,

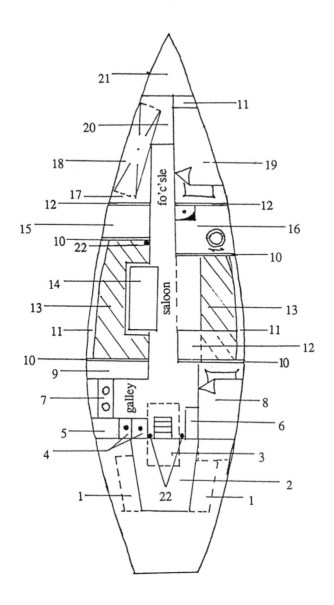

PARTS OF THE BOAT INTERIOR

1. bosun's locker
2. cockpit
3. engine compartment
4. twin galley sinks
5. draining board / locker
6. oilskin locker
7. gimbaled galley stove

8. quarter berth
9. work surface / locker
10. bulkheads
11. lockers
12. chart table
13. double settee berths
14. extending table
15. hanging locker

16. heads and shower
17. workbench and lockers
18. pipe cot
19. fo'c'sle bunk
20. sail locker
21. chain locker
22. fire extinguishers

when the wind goes from north to west, it has backed. See "Veer."

BACKING DOWN   Rowing by pushing forward (instead of pulling backward) on the oars to stop or maneuver a dinghy.

BAGGY WRINKLE   Antisail-chafing device made out of unraveled old rope and hung on shrouds and stays.

BALLAST   Added weight, usually iron or lead, often placed outside on the keel (ballast keel) to improve the stability of monohulls, or, simply, additional weight to stop the boat from falling over at sea.

BARE POLES   Masts without sails on them.

BEAM   (1) the greatest width of a boat, and (2) the athwartships members on which the deck is laid. The ends of these beams are referred to in wind directions, "forward of the beam." A sea which hits the boat on the side hits her beam-on, while a wind forward of the beam is blowing from a direction in the right angle between bow and amidships. Finally, when a boat is heeled far over on her side, she is said to be "on her beam ends."

BEAR AWAY   To alter course farther from the wind or another object.

BEAT   To gain against the wind by sailing zigzag toward it; to tack.

BEAUFORT SCALE   International scale for assessing wind strength from Force 0 to Force 12. (See Appendix C.)

BELAY   To make fast to a belaying pin or cleat.

BELAYING PIN   A short, upright rod of wood or metal fitted through a board or rail for making halyards and sheets fast. Also useful as a small club for repelling boarders.

BELOW   Inside the boat. "One moment, I'll call him, he's down below."

BEND   To fit a sail in place on a boat. So it's congratulations, not sympathy, that are wanted when the skipper says, "I've bent the mainsail."

BERMUDAN RIG   A rig where the mainsail is triangular. The most common yacht rig.

BERTH   (1) a verb meaning to bring a boat into her mooring: (2) the actual place where the boat lies in a marina, sometimes a "permanent berth," and (3) another name for a bunk. In other words, you could say, "Before collapsing into my berth, I berthed the boat in her berth." All quite simple really.

BILGE   The rounded bit of hull, low down under the floorboards where bilge water, leaked gas, and dead rats collect.

BITTS   Mooring posts on the foredeck.

BLOCK   A pulley.

BOBSTAY   A piece of wire or chain underneath the bowsprit to hold it down (most useful for climbing aboard after a swim).

BOLLARD   A circular, upright metal fitting for making lines fast. Large versions are often found on jetties and docks.

BOOM   A spar along the foot of the sail.

BOSUN'S CHAIR   A swinglike seat with line for hoisting crew up the mast.

BOTTLE SCREW   See "Rigging screws."

BOTTOM   (1) the hull below the waterline; and (2) the seabed, "a sandy bottom."

BOW   The front end of a vessel.

BOWSPRIT   The spar which sticks out in front of a sailing boat's stem.

BULKHEAD   Partition separating the interior of the boat into different sections; in a house it's called a wall.

BULWARKS   Extension to topsides above the deck. On small yachts often a toe rail only a few inches high.

BUNK   A bed on a boat.

BURGEE   A small triangular flag showing the emblem of the owner's yacht club. A burgee is hoisted either at the masthead or the starboard spreader.

CANOE STERN   A canoe-shaped pointed stern.

CAST OFF   To free a line from its bollard or cleat.

CATAMARAN   A yacht with two hulls.

CENTER LINE   An imaginary line running down the middle of the boat from stem to sternpost.

CHAIN PLATES   Metal strips bolted to the hull to which rigging screws and shrouds are attached.

CHRONOMETER   An extremely accurate timepiece used for navigation.

CLEAT   A metal, wooden, or plastic fitting for securing a line.

CLEW   The aft, lower corner of a sail.

CLOSE-HAULED   Having the boat sail as close into the direction of the wind as possible.

COCKPIT   A recessed portion of the deck in which one normally sits and also steers.

COMPANION, OR COMPANIONWAY   A permanent ladder on a boat; hence "companionway squatter," someone who insists on sitting on the steps, getting in everyone's way.

CRADLE   A special wooden or metal frame to keep a boat upright when it is pulled ashore.

CROSSTREES, OR SPREADERS   Crossbars placed up the mast to spread the load of the rigging and help keep the mast straight.

CUTTER   A one-masted vessel rigged with two sails forward of the mast. Compare with "Sloop."

DAVITS   Pieces of wood or metal projecting over the water for lifting things. Stern davits lift dinghies; anchor davits lift anchors.

DEAD BEFORE   Sailing with the wind straight behind you or "dead aft."

DEAD RECKONING   An informed estimate of one's position.

DECKHEAD   Underside of the deck, which, viewed from below, forms what in a house would be called the ceiling.

DINGHY, DINK OR TENDER   A small boat carried on a yacht and used for ferrying people and supplies between the yacht and the shore.

DOUBLE-ENDER   Vessel with both bow and stern pointed.

DOWNHAUL   A rope for hauling or pulling down a sail or spar.

DOWN HELM   The command given when the skipper wants the tiller moved away from the wind.

DRAFT   The depth of hull below the waterline. Boats can have deep, moderate, or shallow drafts.

DRAGGING   The slipping of an anchor along the top of the seabed when it should have dug well in. Dragging is often swiftly followed by "All hell breaking loose."

DRY DOCK   A dock where a boat is locked in and then the water pumped out, leaving the boat in the dry.

EBB TIDE   Falling tide, ebbing away from the land.

ECHO SOUNDER   An electrical gadget for measuring the depth of water under the boat.

EYE OF THE WIND   The exact direction from which the wind blows.

FENDERS   Balloon- or sausage-shaped objects made of strong flexible material, often rubber, used to protect the ship's side when against docks or other boats.

FEND OFF   (1) to stop boats from touching when alongside each other or the dock; and (2) the cry of a desperate skipper to his hapless crew when the yacht is about to collide with an immovable object such as a granite quay.

FIDDLES   Narrow lengths of metal bar fitted around stove tops to stop saucepans from slipping off. Same thing around tables.

FLOOD TIDE   Rising tide, flooding in toward the land.

FOOT   The bottom edge of a sail.

FORE-AND-AFT SAIL   The most common type of yacht sail, hoisted along the center, fore-and-aft, line of the boat. The opposite is a square sail, which is hoisted athwartships, or across the boat.

FORECASTLE, OR FO'C'SLE   Forwardmost accommodation.

FOREDECK   Deck at the forward end of a boat.

FORWARD   Toward the front or bow.

FREEBOARD   The distance from the water to the deck of a vessel.

FULL AND BY   Sailing with the sails full and yet as close to the wind as possible without the sails lifting.

FURL   To roll up a sail and secure it.

GAFF   The spar along the upper edge of a quadrilateral gaffsail.

GAFFSAIL   A quadrilateral rather than triangular fore-and-aft sail often found on traditional workboats.

GALLEY   A ship's kitchen.

GALLOWS   A raised rest to keep a boom horizontal when the sail is lowered.

GASKETS   Long pieces of canvas or line used to tie up sails when they are lowered. Also called tiers.

GENOA   A large jib sheeted well aft.

GIMBALS   A swinging arrangement for suspending things on boats so that they remain upright—i.e., stove, table, oil lamp, compass.

GO ABOUT   To pass the bow of the boat through the eye of the wind; to tack.

GREEN WATER   A solid wedge of water, not just spray, coming aboard.

GUNWALE, OR GUNNEL   The flat, upper edge all around an open boat.

HALYARD   Line or wire for hoisting and lowering sails.

HANKS   Metal clips which fasten a sail to a stay.

HATCH   The hole which leads down to the inside of a boat.

HEAD   Marine toilet.

HEAD OF SAIL   The top corner of a triangular sail and the top edge of a gaff-sail.

HEADSAILS   All sails forward of the foremast.

HEAD-TO-WIND   The bow of the boat pointing straight into the wind. One way to stop a sailboat's forward motion is to bring her head-to-wind.

HEAVE TO   To slow a vessel down by making one sail work against another.

HEEL   A verb used to describe what happens when a boat leans over to one side, usually due to the pressure of wind on the sails. "She heeled right over in the heavy gust."

HELM   A wheel or tiller. If asked to take the helm, you are expected to steer not remove it to your bunk.

HOIST   (1) to pull anything up—e.g., a sail, and (2) the vertical edge of a flag to which rope is attached.

HOLIDAY   A polite word to point out to infuriated friends that they have accidentally skipped an area while painting as in "I expect you know you've left a holiday there."

HORSE   A metal, horizontal bar, usually bolted to the deck and running athwartships. It carries the sheet from one side to the other.

HULL   The main body of a boat.

INBOARD   Toward the center of the boat.

JACKSTAY   A wire running the full length of the deck on either side of the boat to which safety lines are clipped.

JIB   The triangular headsail which is set farthest forward on a vessel.

JIBE   To pull the mainsail in and then maneuver the stern of a sailboat so that the wind will strike on the opposite side of the sail while running downwind. An accidental jibe can be dangerous when the boom crashes across the boat, but a controlled one is a normal maneuver to be undertaken with care.

JURY RIG   Rig improvised after damage in order to make land and safety.

KEEL   The lowest part or backbone of the hull running fore and aft. Monohulls often have an extra, ballast keel, bolted under the main keel.

KETCH   A two-masted vessel with a mainmast forward and a mizzenmast aft. See "Yawl" and "Schooner."

KNOT   A measurement of speed equal to one nautical mile per hour. It is not a distance. Therefore, one does not say "five knots per hour" but "We were doing five knots."

LEAD LINE   A line with a lump of lead at the end and special markings indicating different depths along its length. Used for measuring depths every time the echo sounder goes on the blink.

LEECH   The trailing or aft edge of a sail.

LEE SHORE   The coast onto which the wind is blowing. Good captains avoid close contact with lee shores if they can.

LEE SIDE   The side of the boat away from the direction of the wind.

LEEWARD (LOO'RD)   Downwind; try not to be leeward of dragging yachts, bad fish, and town drains.

LEEWAY   The drift a boat makes sideways from her course because of the wind pressure on sails and hull.

LIFELINE   A security wire supported by stanchions and running around the boat to prevent people from falling overboard.

LOG   An instrument for measuring the distance a boat covers through the water.

LOGBOOK, OR THE LOG   An hour-by-hour account of weather conditions, boat's position, speed, etc. while at sea.

LUFF   The leading or forward edge of a sail.

MAINMAST   The tallest mast on a yacht.

MAINSAIL   The principal sail.

MAKE FAST   To secure a line to something solid, such as a cleat, bollard, or pin.

MASTHEAD   The top of the mast (as opposed to the foot). A masthead light is traditionally white and attached to the top of the mast. But see "Navigation" under Chapter 24, "Safety at Sea."

MIZZENMAST   The aft mast of a ketch or yawl.

MONOHULL   A vessel with only one hull—i.e., the vast majority of boats.

MOORED   (1) making a vessel fast to an extralarge anchor, heavy cement block, or length of chain permanently laid in a harbor as a mooring, and (2) holding a vessel firm by two or more separate anchors. In both cases a moored boat needs less swinging space than an anchored one.

NAVIGATION LIGHTS   Lights used on a vessel which is under way at night: red to port (port wine is red); green to starboard; white at masthead and stern.

NEAP TIDE   A small range of tide which comes twice a month at the quarter moon.

OARLOCK, OR ROWLOCK (ROLLUCK)   A stirrup-shaped fitting which acts as a fulcrum for oars when they are in use.

O.B. (OH BEE)   Abbreviation for "overboard."

OGGIN   Nautical slang for the sea, as in "He fell in the oggin."

OUTBOARD   (1) toward the outer edge of a boat or even outside the hull, and (2) a small engine, usually attached to a dinghy and taking the place of oars.

PAINTER   The line on a dinghy for making it fast (tying it up).

PEAK   (1) the highest point of a gaffsail (the peak halyard hoists the outer, or peak, end of the gaff) and (2) to tighten up the peak halyard, lifting the peak higher.

PORT SIDE   The left side of a vessel looking forward ("port" and "left" have the same number of letters, and both are easy to spell).

PORT TACK   To sail with the wind coming over the port side, forward of the beam—i.e., the sails are on the starboard side.

PULPIT   Protective metal or wooden railing about three feet above the deck fixed to bow and stern, (sometimes erroneously called pushpit in the stern).

QUARTER   Between astern and abeam (a quarter of the way from the stern to the bow). A ship on the port quarter would be about forty-five degrees abaft the port beam.

RAFT UP   To tie up alongside another yacht in a crowded anchorage or dock. Raft up only if there is no room to moor on your own, and then always ask permission from the other yacht's skipper.

RATLINES   Pieces of line or wood fixed across the shrouds like a ladder to enable people to climb aloft.

REACH   To sail with the wind approximately on the beam.

REEF   To reduce the amount of canvas showing on a sail by wrapping the lower part along the boom and tying it down. See "Roller reefing."

REEF POINTS   Short pieces of line dangling down in a row on some sails to tie the reefed sail to the boom.

RIDING LIGHT   An all-round white light carried nine feet above the deck when the boat is anchored at night.

RIG   The individual system of masts, booms, and standing rigging used on a yacht—e.g., "She's schooner rigged" or "She's a gaff-rigged ketch."

RIGGING   (1) immovable wires holding the masts in place, known as standing rigging, and (2) lines or wires which move as they hoist or control sails— i.e., sheets and halyards—called running rigging.

RIGGING SCREWS, OR BOTTLE SCREWS OR TURNBUCKLES   Metal fittings usually used to join shrouds to chain plates, so that tension can be adjusted. They can also be used for the same purpose in other parts of the rigging.

ROLLER REEFING   A mechanical device for reducing sail by wrapping the sail around itself on or off a boom or inside either the boom or mast.

ROPE   There are very few "ropes" on board a boat. The most common are (1) bell rope for the bell, (2) bolt rope around the edge of a sail, (3) bull rope for mooring to a heavy metal buoy, and (4) boat rope, as opposed to painter, for towing a dinghy.

RUNNERS, OR RUNNING BACKSTAYS   Wires fitted to some yachts to hold the mast backward. They have to be released very quickly each time the boat goes about—in other words, a pain in the neck!

RUNNING   Sailing with the wind well aft of the beam.

SAILS   (See drawings of the kinds of sails and the parts of the sail on pages 240 and 241.)

SATELLITE NAVIGATION, OR SAT. NAV.   The lazy person's sextant, actually great fun to use but, like all electronics, liable to go wrong on small boats. Take your sextant, too.

SCHOONER   Fore-and-aft rigged vessel usually having two masts with the main-mast aft.

SCUPPERS   Drain holes or pipes leading from deck to sea.

SEA ANCHOR   A strong, openmouthed, parachute-shaped bag, usually of canvas, which is dropped over the stern or bow of a small boat in severe weather to try to bring her bow or stern onto the waves and avoid the boat's being rolled over. Not always very effective.

SELF-STEERING   A mechanical rather than electrical system for keeping a sailing boat on a set course with no one at the helm.

SET   (1) to hoist a sail, and (2) the direction of a current or tidal stream, as in "The current was setting them onto the rocks."

SETTEE   The sofa on a boat, often doubling as a bunk at night.

SEXTANT   An instrument for measuring the angle between stars or planets and the horizon. Used by sailors in conjunction with navigation tables and a chronometer to find out where they are. Most often used for shooting the sun.

SHACKLE   A metal connecting link removed by unscrewing a pin.

SHEER   The up-and-down curve of a vessel running from bow to stern. Sadly missing in many modern yachts.

SHEET   The line attached to the lower, aft corner of a sail or boom to control it—e.g., mainsheet, jib sheet.

SHEET IN OR OUT   To pull in or let out on a sail's sheet in order to alter the sail's angle to the wind and thus improve its efficiency.

SHIP   (1) to take on board, as in "We shipped a heavy sea"; (2) to put oars back inside a row boat after rowing, as in "She shipped the oars as she came alongside the yacht."

SHROUDS   Fixed wires which hold the mast in position on either side.

SIGHT   The measuring of the angle between horizon and a heavenly body using a sextant. Known as "taking a sight."

SLIPWAY   A special hard slope of land running down to the water and used for slipping boats in and out of the water—i.e., for launching and hauling out.

SLOOP   A one-masted vessel which has only one sail forward of the mast. See "Cutter."

SOLE   The deck or floor in the interior of a yacht—e.g., the cabin sole.

SPAR   A long piece of wood or metal, usually rounded and hollow, used for masts, booms, gaffs, etc.

SPINNAKER   A half-balloon sail used for running or reaching.

SPREADERS   See "Crosstrees."

SPRING TIDE   Large range of tide coming twice each month two days after full and new moon.

SQUABS   The long cushions placed on settees and cockpit seats.

STANCHIONS   Upright metal rods or wooden posts on outer deck edge used to support lifelines or bulwarks to stop people from falling o.b.

STARBOARD   The right-hand side of a vessel when one looks forward (both "right" and "starboard" are more complicated to spell than "port" and "left").

STARBOARD TACK   Sailing with the wind coming over the starboard side, forward of the beam. (If it's aft of the beam, then you are on the starboard jibe.)

STAY   A wire which supports the mast in a fore-and-aft direction.

STAYSAIL   A triangular sail set immediately forward of the mast and usually clipped to a stay.

STEM   The farthest forward part of the hull forming the bow.

STERN   The aft end of a vessel.

STERN WAY, TO MAKE   To move a boat backward through the water—that is, stern first. Usually unintentional, as opposed to making stern boards, which is a brilliant maneuver exemplified by West Indian schooner captains who, when commissioning a new ship, make stern boards, or tack backward, stern first through the fleet. Not for beginners.

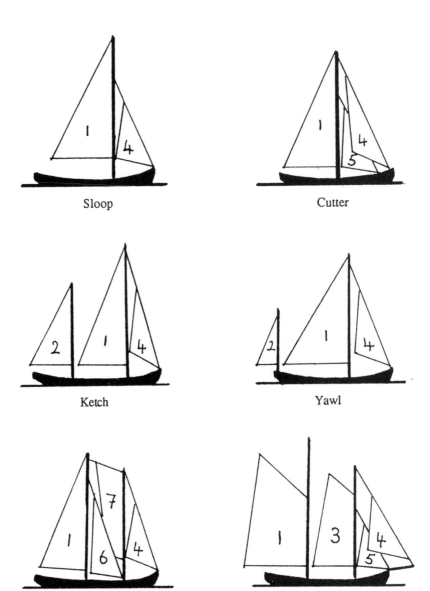

Sloop

Cutter

Ketch

Yawl

Gaff Schooner

Staysail Schooner

KINDS OF SAILS

1. mainsail
2. mizzen

3. foresail
4. jib
5. staysail

6. main staysail
7. fisherman topsail

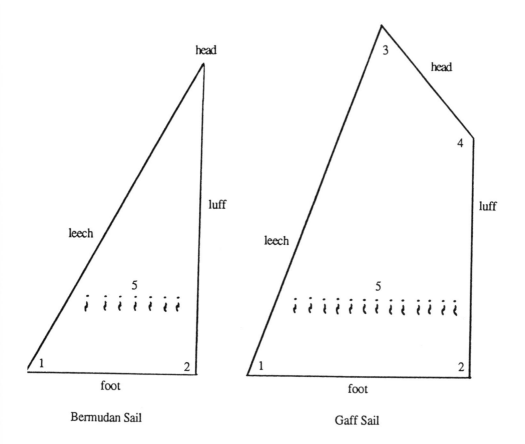

Parts of the Sail

1. clew   3. peak   5. reef points
2. tack   4. throat

Stiff   Refers to a vessel's tendency to stay upright or return quickly to an upright position in rough weather.

Tack   (1) to bring the wind on the other side of sails by passing the vessel's bow through the eye of the wind, and (2) the forward, lower corner of a sail.

Tackle   A line running through a series of pulleys or blocks to give a mechanical advantage.

Tender   (1) Refers to a vessel's tendency to heel over a lot and roll; opposite of "Stiff" and (2) a ship's dinghy.

Throat   The place where the gaff joins the mast. Throat halyards hoist the mast end of the gaff.

Thwart   A plank / seat going athwartships across a dinghy or small boat.

Tight   Not leaking. A good boat is said to be as "tight as a bottle."

Tiller   A bar for steering rather than a wheel.

Topping lift   A line going from up the mast down to the end of the boom to support the boom when sail is lowered.

Topsides   The outside of the hull between waterline and deck.

Transom   The flat piece across the stern of a square-sterned vessel.

Trim   (1) to adjust sails for maximum efficiency and (2) to adjust the distribution of weight in a dinghy or racing craft so that it is well balanced.

Trimaran   A yacht with three hulls.

Turnbuckle   See "Rigging screw."

Veer   A verb describing when the wind changes direction clockwise, e.g., east to south. Opposite of "Back" (see Chapter 29, "Weather").

Warp   To maneuver a vessel using only mooring lines.

Warps   Heavy lines for towing or mooring.

Waterline   (1) the invisible line around a boat's hull where water ends and air begins, and (2) the place where topside paint meets antifouling. The two are seldom the same.

Winch   A mechanical device, giving mechanical advantage, for hauling in sheets and halyards by turning a handle.

Wind, hard on   Sailing as close to the wind as possible.

Windlass   A winch for pulling up the anchor.

Windward   Toward the wind.

Yawl   A two-masted vessel with a very small mizzen aft.

APPENDIX B

Measurements /Conversions

DISTANCE—NAUTICAL

1 fathom = 6 feet
1 fathom = 1.85 meters
1 meter = 0.547 fathoms
1 cable = about 100 fathoms
1 nautical mile = 10 cables
1 international nautical mile = 6076 feet and 1.151 statute miles

1 nautical mile = 1.852 kilometers
1 statute mile = 0.869 nautical mile
1 kilometer = 0.54 nautical mile
3 nautical miles = 1 nautical league
60 nautical miles = 1 degree

DISTANCE—STATUTE

1 inch = 25.4 millimeters
1 millimeter = 0.03937 inch
1 inch = 2.54 centimeters
1 centimeter = 0.3937 inch
1 foot = 30.48 centimeters
1 foot = 0.31 meter
1 meter = 3.28 feet

1 meter = 39.37 inches
1 yard = 0.914 meter
1 meter = 1.093 yards
1 statute mile = 1.609 kilometers
1 kilometer = 0.6214 mile
1 kilometer = 1,094 yards
5 miles = about 8 kilometers

SPEED

1 knot = 1 nautical mile per hour
1 knot = 1.152 miles per hour

1 knot = 1.853 kilometers per hour
1 mile per hour = 1.609 kilometers per hour

WEIGHTS

1 ounce = 28.35 grams
1 gram = 0.352 ounce

1 pound = 0.453 kilogram
1 kilogram = 2.2 pounds

LIQUIDS: U.S.—METRIC

1 fluid ounce = 29.57 milliliters
10 milliliters = 0.338 fluid ounce
1 liter = 0.264 gallon

1 liter = 1.056 quarts
1 gallon = 3.78 liters

OTHER

1 millibar = approximately 0.029 inch   Fahrenheit degrees − 32 × 5/9 =
1 inch = 33.86 millibars   centigrade degrees
watts = volts × amps   Centigrade degrees × 9/5 + 32 =
amps = $\dfrac{\text{volts}}{\text{ohms}}$ Fahrenheit degrees

Europeans use commas instead of periods for decimal points.

COMPARATIVE INTERNATIONAL SIZES

	Women's Dresses						*Women's Shoes*					
American	10	12	14	16	18	20	6	6½	7	8	8½	9
British	32	34	36	38	40	42	4½	5	5½	6½	7	7½
European	38	40	42	44	46	48	36	37	38	39	40	41

	Men's Shoes								
American	5	6	7	8	8½	9	9½	10	11
British	5	6	7	8	8½	9	9½	10	11
European	38	39	40	41	42	43	44	44	45

	Men's Shirts							
American	14	14½	15	15½	16	16½	17	17½
British	14	14½	15	15½	16	16½	17	17½
European	36	37	38	39	40	41	42	43

APPENDIX C

Beaufort Wind Scale

THE BEAUFORT wind scale is a simple, internationally recognized system for recording wind speed.

BEAUFORT WIND SPEED

Force No.	Knots	Description	State of Sea*
0	Under 1	Calm	Sea glassy.
1	1–3	Light air	Tiny ripples without crests.
2	4–6	Light breeze	Real wavelets, still no crests.
3	7–10	Gentle breeze	Bigger wavelets with scattered whitecaps.
4	11–16	Moderate breeze	Small waves and longer, many whitecaps.
5	17–21	Fresh breeze	Moderate waves, their form elongating, foaming white crests, more spray.
6	22–27	Strong breeze	Large waves forming, foaming crests, more spray.
7	28–33	Half gale	Sea piles up, foam streaks from breaking waves.
8	34–40	Gale	Longer, higher waves, crest edges breaking into spindrift, streaks of blown foam.
9	41–47	Strong gale	High waves, crests toppling, heavy streaks foam, spray may hamper visibility.
10	48–55	Storm	Crests overhanging very high waves, great areas of foam blown in thick streaks, sea looks white, reduced visibility.

*State of the Sea, an excellent booklet published by the British government, illustrates the Beaufort wind scale with one photograph for each force of wind. You can order it from Her Majesty's Stationery Office, 49 High Holborn, London, WC 1 V 6HB, England.

Force No.	Knots	Description	State of Sea*
11	56–63	Violent storm	Waves may reach thirty-five feet, hiding small ships; sea a blanket of long areas foam, reduced visibility.
12	64 plus	Hurricane	Air full of spray and foam, sea white, poor visibility.

APPENDIX D

Stars

IF YOU ARE INTERESTED in identifying individual stars, buy a Rude star chart from a chart supplier. Not only is it fun to use, but it is extremely useful for celestial navigation.

SKY AT NIGHT: NORTHERN HEMISPHERE

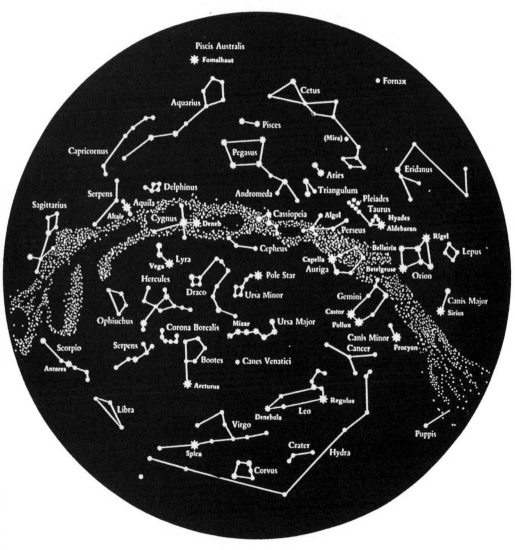

Sky at Night: Southern Hemisphere

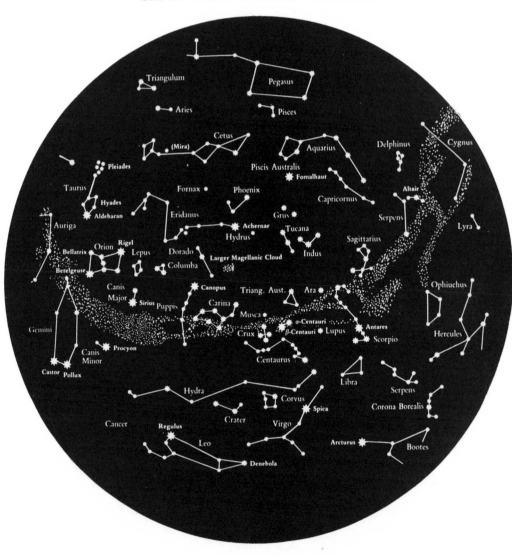

APPENDIX E

Knots

ON BOATS, most knots are called either bends or hitches. A bend joins the ends of two lines together. A hitch makes a line fast to something else (a hitching post maybe?).

Here is a list of the most common bends and hitches used aboard yachts. See the diagrams below for how to tie them:

1. A round turn and two half hitches is probably the most common hitch of all. It won't jam tight and is easy to undo. It is used mainly for securing dinghies or mooring lines to rings on a quay. If you are leaving the hitch for some time, bind the free end to the standing part with string so that it cannot work undone.

2. A sheet bend is used when you make one line fast on a bight (loop) of another line, normally to lengthen the original one. A double sheet bend simply takes two turns around the bight instead of one, to be doubly safe.

3. A figure of eight knot at the end of a line prevents the line from running out through a block.

4. A reef knot is good for tying things up when you are using only one piece of small-diameter line. Never use a reef knot to join two separate lines unless each free end is backed up by a half hitch because a reef knot is inclined to come undone under strain.

5. A bowline (as in "bow" and arrow, plus "lyn"), if tied correctly forms a loop which will not come undone on its own except when constantly lifted in and out of water. If it is too loaded with strain, as when employed to attach a mooring line to a bollard in a gale, the bowline can pull so tight as to be almost impossible to undo.

To Tie a Bowline: Practice a little and you will be able to tie this bowline in a couple of seconds, behind your back, in the pitch-dark. Once learned, this technique becomes automatic, no fear of getting the loop wrong. For this reason it is the method adopted around the world by those who earn their living from the sea.

(1) Take the end of the line in your right hand and the standing part, about two feet farther up, in your left. (2) Hold the line so that it lies between thumbs and index fingers, the latter being stretched out along the line and the loop coming across the palms, which face upward. (3) Put the rope end across the top of the line held in the left hand so that both lines and index fingers are crossed. Move the right-hand thumb so that both parts of the line are held between the right thumb and index finger, the thumb underneath, and both pointing away from the body. Withdraw left index finger. (4) Now flip the right hand in a circle going first away from you and then up inside the main loop toward you. This will throw the rope

1. Round turn and
   two half hitches

2. Sheet bend

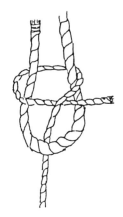

3. Figure of eight

4. Reef knot

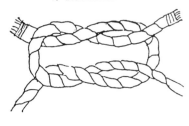

5. Bowline

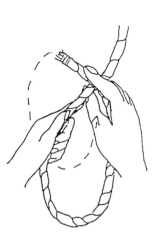

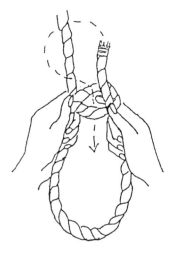

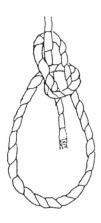

(stage 1)   (stage 2)   (stage 3)

end up in the air between right thumb and index finger, while making a small loop of the standing part around this end. (5) Trap the loop with the left index finger and thumb, thumb on top. (6) Now, with the right hand, go to the end of the rope, and take it around the back of the main standing part and to the left, then down through the center of the small loop held in the left hand. (7) Pull the end through about two-thirds the length of the required loop. Give a final good tug by holding the loop in the right hand and the standing part of the line in the left.

APPENDIX F

Sewn Whipping

I INCLUDE how to make a sewn whipping because it seldom appears in books on sailing and maintenance yet is the only type of whipping which stands the test of time.

Frequently rope that needs whipping has already begun to unravel into its separate strands (a "cow's tail" no less), so first these strands have to be put back into their correct positions. Since the most common rope on board is three-stranded, it is this that I describe here.

Collect together a sail needle; strong thread, preferably waxed; a sailmaker's palm (there are left-handed palms for left-handed sailmakers); and a sheath knife.

First cut off two six-inch lengths of thread, and lay them by, ready for use. Now make the rope fast to something solid on the boat so that the end to be whipped can be pulled taut toward you.

Select two of the three unraveled strands, and pulling firmly, twist each strand up as tightly as it will go on itself without actually buckling over. Now wrap the two, tightly twisted, strands around each other, while holding them taut at the same time. The strands should fall into their old positions on each other.

When they are in place, tie the two firmly together with one of the short lengths of thread already cut.

Take the third strand and wind it up on itself until it, too, is very tight. Holding the other two strands taut in your left hand, wrap the third strand around them, pulling it into its original position next to the others. Remember to keep it twisted tightly up on itself at the same time. All three strands should now be back in their original places. Tie them together with the second thread. They are ready to be whipped.

Depending on the size of rope, you will need about four feet of twine to make the whipping. Thread a sail needle, and knot the two ends of twine together so as to form a double thread. (One should never use a knot when sewing sails, but it is permissible in ropework.)

Starting one and a half diameters from the end to be whipped, push the needle right through one strand of rope. Pull it tight and bend the loose ends of thread toward the rope end so that they will eventually be covered by the whipping.

Now carefully wrap the double thread around and around the line against the lay (i.e., the way the strands are twisted up) and toward the rope end. Carry on until the whipped part is the same depth as the line's diameter.

Next, push the needle straight through the center of the nearest strand of rope so that it comes out *between* the other two strands.

Pull the thread through firmly.

Now, with the thread, follow the direction of the gap between the two strands just separated, going diagonally back to where the gap comes out at the upper end of the whipping. Insert the needle here, between the same strands, and push it through so it comes out at the far side of the next strand.

Thus the thread will have come diagonally across the outside of the whipping as if to redraw the original strands of the rope.

Now go diagonally back down the whipping with the next stitch and push the needle through so that it comes out beside the final strand to be etched in.

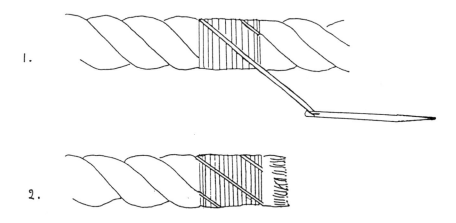

1.

2.

After one more diagonal stitch, finish off the thread by making two overhand stitches, one on the other, and pulling the thread tight. Cut it off flush with the rope.

The whipping is now complete. It should never come undone. Neaten the ends of the rope with a sharp knife. If the rope is nylon or polyproplyne, twist the end over a flame for a moment to give it an extra seal.

If you want to cut a length off a coil of rope, do two whippings either side of the place to be cut. Leave a gap, one diameter of the rope wide, between the two finished whippings. Sew both whippings first; then cut the rope in the middle of the gap thus left.

APPENDIX G

Fish

IN THIS SECTION I have collected together a short list of fish which are not frequently found in supermarkets in the States but which may, with luck, appear on the end of your fishing line. The second part of the chapter describes how to prepare the fish once caught and also how to dry it if you happen to catch a shoal.

KINDS OF FISH

Barracudas ▪ These pikelike creatures remind me of the one that snapped at poor Jeremy Fisher's toe in Beatrix Potter's tale of that name. They do in fact also snap at humans and in some parts of the world are more feared even than the shark. When you know that, it is disconcerting to have one suddenly appear around the edge of a coral head to stare at you. For the barracuda has a large, rather pointed head with a powerful lower jaw which juts out past the upper jaw, giving the whole a most malevolent air. Usually dark green or gray on top with a whitish underbelly, the barracuda has two separate dorsal fins, which are either yellow or gray. Though normally two to three feet long, barracudas over eight feet long and weighing more than a hundred pounds, have been caught. Barracudas normally hunt alone. In the Indian Ocean I saw a barracuda herd a shoal of small fish into a corner and then keep them there, snapping up one or two whenever it felt peckish.

Barracuda meat is firm, white, and excellent—when not poisonous. In some areas, such as those around Antigua in the West Indies, barracuda is notoriously poisonous as we know to our cost. So check before eating one. Barracuda poisoning is always unpleasant and occasionally fatal.

Dorado ▪ Dorados, or dolphins as they are frequently called in the States, should not be confused with the real dolphin or porpoise. Though they sometimes reach six feet in length, dorados are normally two to three feet long but not as thick and powerful-looking as either the barracuda or the tuna. The most distinctive feature of the dorado is its weird, high forehead which makes it look as if it had just crashed head-on into a lead keel.

Dorados often arrive in shoals way out at sea and will follow a boat for miles. Alive, dorados are exquisite, their scales glittering rainbows of turquoise blue and purple, gold and metallic silver. As soon as they are landed, however, their vibrant colors fade, a symbolic mourning for a life just past.

Dorados have a fine white flesh, ideal for drying.

Flying Fish ▪ These are small fish growing, at most, to one and a half feet long. They are metallic blue on top with a silvery underneath, while their little heads are appealingly blunt. The much-enlarged pectoral fins are almost transparent. When chased, a flying fish rises out of the water by swiftly beating its tail while spreading those large pectoral fins to act as gliding wings.

When flying fish are found on deck after a night sail, they are usually so small you can sadly hope for little more than a dainty morsel of the delectable white flesh.

Garfish or Needlefish ▪ These fish have very thin bodies as their second name, needlefish, implies. Generally only a foot or two long, they have elongated beaks and are either silvery blue or sea green in color. Garfish are found in warm waters, including those of the United States and Europe. When being chased by other carnivorous fish, the garfish can travel amazingly fast with most of its long body held upright clear of the water, propelled only by its tail.

The bones of the garfish are an ominous bright green, but don't be put off because the flesh, though sparse, makes good eating.

Groupers ▪ These are usually about two feet long, though they have been known to grow to twelve feet in length and weigh 750 pounds. Groupers come in many colors which each individual fish can change up to eight times for the sake of camouflage. One man, a Dr. Beebe, says he saw a shining blue grouper with three broad vertical stripes of brown swim in between some coral and come out a couple of minutes later "Clad in brilliant yellow, thickly covered with black polka-dots"!

Groupers have large, grumpy mouths and big eyes. Their scales, too, are large and sometimes slimy. If trapped in a cave, a grouper will make a booming noise to frighten people away, and groupers have, in such circumstances, been known to attack. When they are free from fear, groupers may be fed by hand like pets. They are mainly found in warm waters near land.

They have a white flesh, particularly good for fish pies, though occasionally it can be poisonous.

Marlins ▪ These are otherwise known as spearfish because of their long, strong beaks. There used to be on display in the British Museum a marlin beak embedded twenty-two inches into a solid piece of wood; on second thought, maybe it wasn't so solid after all. Marlins are usually deep blue, black, or dark brown on top with the belly yellow, silver, or off-white. The first few spines of the marlin's dorsal fin are tall and thick like a crest, which then, unlike the sailfish's, rapidly diminish in size toward the tail. The actor Lee Marvin once landed a fifteen-foot marlin which weighed twelve hundred pounds. Marlins are extremely fast swimmers and live in warm waters.

If you do manage to land one, marlins are quite edible.

Sailfish ▪ These have been recorded over eleven feet in length and weighing many hundreds of pounds. In the whole animal kingdom only the spine-tailed swift travels faster, a sailfish having recorded an incredible 68 mph. To achieve such speed it lowers its great dorsal fin; the same saillike fin which gives the fish its name and distinguishes it from the marlin. The single fin running about three-fourths of the length of the fish's back is held up by many rays. Sailfish are a wonderful metallic blue or blue-black on their backs with shimmering silver sides and bellies. The upper jaw projects a long way beyond the lower one.

Sailfish steaks, grilled or fried, are magnificent.

Sharks ▪ The shark is familiar to most people, its pectoral fin showing above the water in a slow, gliding movement different from the dolphin's usually brief up-and-down appearance. Sharks are found in most parts of the world. Some, like the mammoth whale shark, can reach sixty feet in length yet not be dangerous to humans (but see "Sharks" in Chapter 23). Sharkskin is very difficult to hack through, but once cleaned and dried, it makes excellent fine sandpaper.

Shark is perfectly good to eat if flaked or cut into small portions and pressure-cooked. It is also delicious smoked. For some reason shark meat keeps longer than that of other fish.

Tunnies or Tunas ▪ These very handsome fish have powerful, well-balanced torpedo shapes. They are covered in tiny scales. Though usually only about two feet long, they, too, can grow to a monstrous size: up to fourteen feet in length and weighing more than a thousand pounds. The tunny has a large dorsal fin, followed by a series of finlets arranged between the main dorsal fin and the tail. There are similar finlets on the underside of the fish. Tunnies are extremely good swimmers, and rare among fish, their temperature is several degrees warmer than that of the surrounding water. Tunnies are usually caught in the open sea, often first spotted as they leap after smaller fish.

Tuna meat is bloody, makes very good steaks and a delicious salad if served cooked and cold, but because of its red meat, it is not so easy to dry.

PREPARING FISH

People seem to imagine that fresh fish are hauled in twice a day, as of right, and preferably one hour before meals. Don't you believe it! One friend claims to navigate by the fish he catches—one every five thousand miles. But if you do stray into a shoal, don't stop when you've caught lunch and supper. Keep going because there are several ways to preserve fish.

As for equipment we are no great fishermen but we have one first-rate ratcheted reel which we use for trolling. With it goes heavy line and trace, though often not heavy enough. In the oceans we've lost more fish than we've caught as line or trace has snapped.

Depending on your speed, try a nice polished spoon, glinting and twisting enticingly about a foot below the surface, or else a handmade lure on which a dash of red cloth mingles with a flash of aluminum foil and a small weight. In calms we've caught dorados one after the other just with a hand-held line and fish-baited hook dangled over the side. When coasting, think about investing in a local fish trap. Each country has its own design, but often traps come in kit form so that they can be erected in some pleasant anchorage and then dismantled again when you get under way. (Otherwise they tend to clutter up the deck.) Our Seychelles fish trap averaged eight fish a day over a quite considerable time, the best haul being thirty-two fish in one trap.

Cleaning Fish ▪ Fish may be eaten raw, cooked, or pickled. They can be dried, salted, and smoked. But for all these one has first to clean the fish. There are many different ways to clean a fish, depending in part on what you plan to do with it afterward. If, for instance, you plan to dry and salt the fish, read "Salting Fish" below before cleaning it.

If you do not want to prepare the whole fish immediately, it is important to remove at least the guts as soon as possible after catching it or the whole thing will go bad. Also, if you are planning to eat the skin, the scales are much easier to remove when the fish is still freshly caught.

I set myself up with two buckets of salt water, one holding the dead fish, the other for rinsing. Then I gather up a large wooden chopping board, and wielding a really sharp sheath knife, I settle myself where the scales will easily wash overboard.

Are you sitting comfortably? (If not, you'll soon get a cramp.) Then we'll begin.

Give the fish a good rinse and place it on the board. Decide now whether you are going to leave the skin on when you cook it or not. Apart from the sometimes excessive store of vitamin A found in fish liver, most of the vitamin content of fish lies in the skin. So I will assume that you have decided to eat the skin in which case the fish wants scaling. If you plan to discard the skin, join us again when we start filleting in (2), below.

1. To scale a fish, hold its tail in your left hand (vice versa if you are left-handed). If the fish is at all hard to grip, make a deep, right-angled cut across the tail down to the bone, and dig your left thumb in there.

Then, with the knife blade slanted slightly away from you so as to catch under the scales but not to penetrate the flesh, push it, parallel with your cut, from the tail toward the head. This way the scales pop off without any danger of the knife's cutting you. Do this carefully all over as scales left behind are cursed as much as fish bones. The fresher the fish, the more easily the scales will flip off.

Watch out for the fish spines since some are poisonous and most others are sharp.

Once the fish is scaled, give both it and the board a thorough rinse to get rid of any loose scales that remain. You, on the other hand, may need a complete swim to be rid of them.

If you want to cook the fish whole, gently slice open the belly from chin to anus, taking care not to slit the guts. Remove them, and wash out the cavity.

Alternatively, if it's fillets you want, leave the guts in place and proceed as follows.

2. Lay the fish on its right side, and make an incision across it from the back of the neck down to the belly, passing just tailward of the side fin. For the first half of the cut go as deep as the backbone, but once you are past it and heading toward the belly, be very careful not to cut too deep or you will pierce the guts.

Now comes the delicate art of actual filleting. Keep the fish on its right side with the dorsal fins toward you. Starting at the head end, cut very carefully just above the dorsal fins for the full length of the fish.

Continue until, approximately halfway toward the belly, the knife comes in contact with the rise of the vertebrae. Lift the fillets so far cut so you can see your way, and cut past the vertebrae.

Now fillet off the last part of the fish down to the belly, taking great care once again, to stay just above the long bones which protect the gut cavity. Congratulations! You've filleted a fillet. All you have to do now is turn the fish over, and this time starting from the tail end, repeat the whole thing all over again on the other side. The fish is filleted, and the backbone is probably still covered with flesh. Don't despair, it takes a bit of practice to do a perfect job. Meanwhile, that head and backbone will make an excellent basis for a nourishing soup, provided, that is, you remember to throw out the guts first. The great joy of this system, though, is that if you decide to throw the bones away, you can hump the whole lot, bones, head, and guts overboard in one piece.

3. So you have your two beautiful fillets. Place them, skin side down, on the board. Now look for a thin, often reddish line running down the center. If not certain of its position, stroke your finger from head to tail down the middle of the fillet, and you will feel a ruffle of little bones. Cut down either side of the bones as far as the skin without cutting through it. Push your index finger under the bony part, between it and the skin, and the whole line of bones should peel off the skin in one piece.

4. If you have decided to remove the skin, this is a good time to do it, though if you plan to poach the fish, the skin comes off very easily when the fish is cooked. Otherwise proceed as follows.

Lay the fillet, skin side down, on the board. Place the knife blade between the skin and the flesh at the tail end. Pressing down and slightly away from you, slowly ease the knife toward the head end, at the same time gently pulling the skin toward you. It takes a little practice to get the tension right. You may also find at first that you cut right through the skin. Never mind. With any luck you will get lots more practice. With some fish it is possible to rip the skin off with ones hands, but this may pull the fillet in two.

At last, the fish is ready to cook, though, of course, if you have caught twenty fish, the process must be repeated twenty times, and by then you will hate the very sight of dead fish. If you are cleaning a lot of fish and planning to dry them or at least to eat the skin, scale them all first and fillet them afterward. Better still, press-gang all hands and turn a chore into a recreation.

Salting Fish ▪ To salt and dry fish, a slightly different approach is needed— plus quite a lot of sunshine.

Remove the scales as in (1) above, only make no cut across the tail for the thumb. In (2) follow instructions, but do not sever the two fillets from the tail end. When the fish is otherwise filleted, bend back the fillets to expose the backbone near the tail. Sever the backbone and save it for soup. You are now left with two flaps of flesh joined by a tail.

Open the fish out, meat uppermost, and rub it liberally with salt. (You can make your own salt by evaporating seawater, but it takes time.) Once the salt has

Hang the salted fish, tail-up.

been well rubbed in, leave the fillets out in the sun for a day, flesh side up. Mop up any excess moisture that is drawn out.

Repeat the salt rubbing the following day, and then put a line between two uprights (in port the lifeline would do), and hang the fish over the line, tails up, so the two fillets dangle down without touching each other.

Leave in the sun all day. Remove from the dew at night. Repeat the salt rubbing for about three days and then continue to lay the fillets in the sun, either hanging or flat, until they are dry and leathery. They will then keep for weeks, provided they never become damp for long and no one takes a sudden fancy to dried fish. One crew member we had found it quite irresistible and must have unconsciously pecked her way through half a dozen large dorados while sitting at the helm.

When a fish is very large, it is better to cut it into thin steaks. Rub each steak with salt; then hang the steaks up to dry, threaded on bits of string.

Some fish are not suitable for salting and drying. These are mainly either oily or red-blooded fish like the tuna, although even tuna, if bled to death first, will dry after a fashion.

When you want to eat some fish, cut off the required amount and cover it with freshwater. After soaking it for four hours, change the water. To regain some of its texture, dried fish should soak for twenty-four hours, though even then it never tastes the same as when fresh. I prefer it cooked either in kedgeree or a sauce. Remember not to add too much salt when cooking.

If we catch a number of oily fish such as mackeral, I pickle them with pickling spice and vinegar. In the tropics they then keep for about a week.

We also keep a small smoker on board which adds yet another variation to the fish dish theme.

APPENDIX H

Dolphin and Whale Sightings

By KEEPING RECORDS of the cetaceans (dolphins, whales, and porpoises) spotted on ocean and coastal passages, yachtsmen can greatly help cetologists collect their data.*

The following method for identifying and recording sightings has been suggested by Lyall Watson in his excellent book *Whales of the World: A Complete Guide to the World's Living Whales, Dolphins and Porpoises:*

1. Date of sighting.
2. Longitude and latitude of yacht at time of sighting.
3. Local time.
4. Height of observer's eye above, or below, the water.
5. Weather conditions; wind speed and visibility most important.
6. Sea conditions, size of waves, etc.
7. Number of observers and how long they kept watch.
8. Duration of sighting, including estimate of cetaceans' diving time.
9. Distance of cetaceans from observer.
10. Movement relative to observer; speed, heading. Also speed and heading of yacht and whether under sail or power. (I have noticed that dolphins seem to be attracted by the sound of engines, loving to play around the bow of fast-moving boats. On the other hand, a becalmed sailboat seems to hold little attraction for them.) Ship's course.
11. If possible, identify cetaceans. Scientific writers differ in the common names they use for whales and dolphins. So to avoid confusion, it is best to identify sightings by their scientific names. After making a tentative identification, or if unable to do so, add (a) size; (b) number, including age and sex; (c) size and shape of dorsal fin; (d) size and shape of blow; (e) color and markings; (f) any visible flukes; (g) presence of tags or markers.
12. Presence of other species: birds of fish.
13. Details of behavior: breaching, spinning; feeding, etc.
14. Reaction of cetaceans to observer or vessel: Did they bow ride, avoid, etc.?
15. Name and address of observer.

*For address to send information, see Appendix J.

APPENDIX I

Seabirds: Feathered Variety

AMONG THE MANY joys of ocean sailing, and coast-hopping come to that, are the birds that skim across the blue water toward you, possibly even perching in the rigging before flying off to you know not where.

Many books are available on birds, so this chapter is a brief introduction to help you identity the most common species.

Albatrosses ▪ Most albatrosses have sturdy bodies finishing at one end in stumpy tails and, at the other, in biggish heads. The whole is carried on fine, elongated wings sometimes with a span of twelve feet. Their bills are also sturdy, with the top mandible well hooked over the bottom. Albatrosses can be black and white, all white, or brownish in color.

When flying, they rise up against the wind, make a large circle, then come down on the wind. Their flight is long and gliding. They land on the water to look for food. Though they are generally found only out of sight of land, I have seen whole flocks of albatrosses following the ferries which ply the narrow Cook Strait between North Island and South Island of New Zealand. Most albatrosses live between 30° and 60° south. The rest are found in the North Pacific. Albatrosses mate for life yet often do not reach breeding maturity for ten years or more.

Auks, Guillemots, and Puffins ▪ These are all small birds with short, stubby necks; small, narrow wings; and very short tails. They also have short legs. In short, they are short. Their bills differ one from another, some fairly elongated but most short and compressed with the puffin's bill looking as if it had been shut in a heavy door by mistake. Normally auks have dark backs and wings with white breasts. When floating they sit up in the water like gulls. Diving under water for fish, they use their wings as highly efficient flippers.

In an attempt to fly, they flap their wings very rapidly like some manic clockwork toy. Most inefficient, they expend an awful lot of effort with very little result, for at least at sea, they seldom rise more than a few feet above the waves. When in danger, they either dive or splash along the surface, plunging through the crests of the waves. However, ashore they nest on cliffs, and for this they manage to rise up in a sweeping curve before crash-landing on braced, outstretched feet. There they stand upright. Because of this, the great auk was once classified as a penguin. Now, after centuries of being hunted for food, the great auk is classified as extinct.

All these birds live in the colder seas of the Northern Hemisphere. In winter they frequent waters close to land.

Cormorants and Shags ▪ These birds have long, graceful necks, slim bodies, and quite long wings. At the end of short legs they sport large, webbed feet. Their tails are often long and wedge-shaped. Their bills are also long with a vicious-looking hook at the tip.

Most Northern Hemisphere cormorants are black while some in the Southern Hemisphere have white plumage underneath. They fly just above the surface of the water with steady, flapping wings and an occasional glide.

To catch fish, cormorants float on the surface; then, rising a few inches in the air, they dive to chase their fishy prey underwater. When there's not much room, they use only their webbed feet. If there's more space, they swim with their wings as well. They appear actually to search out their prey underwater rather than spy it first from the surface. Because their feathers are not very waterproof, they spend a lot of time perched on rocks shaking themselves and holding their wings up to dry, spread-eagle fashion. Cormorants and shags rarely go out of sight of land. They are found in all but the Central Pacific Ocean.

Frigate Birds ▪ Large, tropical seabirds, frigate birds have very long wings, very short legs, and very long, forked tails, which they sometimes open and shut in flight. They are either black or black and white and, to my mind, are the most sinister of all seabirds. They never settle on the water or on flatland. Instead, they ride the thermals high above other birds, swooping down on them like naval frigates on an innocent barque, to grab their food. With vicious pecks from their great, hooked breaks, the frigate birds force the smaller birds to disgorge their catch; sometimes they even break their victims' wings in the process. Only occasionally do they deign to fish for themselves. At night they usually roost in trees or bushes, though sometimes they spend a night or two riding the thermals. So sighting a frigate bird does not necessarily mean you are close to land.

Gannets or Boobies ▪ These medium-large seabirds are about the size of a small goose. Their beaks are strong and conical; their necks, short; their bodies, powerful and sleek, ending in wedge-shaped tails. The young are brown; the adults, mainly white with sometimes some brown areas as well. They, too, are amazing birds. Feeding on fish, they dive expertly from as high as one hundred feet up and have been caught alive in fishermen's nets ninety feet down. Gannets chase and eat fish underwater. They often travel in small groups ten to twenty feet above the water, sometimes forming a single file of birds, their wings working in powerful steady beats. Though found throughout the world, two-thirds of gannets nest around the coast of Britain in vast gannetries, many of which have been going for hundreds of years.

Gulls ▪ These seabirds have long wings attached to medium-sized bodies. Their tails are usually square. Most have bodies and tails white, with wings and backs gray or black. Young gulls are normally mottled brown. Gulls fly with wonderful grace, alternately flapping their wings in steady, metronomic flight and then twisting and turning, soaring and swooping on thermals. They are mostly scavengers, often settling on the water or waddling along the beach in search of food. They do sometimes feed inland on insects. Despite their grace, they are a raucous lot, constantly bickering and fighting among themselves. Coastal birds, they are not found in the tropics or far out to sea.

For a whole different perspective on gulls, read that glorious masterpiece by Richard Bach, *Jonathan Livingston Seagull*.

Pelicans ▪ These birds have large, cumbersome bodies, broad wings and longish necks. The pelican is well known for, and easily recognized by, its extraordinary great bill with its weird food pouch slung underneath. Pelicans normally travel in flocks. Flying high with a fair wind, they just skim the water if the wind is ahead. Their flock formation is very distinctive with a diagonal single file of birds alternately flapping and gliding in incredible unison. Pelicans circle around at some height before spying fish. Then they plunge down into the water as heavily and gracelessly as unleavened dough. They hit the water so hard and unscientifically that eventually they damage their eyes. Because of this, many older pelicans die of starvation, no longer able to spot food.

Penguins ▪ These well-known, and much-loved, flightless birds of the South-

Bird watching: but who's watching whom?

ern Hemisphere have sleek, sturdy black-and-white bodies and short necks. Ranging in size between a duck and a goose, they stand upright on short, webbed feet, looking for all the world like pompous Victorian politicians. Their bills are stout and their tails short. Penguins travel considerable distances underwater, coming up only for breath. When on the surface, they swim very low in the water so only their heads or heads and backs show. Penguins often display the same apparent verve and joy for living as dolphins, leaping and diving through the waves. Many can jump more than a yard out of the water to land on the top of an ice floe.

Penguins move around in flocks and feed on fish. They have a strange, carrying cry which sometimes sounds unnervingly like a donkey braying. They range from the Antarctic to the Tropic of Capricorn and even up to Galápagos.

Shearwaters, Petrels, and Fulmars ▪ These seabirds vary from pigeon to goose size. They have hooked bills and narrow wings and are black, brown, gray, or white. They are also some of the most graceful birds in the world as they glide, skimming low over the waves, often tipping one wing or other down toward the sea. I could watch them for hours. Found far out in the oceans, they settle on the water to rest. They appear all over the world and are normally silent at sea. But when nesting, fulmars in particular should be avoided. In defense of its young the fulmar will attack intruders, whether human or feathered, by ejecting a foul-smelling oil from its mouth. Since it clogs up the feathers and prevents flight, this oil can mean death to other birds. To humans it simply confirms the original version of the fulmar's name, foul mew, or gull.

Storm Petrels ▪ Sometimes known as Mother Carey's chicks and averaging only six inches in length, these are the smallest seabirds around. They have disproportionately long legs and fairly dark plumage often with distinctive white splotch at the base of their tails. Their flight is hilarious but sadly undignified. They flutter along, their wings held up and out while their feet pedal frantically at the water a bit like farmyard hens trying to get airborne. Despite their ungainly flight, storm petrels survive in the roughest seas. In fact, their name, "petrel," is said to come from St. Peter and his ability to walk on water. Storm petrels are found in most parts of the world. They sometimes settle on water.

Terns or Noddies ▪ These birds have short legs, small, webbed feet, and delicate bodies held aloft on long, slender wings. Their tails are usually forked. A few are mainly black, but the rest are white or gray. They often travel in large flocks, seldom landing on the water. They live off small fish. When flying, terns scan the water, their bills pointing down. Once a fish is spotted, the tern hovers over the prey, then shuts its wings and dives, sharp as an arrow, into the sea. After a quick dip it flies off again, fish in beak. Sometimes, instead of diving, it swoops down to just above the water, dips its bill to grab a small surface fish, then flies up again without even getting the tips of its wings wet. Terns live mainly along the coast of tropical countries, but some go north and south. The exquisitely delicate arctic tern spends its life migrating many thousands of miles back and forth from the Arctic north to the Antarctic south. That way it is reckoned to get as much as eight months of solid daylight.

Tropicbirds ▪ These very beautiful white seabirds are found only in the tropics. They have straight beaks, long wings, and short legs ending in webbed feet. Their tails are wedge-shaped with the two central feathers enormously elongated and, in the red-tailed tropicbird, startling scarlet in color. Their plumage is snow white, but sometimes it appears suffused with the hint of a sunset glow of rose. Many tropicbirds have vivid bars of black across their wings. Their wingbeats are unusually rapid but powerful, unlike the auks' feeble flapping. Tropic birds fly fifty feet or more above the water and, when they spot food, dive directly down for it. Tropicbirds do not settle on the water often, but when they do, they hold those fantastic tail feathers fastidiously high out of the sea.

Wherever you sail there are birds. Usually they are just passing by, but sometimes they'll stop aboard long enough to plume their feathers. Occasionally they'll honor you enough to make your boat their home. In Kenya a pair of wagtails built a nest, laid their eggs, and raised their young—all on top of Edward's binocular case.

APPENDIX J

Useful Addresses

INTERNATIONAL YACHT CLUBS

The Cruising Association
Ivory House
St. Katharine Dock
London E1 9AT
England

Ocean Cruising Club
6 Creek Road
Emsworth
Hants
England

The Seven Seas Cruising Association
Suite 220
500 SE 17th St.
Fort Lauderdale, FL 33302

EDUCATION

Calvert School
105 Tuscany Road
Baltimore, MD 21210

Growing without Schooling
Holt Associates
2269 Massachusetts Ave.
Cambridge, MA 02140

WES
Strode House
44–50 Osnaburgh St.
London NW1 3NN
England

Education Otherwise
25 Common Lane
Hemmingford Abbots
Cambridgeshire PE18 9AN
England

DOLPHINS

Dolphin Survey Project
c/o Department of Anatomy
Downing St.
Cambridge CB2 3DY
England

Tinker Tramp
J. M. Henshaw Marine Ltd.
Verrington Lodge
Wincanton, Somerset BA9 8BN
England
(door-to-door delivery)

BRITISH GOVERNMENT PUBLICATION

Unipub
4611F, Assembly Drive,
Lanham, MD 20706-4391

APPENDIX K

Books

NOWADAYS, with so many new book titles appearing on the shelves each year, any attempt at a comprehensive book list is doomed to failure. At the same time how could *The Intricate Art of Living Afloat* be a proper companion without some mention of those greatest companions of all, books. Not only can they transport you to other worlds in times of trouble, but they can also get you out of that trouble and help you to be more self-sufficient. To my mind, self-sufficiency is what cruising is all about.

Below, I have listed books under general categories. The few I have mentioned by name are ones I would go out of my way to look for in a secondhand bookshop if they were out of print.

NAUTICAL

Cruising Under Sail, by Eric Hiscock, is perhaps a little dated now, but it has been, for many years, the bible of the cruising world.

Current *Nautical Almanac.*

Navigation tables. See if you can find Ageton's HO 211. The tables come in one volume one-fourth by ten by eight inches (sic) and cover the whole of the world for the whole of your life. *Sky and Sextant,* by John P. Budlong, published by Van Nostrand Rheinhold, carried the tables as an appendix.

Good pilot books for your cruising area.

Book of radio beacons for radio direction finders.

Book of VHF shore stations and call signs.

Books on: Boat maintenance; Sailmaking and repair; Weather.

State of the Sea (see Appendix C).

GENERAL REFERENCE

One-volume encyclopedia. Puts a stop to many an argument.

Books on: birds; fish; shells; stars.

Foreign-language dictionaries and home-tutor courses.

Dictionary.

A world atlas—for dreaming.

MEDICAL

Book designed specifically for medical crisis at sea.

A family medical encyclopedia which gives help with diagnosis.

An all-round health book emphasizing prevention of illness and outlining sound dietetics.

FAMILY

The Gesell series: The following three books cover the whole physical and emotional development of children. Not only a fascinating read but also very reassuring to isolated parents.

Child Behavior, Frances L. Ilg and Louise Bates Ames

The Child from Five to Ten by Arnold Gesell and Frances L. Ilg

Youth: The Years from Ten to Sixteen by Arnold Gesell, Frances L. Ilg, and Louise Bates Ames

Book on practical child care.

Book of indoor and outdoor games for children.

Book of card and board games.

Haircutting book.

Dressmaking book.

OTHERS

How-to hobby books.

Fat, easy-reading novels for long, hot nights in the tropics.

A selection of classics for long, hot days in the tropics.

One or two books on survival at sea (see those in Chapter 5).

Cookery books or cards. My favorite is *Cooking in a Bedsitter*, by Katherine Whitehorn. Very basic but ideal for a restricted one- or two-burner galley; it is also the only cookery book that has ever made me laugh.

APPENDIX L

Communications

Mail ▪ When sailing off on your annual vacation, arrange either with the post office to hold your mail or arrange with a neighbor to collect it. Bulging letterboxes are dead giveaways to thieves.

Coping with mail on extended foreign cruises is unfortunately a more hit-and-miss affair.

First, you have to persuade someone to volunteer as "collecting box" in your home country. The criteria for the collecting box are threefold: S/he must have a permanent address; considerable perspicacity, if not clairvoyance, in guessing the best place to forward mail to; and, most important of all, the disposition of a saint. My mother has acted as our collecting box for the past eighteen years. We give her address to friends. Then, when she thinks there's a chance of catching us, she forwards all our mail to whatever latest address we have given her.

When a letter arrives at the collecting box by airmail, there is no need for extra stamps. Just forward it on, unopened and redirected, in its own envelope. Only if letters have come on the internal mail service do they require extra stamps stuck on the envelope to make up the extra airmail charge.

For further information ask your post office for the Postal Union mail pamphlet which is extremely helpful and just what the collecting box will need. There are often special rates for small packages (under two pounds) and for printed paper (under four pounds). The same pamphlet may be of some use to you on your travels as well, although regulations, especially those regarding how packages and parcels must be wrapped, do vary from county to country. For instance, in Singapore you are *not* allowed to use adhesive tape on registered mail.

With some developing countries it is best to register everything. In Kenya I discovered that letters sent to me with an enclosure, such as a photograph, never arrived unless they were registered. (In other countries mail gets stolen *because* it is registered) But in most countries, ordinary incoming mail is safe. When mailing letters out of a doubtful country, get the post office to frank the stamp in front of you. That way no one will steam the stamps off and throw the mail away. In fact, if you ever see the stamp seller also franking letters, it is a sure sign of an unreliable postal service, so join the line and get yours franked, too.

The next problem is where to have mail sent. Yacht clubs and marinas around the world are very helpful. Poste Restante service (as far as I know, this is called General Delivery only in the States) varies from excellent (Singapore) to hopelessly corrupt (naming no names).

To collect from General Delivery or Poste Restante, you usually have to show some form of identity; your passport or a credit card will do. It is also an idea to carry your name printed in clear, block capitals on a separate piece of paper.

Ask to look through the mail yourself. If permission is refused, hand over the piece of paper with your name on it. Then, as the postal worker flips through the letters, try to perfect your rapid, upside-down reading—definitely one of the more intricate arts of living afloat.

To avoid confusion, ask friends to put only your initials and surname, in capitals, on the envelope. Different cultures have different orders for writing their given names and surnames. The Chinese, for instance, put their surnames first. So a letter addressed to Daisy Smith might easily be filed under *D* rather than *S*. If mail is missing, look through all the letters filed under each of your initials as well as your surname. A few countries charge a fee for every letter handled by Poste Restante.

A different problem occurs when your arrival is delayed. Then the helpful Poste Restante or yacht club may decide to return all your mail to sender. We've had letters take two years to catch up with us. Most recently, in a tiny town in Turkey, we came across a Christmas card sent from a guy in the States to a man in Chile. Heaven only knows how it got to that one-donkey town in Turkey. The charming Poste Restante man (Turks are wonderful people!) was delighted when we translated "Chile" into Turkish and so cleared up the mystery. He sent the card off—posthaste.

There are two other possible mail-receiving centers: care of the harbor master, if there is one, and American Express if you are a card carrier and there is a convenient office. Embassy officials usually refuse to deal with their travelers' mail; British ones are most reluctant to deal with their travelers as well.

Telephone ▪ Praise be to satellite communications. Gone are the days, or almost, of waiting up to ten hours in a stuffy telephone office to place an overseas call. To telephone from Singapore to the United States is now as simple as telephoning your next-door neighbor. However, there are a few countries still not connected by satellite communications. If you are in one of those and want to call home, then pack a picnic and a book to wear away the waiting hours while keeping your place in the line.

Telex ▪ More and more governments now provide some sort of telex facility for the general public. Ask at the local post office of any large town.

News ▪ If you want news from the outside world, *Newsweek* and *Time* are sold in most towns which have some English-speaking tourist industry. More difficult to find but, for my money, a much better buy is the *Economist*. For years I was put off by the title. I was wrong. Though it does have a section on finance, it also has an intelligent and comprehensive, if rather right-of-center, coverage of the week's events around the world, including a long section dealing exclusively with U.S. affairs. And then there's the bonus of getting, for a fractionally higher cost, twice as much reading matter and half as much scandal as its rivals.

A less well-publicized source of news for the cruising person who lives in a remote part of the world is the scrap of newspaper with which poorer shopkeepers wrap their goods. For some inexplicable reason they are frequently in English.

Once I get my parcels home, I carefully unwrap them and smooth the paper out, shake off the breadcrumbs and sugar grains, and settle down to a good read. I reckon I've really hit the jackpot if the torn sheet includes not only one whole article but is from the current year as well.

Radio • If it's up-to-the-minute news you're after, tune in to shortwave radio. You don't need anything fancy. My present Sony radio has seven shortwave bands, measures five-by-three-by-one inches, cost $150, and gives me adequate coverage all over the world.

The three main English-language broadcasts are Voice of America, Radio Moscow, and the BBC World Service. Each has its virtues. One of the positive results of *glasnost* is the incredible change that has come over Radio Moscow. No longer does it overload the airwaves with a nonstop flow of puerile anti-American propaganda. Now one can hear programs which actually encourage greater understanding between East and West. Soviet broadcasters even mention some of their country's failings. In fact, I am amazed at the courage of the people who speak out honestly in this way. I would be far too worried that another Stalin might be lurking around the corner. Not that even now the revolution is total. Some subjects are still taboo, and the name Solzhenitsyn still draws forth the old invective.

The Voice of America is exactly what it says it is, giving first-class coverage of U.S. news and sports for expatriates overseas. The international news broadcasts are of high quality and wide general interest, though with a U.S. slant. Reception is usually excellent.

The BBC has the largest worldwide audience of the big three, but then it has the unfair advantage of being independent of government interference and so more like a regular radio station. Though it carries programs about its home country, Britain, it also offers coverage on a daily basis of international events from all parts of the developed and developing world. Along with this, it has an excellent arts section featuring concerts, serialized book readings, short stories, and full-length plays performed by some of the best actors. For those with more frivolous interests there are always panel games, comedies, and pop music to listen to. If, that is, you can hear it. Sadly BBC reception seldom compares favorably with its competitors.

APPENDIX M

Languages

THE QUICKEST WAY to make friends when traveling abroad, be it with surly immigration officials or the man hawking squid on the beach, is by having a go at speaking the language. What with the British background of nineteenth-century colonialism and the present accusations of twentieth-century American economic imperialism, English-speaking peoples, more than any others, need to make the effort to speak foreign languages or risk being thought insufferably arrogant.

So don't be shy. Throw away all those useless inhibitions about making a fool of yourself. What in the world does it matter if you do? You don't have to be a linguist or to produce a perfect accent either. All that is wanted is a warm smile (there are far too few of those around) and a willingness to try.

Wherever you go, except perhaps in France, your efforts will be welcomed with open arms. (The French love their language so passionately that some refuse to understand barbarian renderings of their tongue even when the renderings are fairly accurate.)

What fun, though, to go into a small Spanish store with your one month's knowledge of Spanish and your list of purchases carefully translated from the dictionary. You struggle and point while everyone crowds around, eager to help. And then the great moment when the light dawns: they know what you want! Everyone laughs and beams with relief. The sugar is weighed out and the bacon sliced and they pat you warmly on the back, for together you have won a marvelous victory against considerable linguistic odds.

And if you are totally at a loss for words, don't forget that most ancient art: sign language.

In Bulgaria we wanted fresh milk, so I mimed drinking from a glass and then gave a loud "moo." They loved it, but unfortunately they don't sell fresh milk in Bulgaria. In India we wanted eggs. Nothing easier. Circle thumb and forefinger together in an egg shape, make distinctive clucking noises and raise enough fingers to cover your order. It works every time. In Greece recently I crowed and flapped my wings in the butcher's. He at once led me to the door and directed me down the street. No, not to the nearest mental asylum but to the little shop around the corner which sold chickens.

I've only once had a nasty shock. That was in the Seychelles, where I ordered a duck as a birthday dinner treat for Edward. It arrived, squawking and demanding to be set free.

An expressive shrug conveys a wealth of meaning. Thumbs up or down, accompanied by the appropriate smile or turned-down mouth, are fairly universal signs. But beckoning in some countries actually means "Stop" or even "Go back," while the Sri Lankans shake their heads to say yes and the Turks nod theirs upward to say no.

I am told that in southern Italy it is best not to use your hands at all. There so many gestures are suffused with sexual innuendo that the uninitiated are bound to end up in trouble.

If you have a dictionary, find the word in English and point to the opposite entry for the local person to read. But remember, he may not be able to read or he may be unfamiliar with the dictionary's confusing habit of giving, for each word in a foreign tongue, several alternative words, all with totally different meanings, in the local language. Don't do anything which would cause someone to lose face. When on your own, and trying to select one of the list of foreign words on offer, turn to the other end of the dictionary and look up each word's English equivalent until you find the one closest to your meaning.

If sign language and pointing do not work, don't forget pen and paper and very simple drawings. Plans and maps are often incomprehensible to an uninitiated eye.

For those planning only a short visit to a country I include a list of the words which I have found most useful in our travels. Please note that I avoid, as much as possible, those strings of complaints so beloved of phrase books: "Waiter, there's a scorpion in my soup!"; "Manager, my room is full of rats/icicles!"; etc. Why travel at all if you plan to whine all the time?

When making a more prolonged visit, invest in a dictionary and a good home-tutoring course (a local girl or boyfriend is often the best). The effort of learning the language will pay off many times over in the insights you gain into the hearts and customs of the people you visit.

PRONUNCIATION

One language can seldom be rendered perfectly in the phonetics of another, and anyway *The Intricate Art of Living Afloat* is not the place to enter into the intricacies of linguistics, so here are just a few brief tips on pronunciation.

FRENCH

e followed by *r, t,* or *z* is pronounced as in h*e*n. Otherwise it is like *er* in paint*er*. The following consonants are never sounded when they appear at the very end of a word: *d, q, h, n, p, s, t, x, z.*

GERMAN

ei . . . l*i*ne	w . . . *v*eer
ie . . . *sea*	v . . . *f*ear

ch . . . lo*ch* (as in Scots, used when *ch* follows a vowel)

DUTCH

ch tj . . . lo*ch* + *y*awl (lo*ch* as in Scots)

sj, stj . . . *sh*oal

Italian, Spanish, and Turkish are three of the easiest languages to pronounce. Learn a few simple and invariable rules, and you cannot go wrong.

ITALIAN

c . . . *ch*ain (when followed by *e* or *i*)

c . . . *c*leat (when *not* followed by *e* or *i*)

sc . . . *sh*ackle (when followed by *e* or *i*)

sc . . . *sk*y (when *not* followed by *e* or *i*)

SPANISH

j . . . lo*ch* (Scots)

c . . . *th*under (if followed by *e* or *i* except in Central and South America, where it is pronounced as *s*)

c . . . *c*atamaran (when *not* followed by *e* or *i*)

Emphasis in both Italian and Spanish generally falls on the next-to-last syllable.

TURKISH

Ataturk introduced the present phonetic alphabet to Turkey in the 1920s. It has twenty-nine letters, most of which follow common phonetic rules. The exceptions are as follows.

ı . . . cut*ter* (note that this *ı* has no dot over it.)

ö . . . s*ur*f

c . . . *j*ib

ç . . . *ch*annel

ş . . . *sh*rouds

v . . . *w*ater

USEFUL FRENCH, GERMAN, AND DUTCH VOCABULARY

NOTE: Starting on page 282 is vocabulary for Italian, Spanish, and Turkish.

ENGLISH	FRENCH	GERMAN	DUTCH
Frequently Needed Words			
bad	mauvais	schlecht	slecht
bank	banque	Bank	bank

ENGLISH	FRENCH	GERMAN	DUTCH
bus	bus	Bus	bus
drugstore	pharmacie	Apotheke	apotheker
glass of water	verre d'eau	Glas Wasser	een glas water
good	bon	gut	goed
how far?	quelle distance?	wie weit?	hoe ver?
no	non	nein	nee
open	ouvert	offen	open
post office	poste/P.T.T.	Postamt	postkantoor
shut	fermé	geschlossen	gesloten
stamps	timbres	Briefmarken	postzegels
toilet	toilette, WC	Toilette, WC	toilet
when?	quand?	wann?	wanneer?
where is?	où se trouve?	wo ist?	waar is?
yes	oui	ja	ja

Greetings and Thanks

hello	salut	hallo	hallo
good day	bon jour	guten Tag	goeden dag
good-bye	au revoir	auf Wiedersehen	dag
excuse me	excusez-moi	entschuldigung	excuseert u my
please	s'il vous plaît	bitte	alstublieft
thank you	merci	danke	dank u
thank you very much	merci beaucoup	vielen Dank	hartelyk dank
no, thank you	non, merci	nein, danke	nee, dank u
sir	monsieur	mein Herr	meneer
madam	madame	mein Frau	mevrouw

Harbor

bonded stores	sous douane	unter Zollverschlß	belastingvrije goederen
cast off, to	larguer	losmachen	losgooien
certificate of registration	certificat du francisation	Registrierungs-Zertifikat	zeebrief
courtesy flag	pavillon de courtoisie	Gastflagge	vreemde natievlag
customs	douane	Zollabfertigung	douanekantoor
harbor master	capitaine de port	Hafenmeister	havenmeester
immigration	immigration	Passkontrolle	immigratie
make fast, to	amarrer	festmachen	vastmaken
passport	passeport	Reisepasz	paspoort
yacht	yacht	Yacht	jacht

ENGLISH	FRENCH	GERMAN	DUTCH

Short Words

a	un (e)	ein(e)	een
and	et	und	en
at	à	am	aan
but	mais	aber	maar
from	de	von	van
here	ici	hier	hier
how	comment	wie	hoe
in/into	dans	in	in
much	beaucoup	viel	veel
not	ne . . . pas	nicht	niet
now	maintenant	jetzt	nu
of	de	von	van
on	sur	auf	op
over	dessus	über	over
there	là	da	daar
very	très	sehr	erg
what	quoi	was	wat
who	qui	wer	wie
with	avec	mit	met

Short Phrases

I am	je suis	ich bin	ik ben
I am not	je ne suis pas	ich bin nicht	ik ben niet
I like it	j'aime cela	ich mag	daar houd ik van
I have	j'ai	ich habe	ik heb
I have not	je n'ai pas	ich habe nicht	ik heb niet
it is	c'est	es ist	het is
is it?	est-ce que?	ist es?	is het?
I don't understand	je ne comprends pas	ich verstehe nicht	ik begrjp het niet
speak slowly	pouvez-vous parle lentement	sprechen Sie langsam?	langzaam spreken
to go	aller	gehen	gaan

Days

afternoon	après-midi	Nachmittag	middag
day	jour	Tag	dag
evening	soir	Abend	avond
morning	matin	Morgen	morgen
today	aujourd'hui	Heute	vandaag
tomorrow	demain	Morgen	morgen

ENGLISH	FRENCH	GERMAN	DUTCH
week	semaine	Woche	week
yesterday	hier	gestern	gisteren
Monday	lundi	Montag	maandag
Tuesday	mardi	Dienstag	dinsdag
Wednesday	mercredi	Mittwoch	woensdag
Thursday	jeudi	Donnerstag	donderdag
Friday	vendredi	Freitag	vrijdag
Saturday	samedi	Samstag	zaterdag
Sunday	dimanche	Sonntag	zondag

People

baby	bébé	Baby	baby
boy	garçon	Junge	jongen
children	enfants	Kinder	kinderen
friend	ami	Freund	vriend
girl	fille	Mädchen	meisje
he	il	er	hij
husband	mari	Mann	man
my	mon, ma	mein	mijn
she	elle	sie	zij
wife	femme	Frau	vrouw
you	vous	Sie	jij
your	votre	ihr	jouw

Measures

kilo	kilo	Kilo	kilo
liter	litre	Liter	liter
meter	metre	Meter	meter

To Ask and Bargain

how much?	combien?	wie viel?	hoeveel?
it's cheap	c'est bon marché	es ist billig	het is goedkoop
it's too expensive	c'est trop cher	es ist zu teuer	het is te duur
all right	ça va	in Ordnung (OK)	OK
have you?	avez-vous?	haben Sie?	heeft U?
I would like	je voudrais	ich mochte	ik wil graag
I don't want	je ne veux pas	ich mochte nicht	ik wil niet
that's all	c'est tout	das ist alles	dat is alles

ENGLISH	FRENCH	GERMAN	DUTCH

To Select

big	gros	gross	groot
cold	froid	kalt	koud
color	couleur	Farbe	kleur
enough	assez	genug	genoeg
half	la moitiée	halb	half
iced	glacé	mit Eis	met ÿs
little	peu / petit	klein / wenig	klein
more	plus	mehr	meer
small	petit	klein	klein
stop	arretez	halt	stop
that	celà	das	dat
this	ceci	dies	dit

Marketing

bacon	lard	Schinkenspeck	spek
bakery	boulangerie	Bäckerei	bakkerij
beef	boëf	Rindfleisch	biefstuk
beer	biere	Bier	bier
bread	pain	Brot	brood
butcher	boucher	Metzger	slagerij
butter	beurre	Butter	boter
cheese	fromage	Kase	kaas
chicken	poulet	Hähnchen	kip
diaper	serviette	Windeln	luier
eggs	oeufs	Eier	eieren
fish	poisson	Fisch	vis
flour	farine	Mehl	bloem
fruit	fruit	Obst	fruit
grocer	épicerie	Kolonialwaren-händler	kruidenierswinkel
lamb	agneau	Lamm	lamsvlees
market	marché	Markt	markt
meat	viande	Fleisch	vlees
milk	lait	Milch	melk
pork	porc	Schwein	varkensvlees
rice	riz	Reis	rijst
salt	sel	Salz	zout
sanitary napkin	serviette	Monatsbinden	maandverband

ENGLISH	FRENCH	GERMAN	DUTCH
sugar	sucre	Zucker	suiker
supermarket	supermarché	Supermarkt	supermarkt
tampon	tampon	Tampon	tampon
toilet paper	papier hygiénique	Toilettenpapier	toiletpapier
vegetables	légumes	Gemüse	groenten
vegetable man	marchand primeur	Gemüsehändler	groenteboer
yeast	levure	Hefe	gist

Boat Supplies and Shipyard

alcohol (methylated spirit, U.K.)	alcool ethylique	Spiritus	spiritus
aluminum	aluminium	Aluminium	aluminium
drinking water	eau potable	Trinkwasser	drinkwater
diesel	mazout	Dieselöl	dieselolie
fiber glass	fibre de verre	Glasfaser	fiberglas
galvanize, to	galvaniser	Galvanisieren	galvaniseren
gas	gas	Gas	gas
gasoline (petrol, U.K.)	essence	Benzin	benzine
glue	colle	Leim	lijm
hardware	quincaillerie	Eisenwarenge-schaft	ijzerhandel
haul out, to	tier à terre	an Land holen	op de wal halen
kerosene (paraffin, U.K.)	pétrole	Petroleum	petroleum
nails	clous	Nägel	spijker
paint	peinture	Lack/Farbe	verf
sandpaper	papier de verre	Sandpapier	schuurpapier
screws	vis	Schrauben	schroeven
ship chandler	fournisseur de marine	Schiffsausrüster	scheeps-uitrustings winkel
shipyard	chantier naval	Schiffswert	scheepswerf
spare parts	pieces de réchange	Ersatzteile	onderdelen
stainless steel	inox	rostfreier Stahl	roestvrij staal
steel	acier	Stahl	staal
weld, to	souder	schweißen	lassen
wood	bois	Holz	hout

Emergency

accident	accident	Unfall	ongeluk
burn	brûlure	Brandwunde	brandwond

ENGLISH	FRENCH	GERMAN	DUTCH
dentist	dentiste	Zahnarzt	tandarts
doctor	médecin	Doktor	doktor
drown, to	se noyer	ertrinken	verdrinking
fracture	fracture	Fraktur	breuk
help!	au secours!	hilfe!	help!
hemorrhage	hémorragie	Blutung	bloeding
hospital	hôpital	Krankenhaus	ziekenhuis
poisoning	empoisonnement	Vergiftung	vergiftiging
police	police	Polizei	politie
quickly	vite	schnell	vlug
shock	choc	Schock	shock
stop!	arretez!	halt!	stop!
thief	voleur	Dieb	dief
unconscious	inconscient	ohnmächtig	bewusteloos

Numbers

numbers	nombres	zahlen	nummers
one	un	eins	een
two	deux	zwei	twee
three	trois	drei	drie
four	quatre	vier	vier
five	cinq	fünf	vijf
six	six	sechs	zes
seven	sept	sieben	zeven
eight	huit	acht	acht
nine	neuf	neun	negen
ten	dix	zehn	tien
eleven	onze	elf	elf
twelve	douze	zwölf	twaalf
thirteen	treize	dreizehn	dertien
fourteen	quatorze	vierzehn	veertien
fifteen	quinze	fünfzehn	vijftien
sixteen	seize	sechzehn	zestien
seventeen	dix-sept	siebzehn	zeventien
eighteen	dix-huit	achtzehn	achttien
nineteen	dix-neuf	neunzehn	negentien
twenty	vingt	zwanzig	twintig
twenty-one	vingt-et-un	einundzwanzig	een-en-twentig
twenty-two	vingt-deux	zweiundzwanzig	twee-en-twintig
thirty	trente	dreissig	dertig
forty	quarante	vierzig	veertig

ENGLISH	FRENCH	GERMAN	DUTCH
fifty	cinquante	fünfzig	vijftig
sixty	soixante	sechzig	zestig
seventy	soixante-dix	siebzig	zeventig
eighty	quatre-vingt	achtzig	tachtig
ninety	quatre-vingt-dix	neunzig	negentig
hundred	cent	hundert	honderd
thousand	mille	tausend	duizend
million	million	million	millioen

USEFUL ITALIAN, SPANISH, AND TURKISH VOCABULARY

ENGLISH	ITALIAN	SPANISH	TURKISH

Frequently Needed Words

bad	malo	malo	kötü
bank	banca	banco	banka
bus	autobus	autobús	otobüs
drugstore	farmaceria	farmacia	eczane
glass of water	bicchiere d'acqua	un vaso de agua	şişe su
good	buono	bien	iyi
how far?	quanto è distante?	que es la distancia?	ne kadar uzaklikta?
no	no	no	hayir
open	aperto	abierto	açik
post office	ufficio postale	correos	postahane
shut	chiuso	cerrado	kapali
stamps	francobolli	sellos	pul
toilet	toletta	baño	tuvalet, WC
when?	quando	cuando	ne zaman?
where is?	dov è?	donde es?	nerede
yes	sì	si	evet

Greetings and Thanks

hello	ciao	hóla	merhaba
good day	buon giorno	buenas dias	iyi günler
good-bye	ciao	adíos	Allahaısmarladık
excuse me	mi scusi	perdón	pardon

ENGLISH	ITALIAN	SPANISH	TURKISH
please	per favore	por favor	lütfen
thank you	grazie	gracias	mersi
thank you very much	molte grazie	muchas gracias	çok teşekkür ederim
no, thank you	no, grazie	no, gracias	hayir, mersi
sir	signor	señor	beyfendi
madam	signora	señora	bayan

Harbor

bonded stores	magazzini doganali	víveres precintados	gümrük antreposu
cast off, to	mollare	largar amarras	çözermisiniz
certificate of registration	certificato del registro navale	patente de navegación	gemi tasdiknamesi
courtesy flag	bandiera della nazione ospitante	bandera de cortesia	selam sancaği
customs	dogana	aduana	gümrük
harbor master	comandante del porto	capitán del puerto	liman şefi
immigration	immigrazione	inmigración	göçmenlik
make fast, to	ormeggiarsi	amarrar firme	bağlarmisiniz
passport	passaporto	pasaporte	pasaport
yacht	yacht	yate	yat

Short Words

a	un(o)(a)	un(a)	bir
and	e	y	ve
at	a	en	de(a)
but	ma	pero	ama, fakat
from	da	de	den, dan
here	qui	aqui	burada
how	come	cómo	nasıl
in/into	in	en	içine
much	molto	mucho	çok
not	non	no	yok
now	ora	ahora	şimdi
of	di	de	in
on	sopra	sobre	üzeri
over	sopra	encima	üstünden
there	là	allí	orada
very	molto	muy	çok

ENGLISH	ITALIAN	SPANISH	TURKISH
what	che cosa	que	ne
who	chi	quién	kim
with	con	con	ile

Short Phrases

I am	sono	yo soy	ben . . . im
I am not	non sono	yo no soy	ben . . . değilim
I like it	mi piace	me gusta	severim
I have	ho	tengo	benim var
I have not	non ho	no tengo	benim yok
it is	é	es	o . . . dir
is it?	é?	es?	o . . . mudur?
I don't understand	non capisco	no compréndo	anlamiyorum
speak slowly	parli più lentamente	hablé mas despacio	yavas konuşun
to go	andare	ir	gitmek

Days

afternoon	pomeriggio	tarde	ögleden sonra
day	giorno	dia	gün
evening	sera	noche	akşam
morning	mattina	mañana	sabah
today	oggi	hoy	bugün
tomorrow	domani	mañana	yarin
week	settimana	semana	hafta
yesterday	ieri	ayer	dün
Monday	lunedì	lunes	pazartesi
Tuesday	martedì	martes	sali
Wednesday	mercoledì	miércoles	çarşamba
Thursday	giovedì	jueves	perşembe
Friday	venerdì	viernes	cuma
Saturday	sabato	sábado	cumartesi
Sunday	domenica	domingo	pazar

People

baby	bambino	bébé	bebek
boy	ragazzo	niño	erkek çocuk
children	bambini	niños	çocuklar
friend	amico(a)	amigo(a)	dost(um)
girl	ragazza	niña	kiz çocuk
he	lui	el	o

ENGLISH	ITALIAN	SPANISH	TURKISH
husband	marito	marido	koca
my	el mio, la mia	mi	benim
she	lei	ella	o
wife	sposa	esposa	kari
you	lei	usted	siz
your	vostro	vuestro(a)	sizin

Measures

kilo	chilo	kilo	kilo
liter	litro	litro	litre
meter	metro	metro	metre

To Ask and Bargain

how much?	quanto costa	cuanto	kaça
it's cheap	costa poco	es barato	ucuz
it's too expensive	è troppo caro	es muy caro	çok pahali
all right	buono	bien	tamam
have you?	avete?	tiene usted?	. . . var mi?
I would like	vorrei	qu erría	istiyorum
I don't want	non voglio	no quiero	istemiyorum
that's all	basta	eso es todo	tamam

To Select

big	grande	grande	büyük
cold	freddo	frio	soğuk
color	colore	color	renk
enough	abbastanza	bastante	tamam
half	mezzo	medio	yarim, buçuk
iced	ghiaccato	helado	buzlu
little	poco	poco	küçük
more	piú	más	daha
small	piccolo	pequeño	küçük, ufak
stop	basta	alto	dur
that	quello	esto	şu
this	questo	eso	bu

Marketing

bacon	panchette affumi-cato	tocino	beykin
bakery	panetteria	panadería	firin

ENGLISH	ITALIAN	SPANISH	TURKISH
beef	manzo	carne de vaca	siğir
beer	birra	cerveza	bira
bread	pane	pan	ekmek
butcher	macellaio	carnicería	kasap
butter	burro	mantequilla	tereyaği
cheese	formaggio	queso	peynir
chicken	pollo	pollo	piliç
diaper	pannolino	pañal	çocuk bezi
eggs	uove	huevos	yumurta
fish	pesce	pescado	balik
flour	farina	harina	un
fruit	frutta	fruta	meyve
grocer	drogheria	tienda de ultrama-rinos	bakkal
lamb	agnello	carne de cordero	kuzu
market	mercato	mercado	pazar
meat	carne	carne	et
milk	latte	leche	süt
pork	maiale	cerdo	domuz (keçi-goat)
rice	riso	arroz	pirinç
salt	sale	sal	tuz
sanitary napkin	assorbenti igienici	paño higiénico	orkid
sugar	zucchero	azucar	şeker
supermarket	supermercato	supermercado	süpermarket
tampon	tampon	tampón	tampon
toilet paper	carta igienica	papel hygiénico	tuvalet kağidi
vegetables	verdure	verduras	sebze
vegetable man	erbivendolo	verdulero	manav
yeast	lievito	levadura	bira mayasi

Boat Supplies and Shipyard

alcohol (methylated spirit, U.K.)	alcool denaturato	alcohol desnatura-lizado	ispirto
aluminum	allumino	aluminio	alüminyum
drinking water	acqua potabile	agua potable	içilecek su
diesel	gasolio	gasoil	mazot
fiber glass	lana di vetro	fibra de vidrio	fiberglas
galvanize, to	zincare	galvanizar	galvaniʐ
gas	gas	gas	gaz
gasoline (petrol, U.K.)	benzina	gasolina	benzin

ENGLISH	ITALIAN	SPANISH	TURKISH
glue	colla	adhesivo	tutkal
hardware	fabbro ferraio	ferreteria	hirdavat
haul out, to	alare in secco	varar	karaya çekmek
kerosene (paraffin, U.K.)	petrolio	petróleo	gaz yaği
nails	chiodi	clavos	çivi
paint	pittura	pintura	boya
sandpaper	cartaveto	papel de lija	zimpara kağidi
screws	viti	tornillos	vida
shipchandler	fornitore navale	almacén de efectos navales	yat için yedek parça
shipyard	cantiere navale	astillero	tersane
spare parts	parti componenti	pieza de repuesto	yedek parça
stainless steel	acciaio inossidabile	acero inoxidable	paslanmaz çelik
steel	acciaio	acero	çelik
weld, to	saldare	soldar	kaynak
wood	legno	madera	tahta

Emergency

accident	infortunio	accidente	kaza
burn	bruciatura	quemadura	yanmis, yanik
dentist	dentista	dentista	dişci
doctor	dottore	médico	doktor
drown, to	annegare	ahogarse	boğulmak
fracture	frattura	fractura	kirik
help!	aiuto!	socorro!	imdat!
hemorrhage	emorragia	hemorragia	kan almak
hospital	ospedale	hospitale	hastahane
poisoning	avvelenamento	envenenamiento	zehirlenme
police	polizia	policía	polis
quickly	presto	rápido	çabuk
shock	shock	shock	şok
stop!	ferma	pare!	dur
thief	ladro	ladrón	hirsiz
unconscious	inconscio	sin conocimiento	baygin

Numbers

numbers	numeri	numeros	aded
one	uno	uno	bir
two	due	dos	iki

ENGLISH	ITALIAN	SPANISH	TURKISH
three	tre	tres	üç
four	quattro	cuatro	dört
five	cinque	cinco	bes
six	sei	seis	alti
seven	sette	siete	yedi
eight	otto	ocho	sekiz
nine	nove	nueve	dokuz
ten	dieci	diez	on
eleven	undici	once	on bir
twelve	dodici	doce	on iki
thirteen	tredici	trece	on üç
fourteen	quattordici	catorce	on dört
fifteen	quindici	quince	on bes
sixteen	sedici	dieciséis	on alti
seventeen	diciassette	diecisiete	on yedi
eighteen	diciotto	dieciocho	on sekiz
nineteen	diciannove	diecinueve	on dokuz
twenty	venti	veinte	yirmi
twenty-one	venti uno	veinte uno	yirmi bir
twenty-two	venti due	veinte dos	yirmi iki
thirty	trenta	treinta	otuz
forty	quaranta	cuaranta	kirk
fifty	cinquanta	cincuenta	elli
sixty	sessanta	sesenta	altmis
seventy	settanta	setenta	yetmis
eighty	ottanta	ochenta	seksen
ninety	novanta	noventa	doksan
hundred	ciento	cien	yüz
thousand	mille	mil	bin
million	milione	millón	milyon

Index